Qualitative Online Interviews

Second Edition

Dedication

*To Hannah, Zac, Alex, Sammy, and Oliver—keep asking big questions;
you might grow up to be researchers!*

*To all my students and mentees—may you apply all you learn
to build new understandings and a better world.*

Qualitative Online Interviews

Strategies, Design, and Skills

Second Edition

Janet Salmons

*Vision2Lead and Capella
University School of Business*

Los Angeles | London | New Delhi
Singapore | Washington DC

Los Angeles | London | New Delhi
Singapore | Washington DC

FOR INFORMATION:

SAGE Publications, Inc.
2455 Teller Road
Thousand Oaks, California 91320
E-mail: order@sagepub.com

SAGE Publications Ltd.
1 Oliver's Yard
55 City Road
London, EC1Y 1SP
United Kingdom

SAGE Publications India Pvt. Ltd.
B 1/I 1 Mohan Cooperative Industrial Area
Mathura Road, New Delhi 110 044
India

SAGE Publications Asia-Pacific Pte. Ltd.
3 Church Street
#10-04 Samsung Hub
Singapore 049483

Acquisitions Editor: Vicki Knight
Editorial Assistant: Yvonne McDuffee
Production Editor: Jane Haenel
Copy Editor: Megan Granger
Typesetter: C&M Digitals (P) Ltd.
Proofreader: Wendy Jo Dymond
Indexer: Karen Wiley
Cover Designer: Bryan Fishman
Marketing Manager: Nicole Elliott

Printed in the United States of America

Library of Congress Cataloging-in-Publication Data

Salmons, Janet, 1952–
[Online interviews in real time]

Qualitative online interviews : strategies, design, and skills / Janet Salmons, Vision2Lead and Capella University School of Business. — Second Edition.

pages cm
Includes bibliographical references and index.

ISBN 978-1-4833-3267-3 (pbk. : alk. paper)

1. Interviewing. 2. Telematics. 3. Online chat groups. 4. Research—Methodology. 5. Real-time data processing. 6. Telecommunication. I. Title.

H61.28.S25 2014
001.4'33—dc23   2014002903

This book is printed on acid-free paper.

14 15 16 17 18 10 9 8 7 6 5 4 3 2 1

Brief Contents

Detailed Contents

List of Figures

List of Tables

Preface

The use of technology for personal and social, professional and commercial, civic and political communications has continued to grow since *Online Interviews in Real Time* was published in 2010. Through social media sites, blogs, and comment forums, people interact with others they know, with those they know only online, and with complete strangers they will never again encounter. The ease of online access to information in libraries and archives, as well as on websites and blogs, means we can readily find what we need to know—whether a scholarly article in a decades-old publication or a menu for a local restaurant. Internet access through mobile devices means that such communications and information retrieval has become ubiquitous—seamlessly woven into our everyday lives. For many of us, it is becoming harder to see a firm line between our online lives and our offline lives, and challenging to say whether one is more "real" than another.

In parallel to the evolution of information and communications technologies (ICTs) and their increased use, data collection methods for scholarly research are evolving. With readily available online communications tools, we can learn from and ask questions of diverse, global participants to collect data anywhere, anytime, using computers, phones, or mobile devices. We can find, generate, and use audio, visual, and written data to answer our research questions. We are on the cusp of a new era, with exciting new opportunities for qualitative e-researchers.

For the purpose of this book, the term *online interviews* refers to interviews conducted with ICTs. The primary focus is on interviews conducted synchronously or asynchronously with text messaging, video conferencing or video calls, web conference meeting spaces, or immersive virtual worlds or games. Researchers may also complement interview research with other data collected from observations, posts, or documents by or about participants or the phenomena.

Interview research is arguably the most personal form of data collection. The interviewer cannot simply stand back to observe subjects or analyze their survey responses. Whether the subject of inquiry is personal or not, the interviewer must actively engage the interviewee, gaining personal trust and professional respect to elicit information-rich responses. Some level of relationship is inherent in the exchange, if only for the duration of the interview. When interviews occur online, researchers must devise and learn new ways to build trust and motivate individuals to contribute. Researchers also must devise and learn new ways to design studies, recruit participants, and meet ethical research guidelines.

I was—and am—intrigued by the potential for using verbal, visual, and textual elements to build researcher–participant rapport and to extend the usual question-and-answer verbal exchange that characterizes what we call an *interview*. The potential to rethink the *interview* expands with the availability of each new communications technology. As we consider and experiment with possible approaches, we need to rethink and reimagine our qualitative methods and move from "virtual" to "digital." I am referring to Richard Rogers's distinction between what he calls *virtual* approaches, those that import traditional data collection methods into the online milieu, and *digital* approaches that take advantage of the unique characteristics and capabilities of the Internet for research (Rogers, 2009, 2010). Rogers's word choice may not be very descriptive, but the important concept is that emerging *digital* qualitative approaches require the researcher to do more than simply repurpose real-world data collection techniques. In *Qualitative Online Interviews,* I encourage you to look for ways to experiment and demonstrate the potential for meaningful new ways to collect data with interviews.

When options expand, typically the complexity of decision making increases as well. Why would a researcher choose to conduct an interview online rather than in person? What special considerations are needed for the design, the sample, and the analysis? What skills will the interviewer need? What online approach is most suitable for a particular research question? The terms *Internet studies* and *Internet research* have been used primarily to describe research that uses online methods to study behaviors and interactions that occur online (Consalvo & Ess, 2011; Markham, 2005). This book takes a broader view, suggesting that online methods are appropriate for studying behaviors that occur online *or* offline.

Two of my own online interview studies are described throughout the book. These research examples used a groupware meeting platform that allowed me to interview participants across the globe from my office in Boulder, Colorado. These dynamic experiences provided the impetus for the book. The online interview approach to data collection was convenient and low-cost, but those practical reasons are not what ignited my curiosity. Even for someone familiar with online communication, the online research process—from initial recruitment to final follow-up—far exceeded my expectations. The data I collected were categorically richer and deeper than I had anticipated.

Research is conducted to create new knowledge. We need new knowledge—theoretical and practical—that reflects the new realities of our digital age and connected, interdependent world. Online researchers have the opportunity to model the process of global connection and make unique contributions. I hope that *Qualitative Online Interviews* will inspire you to be one of them!

Purpose of the Book

The purpose of *Qualitative Online Interviews* is to encourage researchers to extend the reach of their studies by using methods that defy geographic boundaries. *Qualitative Online Interviews* focuses on designing, conducting, and assessing research that relies on data from interviews and related observations, materials, or artifacts collected online. The emphasis is on the use of in-depth interviews in qualitative research, where relevant, mixed-methods designs are discussed. Whether used in its print or electronic format, this book is meant to be fringed with sticky notes, highlighted, and left open on the side of the desk (or desktop) for ongoing reference—not shelved after a single reading.

Qualitative Online Interviews encompasses the practical how-to information needed to make thoughtful decisions and the scholarly foundations needed to support them.

It is not enough simply to decide to use ICT tools or social media sites as places for exchange with research participants. Online communications vary not only from face-to-face communication but also from one another. An e-mail exchange is qualitatively different from a video call, and in research, those differences matter. *Qualitative Online Interviews* aims to provide the basis for assessing what matters to the research at hand to develop a credible, ethical study.

New Features in the Second Edition

The second edition updates *Online Interviews in Real Time* by doing the following:

- *Using the E-Interview Research Framework as the organizational structure for the book.* The E-Interview Research Framework was introduced in *Cases in Online Interview Research* (Salmons, 2012; see Figure 1). This conceptual framework offers a way to understand interrelationships across key elements of online interview research design and associated design decisions—and implications. The E-Interview Research Framework includes eight categories of questions and design considerations researchers need to think through when designing or evaluating a study with data generated through online interviews. Each category of the framework is covered in-depth in one or more chapters of *Qualitative Online Interviews*.

Figure 1   E-Interview Research Framework

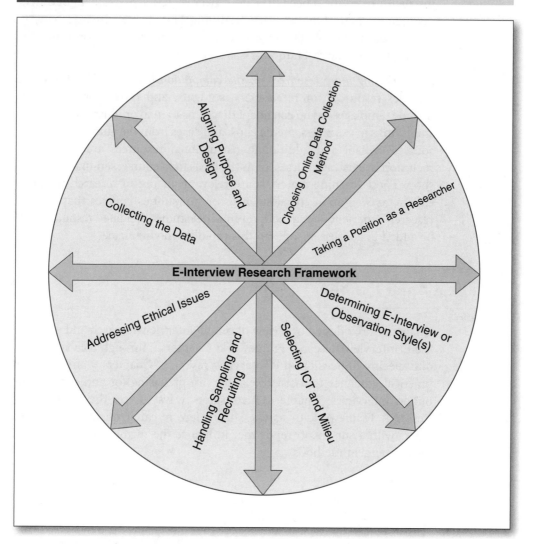

Source: Vision2Lead Inc (2009–2015).

• *Broadening the options for online interviews.* While *Online Interviews in Real Time* focused exclusively on synchronous interviews, this edition considers a full range of synchronous, near-synchronous, and asynchronous options.

• *Adding suggestions for collecting data from online observations and collecting online documents.* Dispersed throughout the book is a discussion of how researchers can complement interviews by collecting data through participant or outsider observations, or by collecting posts or user-generated content, including written material, images or other media, artifacts, or documents.

- *Adding a chapter on e-interview research quality.* Whether as an instructor or editor, a peer student or peer reviewer, assessment of others' research is a part of the scholarly tradition. This chapter discusses emerging standards for quality in e-research and offers steps for using the E-Interview Research Framework as an evaluative tool.

- *Offering more resources on the companion book site.* The book site includes resources for researchers, students, and instructors. Materials include templates so you can adapt diagrams to map or illustrate your own study, links to examples, media clips, and cases from the author or credible sources. Syllabi and additional instructional resources are offered for inclusion in existing courses, or as the basis for a course, seminar, or workshop. These learning materials are relevant for use in research methods classes, as well as in social sciences or humanities courses that include research experiences or a focus on Internet studies. Updated resources will be added to address changes in this rapidly evolving field.

Organization of the Book

Chapter 1 provides an overview of online interview research and explains the E-Interview Research Framework. Chapters 2 through 8 each explore one specific dimension of e-interview research. Chapters 9 and 10 offer practical guidance to assist researchers in preparing for and conducting online interviews. Chapter 11 considers ways to use the E-Interview Research Framework to assess e-interview research quality. The book closes with a survey of trends that influence the further development of these emergent methods.

CHAPTER 1: THE E-INTERVIEW RESEARCH FRAMEWORK

In Chapter 1, you will learn about the E-Interview Research Framework. You will look at the options e-interview researchers have and the decisions they make, and explore how each decision influences the nature of the study and the research design.

CHAPTER 2: ALIGNING PURPOSE AND DESIGN

In Chapter 2, you will examine the need for alignment between epistemologies, theories, methodologies, and methods. You will focus specifically on the implications of the type of online interview for the research design.

CHAPTER 3: CHOOSING ONLINE DATA COLLECTION METHOD AND TAKING A POSITION AS A RESEARCHER

In Chapter 3, you will look at ways the motivation to use e-interviews influences other aspects of the research design, including sampling, recruiting, and selection of technology used in the interview. You will consider how the researcher's insider or outsider position influences the interview style, and the metaphors we use to explain the researcher's relationship to the study.

CHAPTER 4: DETERMINING E-INTERVIEW OR OBSERVATION STYLES

In Chapter 4, you will look at the use of structured, unstructured, and/or semistructured interview styles online. You will consider how interviewers decide what behaviors to observe as part of the interview.

CHAPTER 5: SELECTING INFORMATION AND COMMUNICATIONS TECHNOLOGIES AND RESEARCH SETTING MILIEU

In Chapter 5, you will scrutinize distinctions between different kinds of synchronous, near-synchronous, and asynchronous communications that can be used for scholarly interviews. You will learn ways to align ICT features with the purpose of the study and the nature of the sample population.

CHAPTER 6: VISUAL RESEARCH AND THE ONLINE QUALITATIVE INTERVIEW

In Chapter 6, you will look at technologies that offer researchers and participants the opportunity to communicate using visual modes in online interviews. The Typology of Online Visual Interview Methods is introduced, with alternatives to use in text-based, video conferencing, online meeting spaces, or immersive virtual environments.

CHAPTER 7: HANDLING SAMPLING AND RECRUITING: SELECTING PARTICIPANTS FOR ONLINE INTERVIEWS

In Chapter 7, you will explore types of sampling and selection of research participants for online interviews. Building on prior chapters, this chapter addresses the implications of research purpose for sampling and participant selection.

CHAPTER 8: ADDRESSING ETHICAL ISSUES IN ONLINE INTERVIEW RESEARCH

In Chapter 8, you will delve into research design considerations for online interview research. You will survey ethical issues in online research and determine what ethical issues might need to be addressed depending on interview approach and public or private setting.

CHAPTER 9: PREPARING FOR AN ONLINE INTERVIEW

In Chapter 9, you will look at the preparation of interview questions or prompts, planning for use of communication tools in the interview, and the interviewer's preparation to listen to the research participant.

CHAPTER 10: CONDUCTING THE ONLINE INTERVIEW

In Chapter 10, you will delve into practical steps for carrying out an online interview. Four kinds of interviews are described using text-based, video conferencing, online meeting spaces, or immersive virtual environments. You also will look at steps for following up with interviewees to verify and complete the data collection.

CHAPTER 11: CONTRIBUTING QUALITY E-RESEARCH TO THE LITERATURE

Chapter 11 draws on the preceding chapters in a discussion of e-interview research quality and strategies for assessing proposals or completed studies.

CHAPTER 12: ONLINE COMMUNICATIONS AND ONLINE INTERVIEWS: TRENDS AND INFLUENCES

The book concludes with a discussion of trends in online communication that influence online interview options.

APPENDIX

The Appendix contains a glossary of terms and an overview of qualitative data analysis.

CHAPTER FEATURES

Some consistent features are offered in each chapter:

- *Research Tips* and *Ethics Tips* in the margins point readers to important practical reminders.
- *Key Concepts* summarize main ideas from each chapter.
- *Discussions and Assignments* may be used as the basis for formal or informal learning about online interview research.
- Other ancillary materials, including media pieces related to the topics of the book, are available on the book's companion website. Live hyperlinks will allow readers of the electronic version of this book to connect directly. This site is important to all readers who want access to up-to-date resources.

Janet Salmons, PhD
Boulder, Colorado

Acknowledgments

This book would not have been possible without the loving support of my husband, Cole Keirsey, who patiently discusses the ins and outs of e-interview research ad infinitum. You have my gratitude for your thoughtful insights and encouragement.

A heartfelt thank you goes to Vicki Knight, acquisitions editor at SAGE Publications, for her unflagging support and enthusiasm for this book.

The book benefited greatly from the constructive comments and suggestions provided at various stages of the manuscript by the following people: Anne-Marie Armstrong, Colorado Technical University and Oakland Community College; Sally R. Beisser, Drake University; Suzanne K. Becking, Fort Hays State University; Debra Borie-Holtz, Rutgers, The State University of New Jersey; David Lee Carlson, Arizona State University; Marilyn L. Grady, University of Nebraska-Lincoln; Laura J. Hatcher, Southern Illinois University Carbondale; Louise Murray, College of Saint Elizabeth; Faith Wambura Ngunjiri, Eastern University; and Sherri Oden, Oakland University.

About the Author

Janet Salmons has served since 1999 on the graduate faculty of the Capella University School of Business, where she enjoys working with emerging researchers as a dissertation mentor. She was honored with the Harold Abel Distinguished Faculty Award for 2011–2012 and the Steven Shank Recognition for Teaching in 2012 and 2013. She is an independent researcher, writer, and consultant through her company, Vision2Lead, Inc. Dr. Salmons edited *Cases in Online Interview Research* (2012) and wrote *Online Interviews in Real Time* (2010) for SAGE Publications, along with numerous articles and book chapters.

Dr. Salmons received a BS in adult and community education from Cornell University; an MA in social policy studies from Empire State College, a distance-learning institution in the State University of New York system; and a PhD in interdisciplinary studies (meshing educational, technology, and leadership studies) at the Union Institute and University. She lives and works in Boulder, Colorado.

The E-Interview Research Framework

1

> *We don't receive wisdom; we must discover it for ourselves after a journey that no one can take for us or spare us.*
>
> —Marcel Proust (1871–1922)

After you study Chapter 1, you will be able to do the following:

- Understand interrelated elements of e-interview research
- Use the E-Interview Research Framework to analyze a research design and plan

Interview Research: A Window Into the Lived Experience

Each individual experiences life in a unique way. Each finds significance in life events by interpreting and reinterpreting meaning through lenses of memory and identity, culture, and prior experiences. Researchers who want to understand the complexities of human drama often choose interviews as an entrée into another's inner reflections and thoughts, feelings, perceptions, and responses to the external world. Interview research is distinctive in its reliance on direct, usually immediate, interaction between the researcher and participant.

Successful qualitative researchers draw on the best of human qualities when conducting interviews: They demonstrate empathy and respect, and they inspire trust. Interview researchers use thoughtful questioning, sensitive probing, and reflective listening. When individuals respond and share their stories, observant researchers make note of nonverbal signals and listen to verbal expressions. Implications of physical setting and the interviewer's demeanor are carefully considered to develop the rapport and comfort necessary to collect robust data. The potential fullness of this active exchange has traditionally motivated researchers to choose face-to-face conversations when collecting data for qualitative and mixed-methods research.

Must individuals sit in the same room to have a meaningful dialogue or perform thorough observation? In many areas of life and work, activities that people previously assumed would require physical proximity are now conducted via electronic communications. Scholarly activities are included in this trend. Contemporary researchers expect to use computers when writing about research design, analyzing data, and creating reports of their findings. Researchers routinely use the Internet to study the existing literature in their fields through online journals and databases. Scholars expect to discuss their ongoing work with far-flung colleagues through e-mail lists, **blogs**, social media, and interactive websites. Scholarly meetings are held online, with presentations and discussions carried out on web conferencing platforms. Increasingly, researchers are using the Internet to collect data as well.

ONLINE INTERVIEW RESEARCH

Online interviews are a viable alternative because researchers can choose from varied communication options and easily talk directly with participants anywhere, at any time. For the purpose of this book, **online interviews,** or *e-interviews*, refer to interviews conducted using **computer-mediated communication** (CMC). Such interviews are used for primary **Internet-mediated research**. That is, they are used to gather original data via the Internet with the intention of subjecting these data to analysis to provide new evidence in relation to a specific research question (Hewson, 2010).

Emerging **information and communications technologies** (ICTs) offer diverse ways to conduct research interviews, observe participants, and/or obtain related documents. Scholarly online interviews are further defined as *any* dialogue or observation carried out for the purpose of data collection. An online interview may be a verbal or written, carefully planned or casual interchange. In other words, even a short text message exchange or quick chat via a **social media** site is treated as an interview with a participant if data are collected. Importantly, if the communication is recorded, noted, or saved for research purposes, it must be conducted in accordance with ethical research guidelines. This means verifiable research participants must provide informed consent before participating in any interview. (See Chapter 8 for more about ethical issues.)

ONLINE INTERVIEWS AND MULTIMETHOD RESEARCH

Interviews, observations, and documents may be used as single types of data or combined in multimethod or multimodal research. Online, the

Table 1.1	Collecting Qualitative Data Online
Online interviews	Interviews carried out with computer-mediated communication (CMC) to collect data. CMC may occur using computers, cell phones, or mobile devices. Locative technologies, such as global positioning systems (GPS) or geographic information systems (GIS) can complement such interviews when mapping to place is relevant. Online interviews may entail communication with one or more participants using text chat or messaging, multichannel web conferencing spaces, video conferencing, or interactions in virtual worlds or games.
Online observations	External or participant observation of online dialogues, behaviors, interactions, events, or activities conducted for the purpose of data collection.
Online document analysis	Posts, digital records, and/or artifacts from websites, blogs, social media sites, and/or e-mail lists gathered for the purpose of data collection. Online "documents" can take the form of drawings, graphics or other images, photographs or media, or written or audio data.

choice is less clear-cut; it may not be possible to fully separate these types of data when collection occurs over the Internet. Data are not neatly differentiated, because CMC may mesh written chat or comments, recorded or live video, images or photographs, or links to other online materials. Depending on the research purpose and design, online interviews may include some observations from the interviewees and/or some review of participants' user-posted material from the participant. Online interview research, then, is to some degree inherently multimethod. This being the case, the researcher is "challenged to find multimodal ways to expand our methodological toolbox" (Beneito-Montagut, 2011, p. 717). As a result, while interviews are central to *Qualitative Online Interviews*, other types of data collection are included throughout the book to allow for a multifaceted examination of the research problem.

A Conceptual Framework for E-Interview Research

What kind of online interviews, observations, and/or documents fulfill the purpose and design of a study? This simple question belies the complexity of online research design. While e-researchers need to address concerns common to any study, we additionally must inquire about the influences of the technology on the research design, conduct, and, ultimately, the study's conclusions. However, since online interview research is an emergent method, a widely accepted set of design specifications or criteria does not currently exist. Where to begin? What questions should be asked? The E-Interview Research Framework offers a conceptual system of key questions about interrelated facets of online interview research. When introduced in *Cases in Online Interview Research* (Salmons, 2012), the central focus was on data collection with online interviews; however, the updated E-Interview Research Framework encompasses related primary (i.e., questionnaires, observations) and secondary (i.e., posts, sites, documents, images, or media) online data collection (see Figure 1.1).

The E-Interview Research Framework is displayed as a circular system because examining design decisions in isolation is inadequate. In many

| Figure 1.1 | The E-Interview Research Framework for Understanding E-Interview Research |

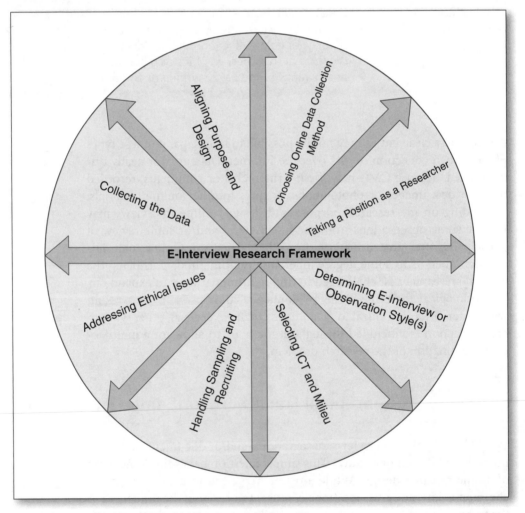

Source: Vision2Lead Inc (2009–2015).

areas of qualitative research design, there are no hard-and-fast rules and "it depends . . ." is a common answer to how and why questions. This "it depends . . ." nature is, if anything, more pronounced in e-interview research design, where technology choices are interrelated with data type, method of collection, and ethical considerations. Hence, a holistic approach is needed, as presented in this E-Interview Research Framework.

The E-Interview Research Framework comprises eight interrelated categories, each with a set of questions and models. This framework can be used whether one is designing original research, analyzing a study proposed or conducted by another researcher, or reviewing a published study. Treatment of these categories begins with *aligning purpose and design*. While this may indeed be the first step, the E-Interview Research Framework suggests that once the other categories have been examined, it may be necessary to circle back to the beginning and make sure all pieces of the design fit. This Chapter 1 overview introduces the categories of the E-Interview Research Framework; each will be thoroughly explored in one or more chapters of the book.

ALIGNING PURPOSE AND DESIGN

Key Questions

- Are theories and epistemologies, methodologies, and methods appropriate for the study and clearly aligned?
- How will qualitative data collected online relate to theories? Does the researcher want to explore, prove, or generate theory?

Any study is strengthened by coherent discussion of research purpose, theories, methodologies, and methods. By exploring elements of the research design, we can understand how the intended use of online data collection methods aligns with the overall purpose and theoretical framework of the study. Importantly, we can learn whether the researcher intends to explore or test extant theories or generate new theory. We can also ascertain whether the researcher is working within, across, or outside of disciplinary approaches.

When designing a study based on online data collection, greater attention to alignment among key elements is needed. The rationale for the electronic methods needs to be comprehensive and precise. Some design questions and relationships are illustrated in Figure 1.2. When a study is mapped in this way, it should be clear that the theories and epistemologies are appropriate to the methodology, and that online methods fit the methodology. Learn more about aligning purpose and design in Chapter 2.

Figure 1.2   Design for Clarity and Coherence

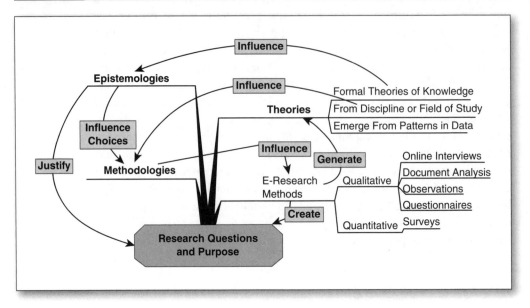

Source: Vision2Lead, Inc (2009–2014).

Components of Research Design

Four interrelated elements of research design—epistemology, theory, methodology, and method—are defined for our purposes as follows:

- **Epistemology** refers to the study of the nature of knowledge, or the study of how knowledge is justified.

- **Theory** refers to an explanation that is internally consistent, supportive of other theories, and gives new insights. An important characteristic of theory is that it is predictive.

- **Methodology** refers to the study of, and justification for, the methods used to conduct the research (Loseke, 2013). Methodologies emerge from academic disciplines in the social and physical sciences, and although considerable cross-disciplinary exchange occurs, choices generally place the study in a disciplinary context.

- **Method** refers to the practical steps used to conduct the study, including sampling, collecting, and analyzing data.

CHOOSING ONLINE DATA COLLECTION METHOD FOR THE STUDY

Key Questions

- Does the researcher offer a compelling rationale for using online interviews and any related observations or documents to achieve the research purpose?
- Is the rationale aligned with methodologies, the research problem, the purpose, and questions?
- Does the researcher explain whether online interviews are chosen to investigate real-world phenomena or online phenomena?

With a clear picture of the overarching contours of the study, next we look at why online interviews and related observations or documents are appropriate for the study. What is the researcher's motivation for conducting the interviews online rather than in person or over the telephone? Does the researcher describe data collection strategy in a way that others—even those with little background in online research—will understand? What compelling rationale supports the online data collection strategy?

Some researchers want to study behaviors or phenomena that take place online by exploring them in the kind of setting where they occur. Patterns of technology use, modes of participation in online communities, or human–computer interaction can best be studied by using ICTs to conduct the interview. In such circumstances, the technology itself may be a part of the phenomenon under investigation.

CMC also allows researchers to explore behaviors, life experiences, or phenomena unrelated to the Internet. The researcher may decide to conduct interviews online because it is a convenient way to meet participants or because participants are geographically dispersed. Online interviews may be selected over telephone interviews because researchers want to see the participant or collect visual data. In such studies, technology is a means to communicate but is not part of the phenomenon under investigation.

As we will see in Chapter 3, each of these choices has implications for the other areas of the research design, including the choice of communications technology and research setting, use of visual methods, and position of the researcher in relation to the study.

TAKING A POSITION AS A RESEARCHER

Key Questions

- Does the researcher clearly delineate an insider or outsider position? Does the researcher explain implications related to that position, including any conflicts of interest or risks of **researcher bias**?
- Is the researcher looking at **emic** issues, revealed by actors in the case (Stake, 1995)? Or is the researcher positioned as an outsider who brings questions in from outside the case, looking at **etic** issues (Stake, 1995)?
- Can the researcher's role be described as miner, traveler (Kvale, 2007; Kvale & Brinkman, 2009), or gardener (Salmons, 2010)?

At this point, we should understand the overall purpose and design of the research and the researcher's motivation for conducting the study online. Now we are ready to explore whether the researcher's motivations are based on the researcher's personal connection to the phenomenon or participants being investigated, or whether the researcher is motivated by scholarly interests or a gap identified in the literature. Online, where people tend to be connected formally and informally to social and professional networks, researchers may have various degrees of relationship to the phenomenon or participants. The distinction between *insider* and *outsider* is not unique to online interview research. The researcher may look at *emic* issues revealed by actors in the case or at *etic* issues drawn from outside the case (Stake, 1995). In qualitative studies, the researcher is the instrument of data collection; so being forthright about any potential biases or conflicts of interest lends credibility to the study.

Another way to describe the standpoint of the researcher is through the metaphorical stances of the miner, traveler (Kvale, 2007; Kvale & Brinkman, 2009), and gardener (Salmons, 2010). According to these metaphors, the researcher who digs out facts and feelings from research subjects is characterized as a *miner*. The *traveler* journeys with the participant. Most common interview practices lie between these two extremes. The metaphor of the *gardener* suggests that the interviewer uses questions to plant a seed and then cultivates the growth of ideas and shared perceptions through extended dialogue with participants.

By understanding the purpose, motivations, and other considerations involved in choosing to collect data online, we can better grasp how the methods and approaches align with other elements of the research design. By understanding the etic or emic stance of the researcher and the intention to travel, garden, or excavate data, we can learn more about the way the researcher relates to the phenomenon and potentially to the research participants.

Learn more about choosing online interviews and taking a position as a researcher in Chapter 3.

Key Questions

- Does the researcher plan to use *structured, semistructured, unstructured*, or a combination of styles for the interview(s)?
- How does the researcher align ICT functions, features, and/or limitations with the selected e-interview style(s)?
- What observations or posted materials will complement the interviews?

DETERMINING E-INTERVIEW OR OBSERVATION STYLE(S)

Any interview researcher must decide whether a structured, unstructured, or semistructured interview best achieves the purpose of the study. By understanding the level(s) of structure the researcher intends to use, we can learn more about preinterview preparation. Some types of CMC are more natural and allow for spontaneity, while others require more forethought or setup prior to an interview. This means an e-interview researcher must also consider alignment of interview structure and questioning style with choice of technology used to communicate with participants, data type, and online research setting (see Figure 1.3).

Structured interviews usually consist of the same questions posed in the same sequence to all participants. They may include closed-ended or limited-response questions or open-ended questions designed to elicit short narrative answers. Interview respondents do not have the option to redirect questions or elaborate on responses. To prepare for structured interviews, the researcher determines the exact wording of all questions in advance. Because the role of the interviewer is meant to be as neutral as possible, the researcher may recruit and train others to implement the interview.

Semistructured interviews balance the preplanned questions of a structured approach with the spontaneity and flexibility of the unstructured interview. The researcher prepares questions and/or discussion topics in advance and generates follow-up questions during the interview.

Unstructured interviews are used to collect data through what is essentially a conversation between the researcher and participant.

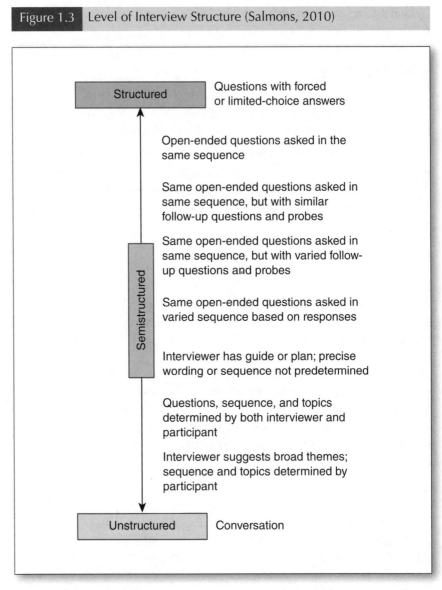

Figure 1.3   Level of Interview Structure (Salmons, 2010)

Source: Vision2Lead, Inc (2009–2014).

Structured interviews can be conducted with almost any ICT since answers may be yes/no or simple statements. Semistructured and unstructured interviews, however, require more careful thought because in some kinds of ICTs, pausing to craft and type questions may disrupt the flow of the interview. Learn more about choosing online interview styles and levels of structure in Chapter 4.

SELECTING ICT AND MILIEU

Key Questions

- Will the interview use text-based, audio, and/or visual communication options?
- Will the interaction take place synchronously, asynchronously, or with a mix of time-response communication options?
- Will the interview setting be in a public or private online milieu?
- Is the choice of ICT aligned with research purpose, interview style, and access/preference of the research participants?

Researchers may choose a particular interview technology and setting for a variety of reasons, including the researcher's preferences or expectations for access and ease of use by participants. Some researchers are looking for specific communications features in the ICT. The desire for observation as a part of the interviews, or in addition to interviews, also influences the choice of research setting. Timing and degree of immediacy possible between question and response are additional considerations.

For the purpose of this book, brand names are generally avoided, and ICTs are described by the features that facilitate communication. The main types are text-based communication in writing; video conference with ability to see communication partners; and web conferencing meeting spaces that allow for text, video conference, and visual interactions with **shared applications**, documents, and/or **whiteboards**. Immersive virtual environments, including **virtual worlds** or games, allow for text, verbal, and visual exchange. These features are available in singular or combined ways through various social media, web, software, and proprietary applications. Learn more about the process for choosing data collection technologies and research settings in Chapter 5.

Using Visual Research in Online Interviews and Observations

The choice of ICT may also involve decisions about whether and how to use visual methods for interviews and/or observations. Increasingly, communication technologies enable the researcher and participant to see each other and to view, share, or create images. How will such data enable the researcher to achieve the study's purpose? Learn more about design options and implications for visual methods in online data collection in Chapter 6.

HANDLING SAMPLING AND RECRUITING

Key Questions

- What sampling approaches are appropriate given the purpose of the study and e-interview approach?
- How will the researcher assess whether the target population has access to the interview technology and the capability and willingness to use it as research participants?
- How can the researcher locate credible research participants? How will the researcher verify the identity and age (or other relevant criteria) of research participants recruited online?

Qualitative researchers often use what is broadly defined as purposive or purposeful sampling when selecting participants, meaning the **sample** is intentionally selected according to the purpose of the study. Additional criteria may be needed to identify appropriate participants with abilities and availability necessary for the online interview. Online recruitment requires additional steps to ensure credibility. Learn more about sampling and recruiting in Chapter 7.

ADDRESSING ETHICAL ISSUES

Key Questions

- Has the researcher taken appropriate steps to protect human subjects and, where appropriate, their avatars or online representations?
- Has the researcher obtained proper informed consent?
- Does the researcher have permission to access and use posts, documents, profiles, or images?

Ethical issues abound in any interview research. In the case of online interview research, there are some particular factors to address. For example, the consent that participants sign should include agreements for use of any user-generated content, images, or artifacts the interviewer wants to include as data. Care must be taken to avoid circumstances where the participant unwittingly reveals more than he or she intended to share as data for the study. Learn more about the complexities of e-research ethics in Chapter 8, and in the "Ethics Tips" sprinkled throughout the book.

COLLECTING THE DATA

> ### Key Questions
>
> - Is the researcher experienced with all features of the selected technology? Has the researcher conducted practice interviews?
> - Does the researcher have a plan for conducting the interview with either prepared questions or an interview guide?
> - Does the researcher have a plan for the four interview stages: opening, questioning and guiding, closing, and following up?
> - Does the researcher have a contingency plan in case there are technical difficulties?

Once designs and plans are complete, the researcher must be able to carry out the interview, with all the messy realities intrinsic to any communication. Does the researcher have the preparation, skills, and abilities needed to conduct the interview and any related observations? Can the researcher bring together purpose and process when faced with the individual research participant or group of participants? What will the researcher do if the interview does not proceed as planned or if there are technical problems? These are some of the questions researchers need to address to actualize the interview and answer the research questions. Learn more about preparing for the interview in Chapter 9, and learn more about collecting data in Chapter 10.

Closing Thoughts

The E-Interview Research Framework can be used as a tool for planning and designing, as well as dissecting and analyzing, research that utilizes online qualitative data collection methods. The chapters of this book examine each respective part of the framework in depth. Taken together, the chapters offer the theoretical and methodological context needed to develop a coherent design and compelling rationale for the study. Practical suggestions and examples are offered to help the researcher carry out the study. Chapter 11 synthesizes key ideas into a discussion of e-interview research quality, and Chapter 12 discusses trends and influences on qualitative e-research. The content of the book is extended with material posted on the companion website.

2 Aligning Purpose and Design

After you study Chapter 2, you will understand the following:

- The importance of aligning research purpose and questions with theories and epistemologies, methodologies, and methods

- The use of interviews and observations to achieve the purpose of empirical research

- Components of a coherent rationale in support of a research design that uses qualitative data collected online

Research: New Knowledge and Understandings

Empirical research is conducted to generate new knowledge and deeper understanding of the topic of study. Research results inform other scholars who may build on the work, as well as decision makers and practitioners looking for reliable information. An understanding of methodologies and methods of **qualitative research** is essential to online researchers for several reasons. The study-specific goals for collecting data with interviews may influence the overall **research design** as well as the choice of communications technologies. The researcher needs to understand the options when deciding whether one or more methods of data collection are needed to achieve the purpose of the qualitative, multimethod, or mixed-methods study. At the same time, knowledge of available communications

Figure 2.1	E-Interview Research Framework: Aligning Purpose and Design

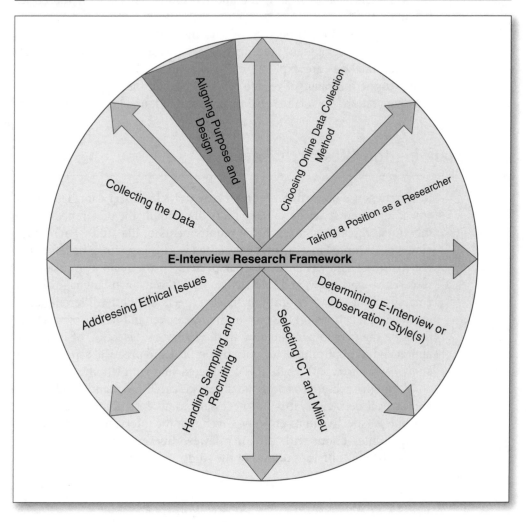

Source: Vision2Lead, Inc (2009–2014).

technologies may influence choice of research methodologies. These decisions need to be made in a coherent way to develop thoughtful rationales and proposals that show alignment of all elements of the research design.

This chapter offers a broad overview of major approaches to data collection to provide essential background that researchers need to grasp the relationship between research tradition, problem, purpose, and design. These principles can be applied in various ways to studies using online interviews and observations. E-research issues for each stage of the design are covered in coming chapters, including data collection styles (see Chapter 4); choices about the information and communications technology (ICT), electronic research setting, and use of visual approaches (see Chapters 5 and 6); sampling and recruiting (Chapter 7); and ethics (Chapter 8).

Each epistemological perspective and methodological approach has its own history, development, and disciplinary focus, and qualitative, mixed, and multimethods are explored extensively in the literature. Doing each justice to the full range of related topics is beyond the scope of this book; thus, suggestions for further reading on research foundations are provided.

Understanding the "Research Interview"

Researchers use many different interview styles to collect data. The diversity of interview styles pertains to more than simply the preferences of the individual researcher or even the requirements of the study. Each interview style is rooted in a distinct view of the world, a system of beliefs about the nature of knowledge, and a perspective on the relationships among researcher, worldview, and knowledge. Each has its own language, with a corresponding set of definitions. Each expects a slightly different set of attitudes and actions on the part of the researcher and has its own way to describe the person participating in the interview. Selection of interview approach has implications for both theoretical and practical aspects of the study—why, how, and where it is conducted, and with whom.

Although each approach to interview research has staunch advocates and critical detractors, it is not necessary to accept an either/or view or any one perspective in its entirety. Given that the interviewer typically has multiple interactions with the interviewee, different approaches may be appropriate for different phases of the study.

WHAT IS AN IN-DEPTH RESEARCH INTERVIEW?

The word *interview* originates from the Latin terms *inter-* (meaning "between, among" or "mutually, reciprocally") and *view* (meaning "the ability to see something") (Soanes & Stevenson, 2004, p. 7). The word *interview* came to English by way of the French word *entrevoir*—meaning "to see each other." A literal interpretation might define the term as "to see something between" people in a "mutual, reciprocal" exchange.

An early, frequently quoted definition calls the research interview a "conversation with a purpose" (Webb & Webb, 1932). Kvale (2007) says that production of knowledge is that purpose and calls for a particular kind of relationship: "The interview is a specific form of conversation where knowledge is produced through the interaction between an interviewer and interviewee" (p. vii). Holstein and Gubrium (2004) define interviewing as a way to "generate empirical data about the social world by asking people to talk about their lives" (p. 204). Seidman (2006) suggests that the goal of an in-depth interview is to "have the participant reconstruct his or her experience within the topic under study" (p. 15).

Although the interview cannot provide a "mirror image of the social world," Miller and Glassner (2004) point out that it does "provide access to the meanings people attribute to their experiences and social worlds" (p. 126). Holstein and Gubrium (1995) see a story emerging from each interview, which is "an interpersonal drama with a developing plot" (p. 16). Denzin (2001) sees significance beyond the immediate players and their interactions:

> The interview is a way of writing the world, a way of bringing the world into play. . . . The interview functions as a narrative device which allows persons who are so inclined to tell stories about themselves. (p. 25)

The interviewer "starts with the participant's story and fills it out by attempting to locate it within a basic social process" to determine what is happening in the interviewee's world (Charmaz, 2003, p. 314). As Rubin and Rubin (2012) describe it, "qualitative interviewing helps reconstruct events the researchers have never experienced" (p. 3). Neuman's (1994) definition describes the relationship between interviewer and interviewee as one with an intrinsic power differential: "a short-term, secondary social interaction between two strangers with the explicit purpose of one person obtaining specific information from the other" (p. 246). Rubin and Rubin (2005) say the interviewer's power entails responsible and respectful actions to "gently guide a conversational partner . . . to elicit depth and detail about the research topic" (p. 4).

As the previous descriptions illustrate, when trying to define the research interview, writers often wax poetic. But their sometimes flowery characterizations contain practical principles. At its simplest, the **in-depth interview** involves interrelationships among the following factors:

- *The interviewer,* who, regardless of interview style, is responsible for ethical, respectful inquiry and accurate collection of data relevant to the research purpose and questions. As a *researcher,* the interviewer places the interview exchange within a scholarly context.

- *The interviewee,* who responds honestly to questions or participates in discussion with the researcher to provide ideas or answers that offer insight into his or her perceptions, understandings, or experiences of personal, social, or organizational dimensions of the subject of the study. Depending on the nature and expectations of the research, he or she may also be called a *subject, respondent,* or *research participant.*

- *The research purpose and questions,* which serve as the framework and offer focus and boundaries to the interactions between researcher and interviewee.
- *The research environment,* which provides a context for the study. Depending on the nature of the study, the environment may be significant to the researcher's understanding of the interviewee. Cyberspace is the research environment for online interviews.

A working definition for the purpose of this book is as follows:

An in-depth interview is a qualitative research technique involving a researcher who guides or questions a participant to elicit information, perspectives, insights, feelings or behaviors, experiences or phenomena that cannot be observed. The in-depth interview is conducted to collect data that allow the researcher to answer research questions, thus generating new understandings and new knowledge about the subject under investigation.

INTERVIEWS IN AN INTERVIEW SOCIETY

The purpose of the research interview is to collect data—data that will be carefully and critically analyzed to generate credible findings. Interviews are widely used for other business purposes, including for hiring or marketing; political purposes, including opinion polling; and also journalism and entertainment. Another important use of interviews in our society is legal—by police, defenders, prosecutors, and congressional investigations. The interview, in its many permutations, has become so pervasive that the term *interview society* is sometimes used to describe it:

We see the interview society as relying pervasively on face-to-face interviews to reveal the personal, the private self of the subject. (Atkinson & Silverman, 1997, p. 309)

In such a society, selves and identities are constructed through interviews. (Schwandt, 2007, p. 164)

Perhaps we all live in what might be called an interview society in which interviews seem central to making sense of our lives. (Silverman & Marvasti, 2008, p. 146)

Professional interviews compare and contrast with those conducted for academic research. The researcher's purpose—to generate reliable knowledge—is somewhat different from the purpose for other types of interviews. By contrast, in a hiring interview, the purpose is clear to both parties and the interviewer aims to draw out responses to specific questions—usually the same questions posed to other applicants. Journalistic interviews are typically conducted to elicit opinions or feelings and may disregard the interviewee's privacy. Casual interviewers may not see the need to objectively screen for less-than-truthful, or unrepresentative, views. Indeed, an extreme view may be the one given time on a television program or in print, because it is more likely to stir controversy and attract more viewers or readers. The common thread in all these interview uses is that the power is firmly in the interviewer's hands and the questioning may be challenging, or even confrontational (King & Horrocks, 2010).

The ubiquity of the casual interview in contemporary media culture places a responsibility on the researcher, who must be able to distinguish for participants how scholarly interviews differ from others in their experience. Unlike other contemporary interviewers, the researcher must work within ethical bounds, under the review of institutional, disciplinary, or professional ethics authorities. The scholarly researcher must be able to justify and defend methods, data, analysis, and conclusions generated by the study, and must also be able to build trust and credibility with individuals who may suspect that anyone who wants to ask about their views has ulterior motives or disrespects their privacy.

Research Epistemologies, Methodologies, and Methods

Although all scholars conduct research to generate knowledge and deeper understandings, each scholar thinks about this process in a unique way. Space does not permit full review of the possibilities here, but it is important to establish a basis for research design that makes sense for studies that utilize interview methods in general and online interview methods in particular. Four interrelated facets of research—epistemology, theory, methodology, and method—are defined for our purposes as follows (see Figure 2.2):

- **Theory** refers to "a unified, systematic causal explanation of a diverse range of social phenomena" (Schwandt, 2007, p. 293).

- **Epistemology** refers to the study of the nature of knowledge, or the study of how knowledge is justified (Crotty, 1998). In qualitative interview research, the constructive nature of social interaction—the view that knowledge is constituted through conversation—is an epistemological position.

- **Methodology** refers to the study of philosophies and systems of thinking that justify the methods used to conduct the research. Methodologies emerge from academic disciplines in the social and physical sciences and, although considerable cross-disciplinary exchange occurs, choices generally place the study in a disciplinary context (Pascale, 2011).

- **Method** refers to the practical steps used to conduct the study (Anfara & Mertz, 2006; Carter & Little, 2007).

Figure 2.2	Interrelated Facets of a Research Design

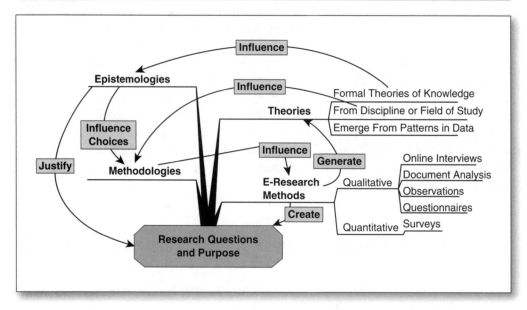

Source: Vision2Lead, Inc (2009–2014).

THEORIES AND RESEARCH DESIGN

Theories, whether they are theories of knowledge or theories from the discipline or field of study, underpin the research design. In some studies, the purpose may be to generate new theory. Theories are interrelated with the epistemology that guides the study and will ultimately be used to justify and explain the new knowledge that emerges from the study. Theories also influence the choice and form of research methodology, which in turn influences the methods used to carry out the study.

Theory plays different roles in qualitative and quantitative studies. Some qualitative researchers frame the study in theoretical terms, while others aim to discover and "ground" theoretical principles in the data. In

quantitative research, theory "is an inter-related set of constructs (or **variables**) formed into propositions, or hypotheses, that specify the relationship among variables" (Creswell, 2014, p. 54). Quantitative researchers start with a theory, develop a hypothesis, and collect data to refine or contradict the theory.

Theories from the discipline or field of study may influence not only the choices of methodology but also the nature and questions of the inquiry. Education, sociology, psychology, business, or science researchers will turn to established disciplinary theories—and to previous studies that explored and tested them—when establishing a basis for knowledge and practice in their respective fields.

When researchers choose epistemology, methodology, and methods, they draw on accepted concepts and practices to create their own frameworks to use in designing, planning, conducting, analyzing, and reporting on the study. (See the template on the book website to map your own research framework.)

EPISTEMOLOGIES INFLUENCE DESIGN CHOICES

Qualitative researchers often base studies on *interpretivist* or *constructivist* epistemologies. The premise of interpretivism, often used synonymously with **constructivism**, is that we "interpret" our experiences in the social world to produce and reproduce meanings (Blaikie, 2004). From this view, we "locate knowledge in the rationality of the knowing subject, rather than external phenomena," thus assuming that knowledge is "not limited to observable phenomena but encompasses a deeper reality which underpins observable appearances" (Sumner, 2006, p. 93). Knowledge acquisition occurs when people interpret their observations of the world and invent concepts, models, and schemes to make sense of experience, and continually test and modify these constructions in the light of new experience (Schwandt, 2007). Subjects construct and interpret their own meanings in different ways, even in relation to the same phenomenon (Gray, 2009).

Another set of epistemologies is loosely described as **critical theory**, a perspective that understands people as historical agents who are participants in action as well as subjects to action (Budd, 2008, p. 175). Researchers who work from these worldviews see research as a means for change and advocacy to "bring about reform that will change the lives of the research participants, the institutions and communities in which individuals live and work" (Bloomberg & Volpe, 2012, p. 29).

Researchers operating from a stance influenced by constructivism (or interpretivism) or critical theory believe that knowledge arises in an individual based on experience and reason. Knowledge and meaning exist in communities of people and define what they share as values, culture, or in their relationships to their environment. The researcher can justify the selection of interview methods based on the desire to uncover the interviewee's knowledge on a topic—or to create new understandings with the interviewee through the research process. The researcher may also want to observe how individuals or groups interact with one another and their environments.

Research justified by interpretivist epistemologies typically uses **inductive reasoning** to come to conclusions. Inductive reasoning works from the specific to the general, from a "particularity (typically a set of observations of some sort) to a broad statement, such as a theory or general proposition concerning a topic" (Fox, 2008a, p. 430). Using inductive reasoning, the researcher looks for patterns, relationships, and associations in the data and constructs generalizations. Researchers use inductive reasoning when they examine how people integrate fragmented phenomena into meaningful explanations of experiences. Qualitative researchers may also use **abductive reasoning**. Abduction is "a practical reasoning mode whose purpose is to invent and propose ideas and explanations that account for surprises and unmet expectations" (Locke, 2010, p. 4). Researchers use abduction to apply an observation or case to a theory (or vice versa) to generate a plausible interpretation (Schwandt, 2007). A third type, **deductive reasoning,** works from the general to the specific. When researchers use deductive reasoning, they state a hypothesis, then gather data (evidence) to support or refute that hypothesis (Shank, 2008). Deductive reasoning is typically associated with quantitative research.

Quantitative researchers often base studies on *objectivist, positivist,* or *postpositivist* views. An objectivist, positivist epistemology describes a worldview that presupposes an objective reality that exists apart from the perceptions of those who observe it. It makes a separation between the consciousness of the observer and the nature of the objects observed. Knowledge is generated by recognizing patterns in the environment that exist independently of individual perception. The goal of research is to discover this objective truth, to better understand this reality (Creswell & Clark, 2007; Schutt, 2006). The positivist view of social reality is that it is "knowable" by researchers using valid forms of measurement (Hesse-Biber & Leavy, 2006). **Positivism** is the basis of fact-based investigation.

Critics of positivism think it ignores context and too narrowly excludes "sources of understanding of the world including those deriving from human experiences, reasoning, or interpretation as inappropriate for scientific enquiry" (Fox, 2008b, p. 660). Social researchers have largely rejected strict interpretations of positivism in favor of **postpositivism.** While positivists aim to prove causal relationships, postpositivists rely on deductive logic to build evidence in support of an existing theory (Creswell, 2003; Hesse-Biber & Leavy, 2006). The postpositivist view challenges earlier positivist notions by recognizing that we cannot be "positive" about our claims of the existence of a common objective reality when studying the behavior and actions of humans because of biases and other limitations of researchers (Creswell & Clark, 2007; Schutt, 2006). The scientific method is the foundation of both positivist and postpositivist views. According to Creswell and Clark, postpositivist researchers make knowledge claims based on the following:

- Determinism or cause-and-effect thinking
- Reductionism or narrowing and focusing on select variables to interrelate
- Detailed observations and measure of variables
- Testing and refining theories (2007, p. 22)

Postpositivists fully acknowledge the role of the researcher as interpreter of data and recognize the importance of reflexivity in research practice (Fox, 2008b, p. 660).

MIXED METHODS, MULTIMETHODS, AND MIXED EPISTEMOLOGIES

The term **mixed methods** describes ways to design studies with qualitative and quantitative approaches used at different stages of the research process (Bryman, 2006; Hesse-Biber, 2010; Johnson, Onwuegbuzie, & Turner, 2007). Mixed methods studies typically use a mix of qualitative and quantitative methodologies and methods for data collection *and* analysis. In such studies data collected with qualitative interviews could be complemented by data collected from quantitative **surveys** or experiments.

Multimethod or *multimodal research* uses more than one qualitative method or more than one quantitative method but stays within the respective qualitative or quantitative methodological framework (Brewer & Hunter, 2006). Given the qualitative focus of this book, the emphasis is on studies that might include a mix of online data collection and interviews, observations, and documents.

Mixed methods may mean mixed epistemologies; researchers must reconcile seemingly disparate views of the world. They need to identify a worldview that encompasses all their methods. They may need to use epistemological bricolage, piecing together different ways to make sense of the inquiry and its findings (Freeman, 2007). From a positivist or postpositivist view, they want to understand social reality, while from an interpretivist view, they want to understand the meanings people give to reality.

Mixed-methods researchers can draw on the theorist Edmund Husserl, who distinguished between "noema," that which is experienced, and "noesis," the act of experiencing, in his 1931 book, *Ideas*. This paradigm may be useful for researchers interested in looking through different lenses to explore factual information or realities of the phenomenon and at the same time understand people's experiences of it. Data about the phenomenon in question may be collected through methods such as document review, observations, surveys, or scientific experimentation. Perceptions and experiences may be explored through interviews with people who have experienced the phenomenon. Thinking in these terms may allow the researcher to appropriately mix strategies and/or methods as needed to find robust answers for inquiries that encompass multiple dimensions.

Mixed-methods researchers can also take a pragmatic stance. **Pragmatism** holds that meaning is determined by the experiences or practical consequences of belief in or use of the idea (Johnson & Onwuegbuzie, 2004). The pragmatic approach looks for plural, rather than polar, positions. Pragmatists take intersubjective attitudes, moving between objective and subjective viewpoints. They rely on abductive reasoning by moving back and forth between inductive and deductive reasoning, "first converting observations into theories and then assessing those theories through action" (Morgan, 2007, p. 71). Pragmatic researchers develop models that match their observations, check them for logical consistency, and test them through further observation and action. Because they believe that research approaches should be mixed in ways that offer the best opportunities for answering important research questions, pragmatists mix epistemologies, methodologies, and methods.

Researchers from diverse epistemological and theoretical viewpoints may choose to collect data through interviews conducted online:

> It becomes clear that what counts as knowledge, and how that knowledge is generated and understood, carry real implications for qualitative interviewing. Methods and methodologies do not exist in a vacuum; rather they are subject to new and extended ways of thinking about the world. (King & Horrocks, 2010, p. 17)

The focus of this book is on using interview methodologies and methods for online interviews in the context of what King and Horrocks refer to as "new and extended ways of thinking." With this premise in mind, *Qualitative Online Interviews* focuses primarily on epistemological influences on design of interview and related observational research studies and will leave to other philosophers and writers broad questions about the nature of knowledge.

METHODOLOGIES AND METHODS: KEY PRINCIPLES AND DISTINCTIONS

The belief that people create, maintain, and live in meaningful worlds is common to most researchers. Literature on the subject describes many ways to collect data about those worlds and meanings by surveying, experimenting, observing, reading documents, or asking people to talk about their experiences. Scholars offer very different approaches to accomplish this seemingly simple task. Some qualitative methodologies align more with research interests in individuals, groups, crowds, or the global society. *Research methodologies* provide conceptual and theoretical frameworks used to design, organize, and explain a study. *Methods* are the techniques used to conduct the collection and analysis of data. Researchers look at the interview as a method to obtain information from *respondents* or construct knowledge with *research participants*.

Each qualitative methodology offers a different vantage point from which to view the research phenomena. Some methodologies allow for study of the practices, activities, or patterns of behavior in groups, while others enable researchers to study attitudes, perceptions, or feelings of individuals. A brief overview of methodologies and design considerations is offered in Table 2.1.

Interviews and Observations in Qualitative and Mixed-Methods Studies

The in-depth interview is a method researchers use to collect data for qualitative or mixed-methods studies. Researchers with a predominantly qualitative orientation may decide that some aspect of the study would benefit from numerical measures or statistical analysis. Researchers who come from a quantitative orientation may find that it is not possible to control variables in social research involving human subjects. They may also realize that a deeper explanation of the meaning and purpose of participants' behavior would enhance study findings. Such researchers may choose to mix qualitative and quantitative methods. The central inquiry for mixed-methods researchers is concisely articulated by Yoshikawa, Weisner, Kalil, and Way (2008): "How does knowledge gleaned from words complement knowledge gleaned from numbers, and vice versa? How and when does the combination of quantitative and qualitative data collection and analytic methods enrich the study results?" (p. 344).

Data collection and analysis methods can be mixed in a number of ways: Qualitative data can be analyzed through either qualitative or quantitative **data analysis** techniques, as can quantitative data. Interview researchers can code responses and then use statistical techniques to analyze data drawn from the transcript codes (Yoshikawa et al., 2008).

In a mixed-methods study, interviews can be conducted as a preliminary step when researchers are defining variables and their relationships. Interviews in the first stage can help identify and define questions to explore more broadly in a subsequent quantitative study. For example, researchers using **Q method** may begin with interviews to collect a large sampling of statements about the questions under investigation (Wilson, 2009). A factor

Table 2.1 An Overview of Qualitative Research Methodologies and Methods

Methodology	Unit of Analysis	Methods for Collecting Data	Methods for Analyzing Data
<u>Action research</u> Applied research involves a process of collaboration between researchers and participants (Newton, 2006, pp. 3–4). Studies aim to identify and develop interventions and change.	Organization(s) or group(s)	Multiple sources of data may be collected through multiple interactions with participants, including online observation, participant observations, one-to-one or group interviews, or focus groups. Action research may also use records or documents, artifacts, and/or online posts or archives.	Inductive or abductive reasoning is used in content analysis.
<u>Case study</u> A study of one or more "cases," clearly defined and bounded exemplars of the research phenomenon	Organization(s) or group(s)	Multiple sources of data may be collected through face-to-face or online observation, participant observations, one-to-one or group interviews, focus groups, documents, artifacts, and/or online posts or archives. Data types may include written field notes, interview transcripts, and/or visual data such as photographs, diagrams or other media, reports, documents, posts, or archival materials.	Inductive or abductive reasoning is used. Yin (2009) identifies five techniques for data analysis in qualitative case studies: pattern-matching, explanation building, time-series analysis, logic models, and cross-case synthesis.

Delphi	Group(s)	One or more types of qualitative data collected in multiple iterations, or "rounds," of inquiry that allow for a series of feedback processes (Hsu & Sandford, 2010, pp. 344–347). Questionnaires with open-ended questions are typically used for the first round, with additional questionnaires or interviews used in subsequent rounds. Questionnaires are typically carried out online, face-to-face, or by telephone. Data types may include written responses to questionnaires and/or interview transcripts.	Data from each round are analyzed and used to craft open-ended questions for the next round.
A study designed to find consensus from a group of experts on a present or future issue or topic			
Ethnography	Organization(s) or group(s), and individual members	"Ethnography unites both process and product, fieldwork undertaken as participant observation, and written text" (Schwandt, 2007, pp. 97–98). Online ethnography and netnography are e-research variations that	Inductive or abductive reasoning is used in content analysis or discourse analysis.
A study of culture(s), cultural influences, or cultural sense making. Studies aim to describe and interpret cultural behavior (Schwandt, 2007, pp. 97–98)			

(Continued)

Table 2.1 (Continued)

Methodology	Unit of Analysis	Methods for Collecting Data	Methods for Analyzing Data
		typically focus on observation and collection of posted data (Hine, 2000; Kozinets, 2010).	
		Formal and informal one-to-one or group interviews conducted throughout the project can contribute data to an ethnographic study.	
<u>Exploratory qualitative study</u> Designed to maximize the discovery of generalizations leading to a detailed and profound understanding of the group, process, or activity under study (Stebbins, 2001, p. 3)	Organization(s) or group(s), or individuals	Exploratory studies may draw methods and approaches from other methodologies as needed. Studies use interviews, observations, and/or documents for data.	
<u>Grounded theory</u> A study designed to generate a new theory, new theoretical constructs, or models	Group(s) and/or individuals	One or more types of qualitative data collected primarily from face-to-face or online one-to-one or group interviews; may also include questionnaires, observations, participant-generated narratives, or documents.	Inductive or abductive reasoning is used from the start of data collection, with substantive coding in comparative constant analysis of data (Charmaz, 2006).

		Data types may include written field notes, interview transcripts, and/or visual data such as photographs, diagrams or other media, reports, documents, posts, or archival materials.	Situational analysis looks at the social *situation*, while grounded theory looks at social *process* (Clarke, 2005).
Phenomenology A study of the ways individuals experience and give meaning to an event, concept, or phenomenon (Moustakas, 1994).	Individuals	One or more types of data may be collected through multiple interactions with participants, typically through in-depth face-to-face or online interviews. Data types may include interview transcripts and research memos.	Inductive reasoning is used. Analysis as described by Moustakas (1994) involves three steps: phenomenological reduction, imaginative variation, and synthesis.

analysis allows researchers to investigate subjectivity of these statements in a systematic way (Brown, 1980, 1993). Researchers may verify and deepen understanding of the statistical analysis through follow-up interviews.

In another example, in a mixed-methods online study (Castaños & Piercy, 2010), semistructured interviews allowed the researchers to identify various perspectives. These perspectives were brought together in the form of a mixed qualitative and quantitative online questionnaire that contained nine general questions participants could answer with a Likert-type scale and also with narrative comments. In a third, qualitative, stage the researchers created a wiki where they could observe participants' interactions.

Alternatively, interviews allow the researcher to collect data to clarify, enhance, or follow up on data collected with a quantitative method. One research team remarked,

> The interview method was used to supplement our previous survey findings, and to gather first-hand, self-reported verbal data from our subjects. Interviews provide access to participants' own language and concepts. We expected that the qualitative nature of this study would provide more in-depth and richer descriptions, such as "how" and "why" . . . and would enable us to draw a holistic, and thus more complete, picture of our subjects. (Chin-Sheng & Wen-Bin, 2006, p. 763)

Mixed strategy is another term that can be used to describe research studies. It is argued here that qualitative and mixed-methods studies both use a mix of strategies. Different levels of structure and varied communication modes and technologies may be used to implement each research strategy.

The interview is not usually a single event—the researcher interacts with the interviewee during the sampling process (see Chapter 7), discussion of informed consent or other agreements needed for research participation (see Chapter 8), explanation of the research purpose and logistics, and then to follow up after the interview (see Chapter 9).

Researchers complement in-depth interviews with other qualitative data collection such as observations, group interviews or focus groups, or review of documents. Document analysis may include the following: review of reports, records, correspondence, diaries, and related items. Observations may include the following: fieldwork descriptions of activities, behaviors, actions, conversations, interpersonal interactions, organizational or community processes, or any other aspect of observable human experience (Patton, 2002, p. 4).

While observers view the subject of the study from the outside—*etic* observation—participant observers adopt an inside view—*emic* observation (Stake, 1995). Participant observers take part in the activity being studied or choose to conduct research on their own activities.

The key to integration of methods—whether within qualitative or with qualitative and quantitative—is to establish a credible rationale for what you are trying to do. In other words, you need to determine and be able to articulate the framework for your inquiry.

Closing Thoughts

This chapter provides a broad overview of profound issues that every researcher must grapple with before beginning the research design. More reading will be needed to fully understand qualitative methodologies; please see the suggested readings listed on the companion website.

Figure 2.3 is a graphic representation of the concepts discussed. A researcher's ability to draft useful conclusions as a result of a study will depend, in large part, on thoughtful and coherent consideration of the four basic aspects of the research framework:

- What *epistemic* views justify and guide my choices of methodology and methods?

- What *theories* of knowledge and what disciplinary theories have been applied to explain key principles related to my subject of inquiry in past research?

- What *methodology* corresponds to the purpose of the study?

- What *method* will allow me to collect and analyze the data I need to answer the research questions? For researchers who intend to collect data with interviews, what interview methodology will inform the choice of a structured, semistructured, or unstructured approach?

Coming chapters will build on these ideas and explore ways you can apply them to design and conduct online research.

Researcher's Notebook

THE E-INTERVIEW RESEARCH FRAMEWORK: CREATING A COHERENT DESIGN

Alignment of purpose and design involves a complex set of decisions in any research. Given that research using emerging approaches often invites additional scrutiny, the researcher who intends to use online interviews for data collection must make careful choices and be prepared to support them. These choices include all areas of the E-Interview Research Framework, as summarized in Table 2.2 and examined in-depth in coming chapters.

(Continued)

Figure 2.3 A Research Knowledge Framework

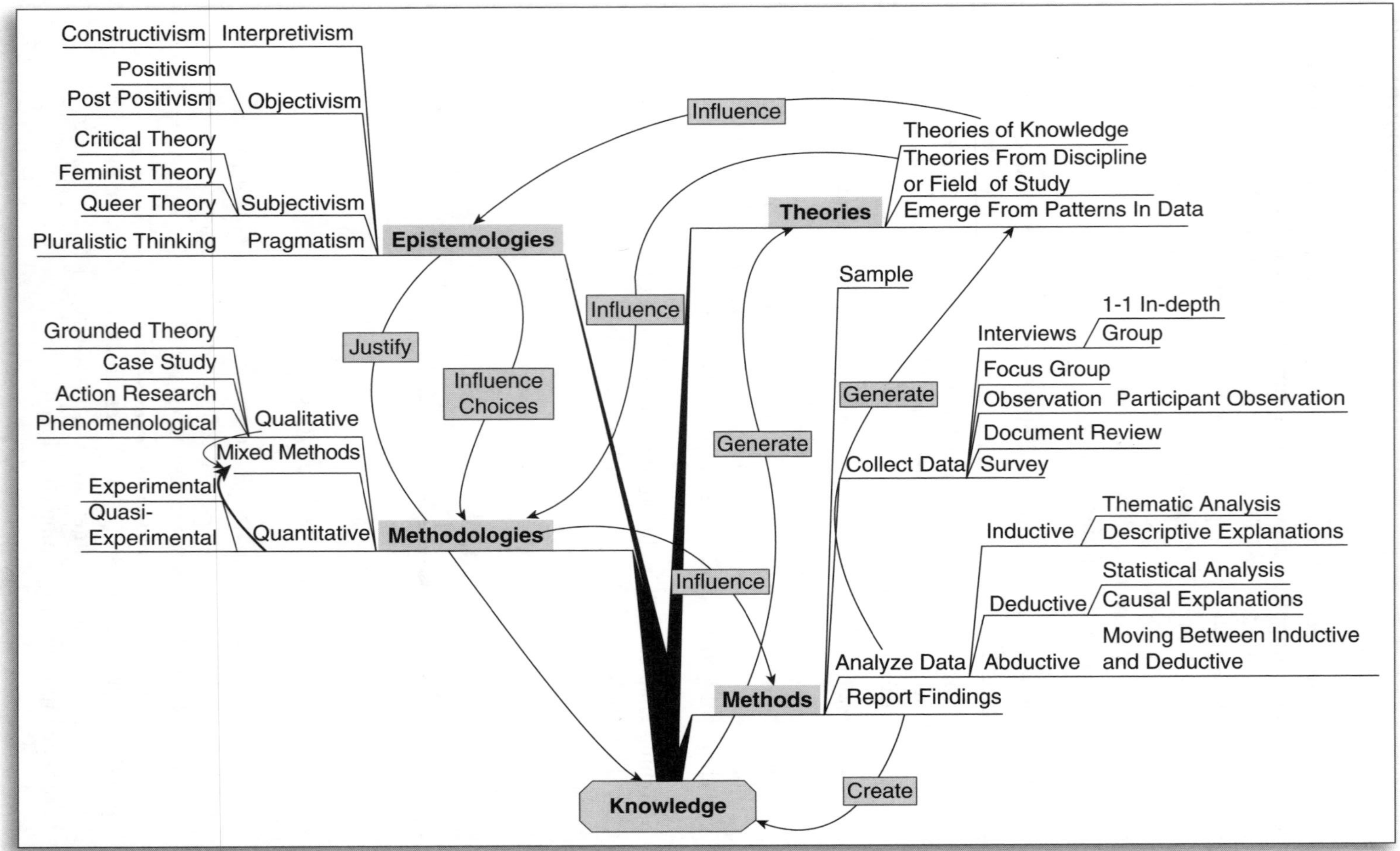

Source: Vision2Lead, Inc (2008–2014).

Table 2.2	Applying the E-Interview Research Framework: Aligning Purpose and Design
Aligning Purpose and Design	
Aligning purpose and design	• Does the researcher make a coherent case for how the purpose, theories, and epistemologies, methodologies, and methods are aligned?
Choosing online data collection method	• Does the researcher offer a clear rationale for choosing online interviews to investigate real-world phenomena or online activities or behaviors?
Taking a position as a researcher	• Does the researcher reveal how his or her position furthers (or conflicts with) the purpose of the study?
Determining e-interview or observation styles	• Does the researcher explain how the style of interview (and if used, observation) aligns with the research purpose? • How will data collected from e-interviews relate to theories? Does the researcher want to explore, prove, or generate theory? Will the selected interview style(s) enable the researcher to make the intended theoretical contribution?
Selecting ICT and milieu	• Does the researcher explain how the style of interview (and if used, observation) aligns with the research purpose? • How will data collected from e-interviews relate to theories? Does the researcher want to explore, prove, or generate theory? Will the selected interview style(s) enable the researcher to make the intended theoretical contribution?
Handling sampling and recruiting	• Does the researcher show how sampling approaches are appropriate given the purpose of the study and e-research approach?
Addressing ethical issues	• Does the researcher explain and address potential ethical dilemmas in the research design? • What benefit to individual or public good will this study generate?
Collecting the data	• How does the researcher plan to work within methodological traditions and paradigms when conducting the interview and other related observations or document retrieval? • How does the researcher plan to maintain a focus on the research problem during the e-interview?

(Continued)

(Continued)

ALIGNING PURPOSE AND DESIGN
ACROSS QUALITATIVE METHODOLOGIES

Most research problems can be studied many different ways—with vastly different approaches and results. In this Researcher's Notebook entry, I explore and sketch out ways to develop the same research topic, using online data collection with qualitative approaches outlined in Table 2.1. The general topic "employee adoption of new technology tools" will be used for the purpose of this exercise.

The Research Problem. When new technologies are introduced, employee resistance can reduce productivity or cause conflict between the early adopters and those who struggle to learn and change from familiar ways of working as needed to use new hardware or software. Scholars studying organizations need a better understanding of the ways employees respond and adapt to changing technologies and related changes in the nature of their work and relationships with others in the organization (Ayyagari, Grover, & Purvis, 2011; Boothby, Dufour, & Tang, 2010; Milliou & Petrakis, 2011; Yu & Tao, 2009).

Action Research. This action research will study the adoption of a new web conferencing platform used by one geographically dispersed department within a large, multinational company. The study will aim to identify the strategies that cause the least disruption and employee stress. These success strategies will be used to develop an organizational change plan for the entire company. Given the phenomenon—adoption of a web conferencing system—the researcher will use this technology as a setting for interviews with meeting conveners during a 3-month period when they are learning and using it. The researcher will conduct online interviews with purposefully selected meeting participants. The researcher will also collect data by observing online meetings held using the web conferencing system. The researcher will analyze data throughout the study and use abductive reasoning to develop explanations for why particular adoption practices work, or do not work, from the perspectives of both meeting conveners and participants.

Case Study. This multiple-case study will aim to compare and contrast how multiple units of an organization plan implement and evaluate adoption of a new online record-keeping system. The researcher will use stratified purposive sampling to select specific subgroups within each unit. To reach the geographically dispersed participants, the researcher will conduct interviews with consenting leaders, managers, employees, and/or IT and tech support staff to explore views of those with varied responsibilities in the implementation. Observations will include online meetings of decision makers during a period when a new technology is introduced and adopted. The researcher will review records, such as rates and nature of calls to tech support, over the period when the new technology is introduced. The researcher will also follow the internal social media to observe and track participants' views and experiences.

Delphi. This Delphi study will aim to reach consensus with a diverse group of experts on the best way to plan the future roll-out of a new technology. The researcher will use maximum-variation purposive sampling to select a highly diverse group of CIOs from different organizations. The iterative rounds will include **online questionnaires**, online interviews, and a focus group with the participants.

Grounded Theory. The grounded theory study will aim to develop a model organizations can use to improve adoption of new technologies. The researcher will use theoretical sampling (Charmaz, 2006), first identifying characteristics based on theoretical constructs and then looking for participants who have those characteristics. Multiple online interviews will be conducted with each participant to learn about successful techniques used initially and habits developed once the technology has become familiar. The interviews will be conducted using the ICT identified by each participant based on his or her communication preferences.

Phenomenology. To explore individual virtual team members' perspectives and experiences of the phenomenon of using a new technology tool, participants will be selected using criterion-based purposive sampling. Criteria will specify research participants' level of experience, technical literacy, type of position, and/or level of authority. Multiple online interviews will be conducted with each participant during the period when a new technology is introduced and adopted to learn about their experiences and perceptions.

Selection of appropriate qualitative methodology allows the researcher to focus the study so it more clearly specifies whose lived experience of what event, activity, or issue will be investigated from what perspective. With this selection, the researcher can go on to look at how other design elements—including online data collection—support the methodological choice.

Key Concepts

- Scholars have developed methodologies and methods that are guided by epistemologies and theories.

- Like any researcher, those who intend to use online interviews need to carefully consider options and choose the appropriate methodology given the research purpose. E-researchers need to be able to explain and support data collection plans in the context of the overall study.

Discussions and Assignments

1. Choose a research problem or topic. Using the methodologies in Table 2.1, sketch out design ideas as was done in the Researcher's Notebook entry.

2. Using your library database or open access scholarly journals, find two peer-reviewed articles based on data collected through interviews. Select one example of a study based on data collected in live, face-to-face interviews and one based on data collected through online interviews.

   - Identify the epistemology, main theories, methodologies, and methods used for each study. Assess whether these elements were aligned in this research design. What would you recommend to improve alignment?
   - Compare and contrast the methodologies and methods in the two studies. Do you believe they made the right choices? What would you recommend?
   - Describe how each study would have been different if the researcher had used another methodology.
   - Describe online options for the researcher who collected data with face-to-face interviews.

On the Web

www.sagepub.com/salmons2e
You will find a media pieces Knowledge Framework template and links and references to additional resources on interview and online interview methodology.

Choosing Online Data Collection Method and Taking a Position as a Researcher

3

After you study Chapter 3, you will be able to do the following:

- Describe how interviews contribute to scholarly studies
- Analyze reasons why researchers choose to conduct interviews over the Internet
- Evaluate the researcher's options in relation to the study
- Consider ways to take a reflexive stance throughout the design and conduct of the study

Researchers make choices at the design stage and throughout the conduct of the study, and every choice influences the direction of the research in subtle or profound ways. Once a determination has been made to conduct interviews online, a number of other related decisions await. Choices explored in this chapter include those associated with crafting a rationale for online data collection methods and reflecting on the position of the researcher in relation to the study. These methods may include collecting data with observations and documents to complement the interview. Chapter 3 explores the basis for choosing online interviews and, once the choice is made, the position of the researcher in relation to the study. In coming chapters, we will consider related choices for interview style (Chapter 4), technology (Chapter 5), and visual research (Chapter 6).

 Researchers opt to conduct interviews online for a variety of reasons. One obvious reason common to almost all online researchers is cost, since online interviews can be planned and conducted without the time and expense of travel. However, cost is just one among many considerations for this important decision. The choice comes down to one or more of three broad possibilities (see Figure 3.2).

| Figure 3.1 | E-Interview Research Framework: Choosing Online Data Collection Method and Taking a Position as a Researcher |

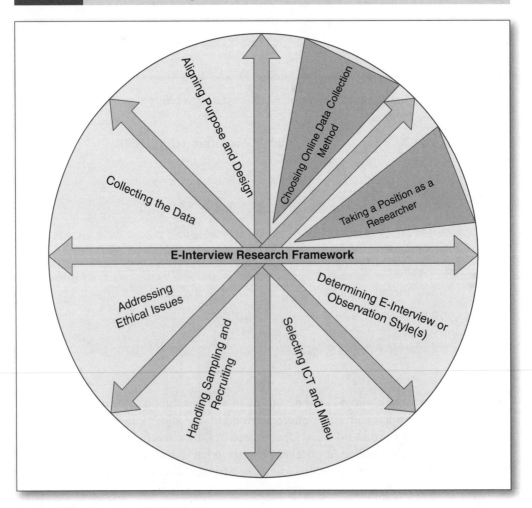

Source: Vision2Lead, Inc (2009–2014).

Choosing to Collect Data With ICTs Based on Medium, Setting, or Phenomenon

1. *Medium:* Information and communications technologies (ICTs) are chosen as a medium for communication with participants. In such studies, researchers and participants use text, audio, or multimedia communications tools. The focus of the inquiry could be any aspect of the lived experience—online or in person.

2. *Setting:* In addition to functioning as the communication medium, the ICT serves as the electronic research milieu. Data collection occurs in an online community, social media site, web conferencing space, virtual world, or game. Again, the focus of the inquiry could be any aspect of the lived experience—online or in person.

3. *Phenomenon:* The purpose of these studies is to analyze activities, experiences, and behaviors on or with ICTs.

Researchers may make the design choice in favor of ICTs as a medium for interviews because online communications allow for significant reduction or elimination of constraints that would make in-person interviews impractical. An increased pool of study participants is possible, including geographically dispersed, international, disabled, or socially isolated individuals and hard-to-reach populations. Researchers can use a virtual presence in settings where a physical presence would not be allowed, such

Figure 3.2   Reasons for Choosing to Use ICTs to Collect Data

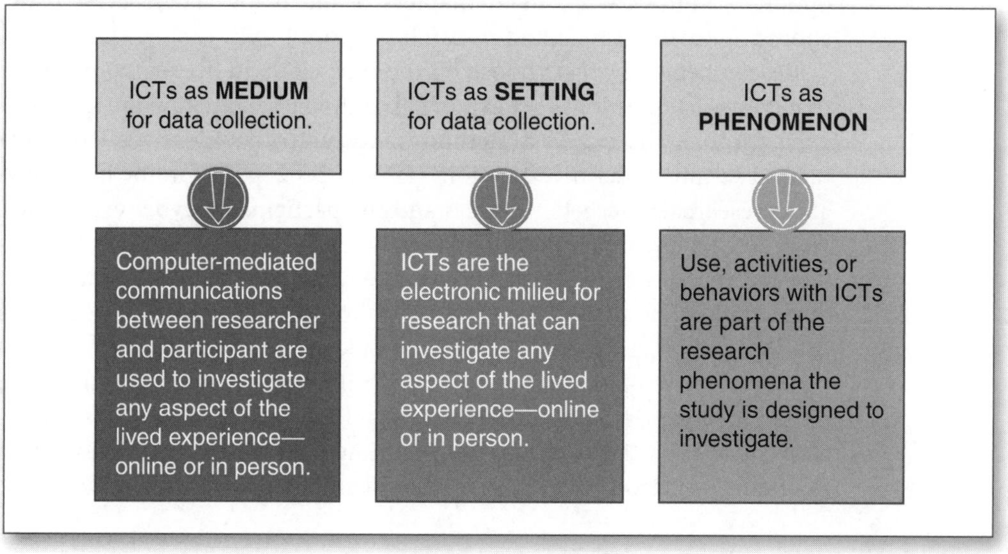

ICTs as **MEDIUM** for data collection.	ICTs as **SETTING** for data collection.	ICTs as **PHENOMENON**
Computer-mediated communications between researcher and participant are used to investigate any aspect of the lived experience—online or in person.	ICTs are the electronic milieu for research that can investigate any aspect of the lived experience—online or in person.	Use, activities, or behaviors with ICTs are part of the research phenomena the study is designed to investigate.

Source: Vision2Lead, Inc 2013.

as hospitals or closed workplaces, or in settings where the presence of an outsider might be disruptive.

Participants may find such methods less stressful and more convenient because they can be interviewed at home or at work, in a familiar and nonthreatening physical environment (Gruber, Szmigin, Reppel, & Voss, 2008, pp. 257–258). They may be more relaxed because they are communicating with the researcher in the comfort of a familiar online setting. More social and personal, as well as business, communications now occur online. Those who spend much of their free time online may not be willing to make the time for or to travel to another location for a personal face-to-face interview but may agree to an online interview (Gruber et al., 2008).

Conducting an interview in a milieu commonly used to connect with family and friends may help some participants be more forthcoming in response to questions. As a result, participants may be more willing to discuss sensitive or personal matters, such as emotions, addictions, sexuality, or disorders that are hard to reveal in person (Ayling & Mewse, 2009; Bjerke, 2010; Cabiria, 2008, 2012; McDermott & Roen, 2012; Paechter, 2013).

Researchers may decide to use varied features of the online setting depending on each participant's preferences—or to use the same features with all interviews. Researchers may make the choice of communications medium because they want to be able to see each participant using video conferencing, to share research-related images or files, and/or to record the interview. People who have difficulties with spoken language or who speak in different languages can participate more easily in written interviews (Bishai, 2012). If specific features are less important, researchers can afford the participants a degree of control over the research process by allowing them to choose between online and telephone or face-to-face options (Hanna, 2012). (See Chapters 5 and 6 for detailed discussion about alignment of ICTs and research purpose.)

Researchers may also choose online interviews to honor the principle that "research questions that explore an online phenomenon are strengthened through the use of a method of research that closely mirrors the natural setting under investigation" (Geiser, 2002, p. 3). Online interviews allow researchers to better understand the participant's cyber experience. As one early researcher described the choice, "Online rather than face-to-face interviews were adopted because the researcher decided to query our target population directly within the context of their (and our) interest in Internet use" (Chou, 2001, p. 574). People who are actively involved in virtual communities, social media, or immersive environments have online identities, friends, and colleagues. Indeed, *virtual methods*—using conventional methods online—are not adequate when the phenomenon of interest is natively digital, grounded in and inseparable from the online world. A qualitative interpretation of what Rogers (2010) calls *digital methods*, those that take advantage of the full dimensionality possible in computer-mediated communications, is appropriate for studying online phenomena. In such interviews, exchanges between the researcher and participant may use the same type of technology or setting represented in the research problem or phenomenon. A study about virtual worlds is conducted in a virtual world; a study about social media is conducted using social media.

Not all researchers will prefer online interviews to face-to-face interviews or other means—nor should they. Some researchers simply believe that recruiting participants and carrying out the data collection online is inadequate for the study. Common reasons for researchers to eschew online interviews include the following:

- The researcher needs to be able to observe the interviewee and/or the research setting throughout the entire interview. Observations of a full range of verbal and **nonverbal communication**, only available when people are physically present, are essential to the study.

- A controlled, private interview setting is necessary to collect private or sensitive information, and the researcher is concerned that others could be present even if they are not visible on the webcam.

- The subject matter is highly sensitive, and physical proximity is needed in case the researcher needs to comfort the research participant.

- The target research demographic lacks access to ICTs.

Certainly, some types of research do require interviews with close or on-site observation, management of the surroundings, and communication options available only when people are face-to-face in the same room. However, even when researchers choose to conduct interviews in person, they may find that online communication is useful for other research steps, including recruiting or screening participants. Online interactions may complement the face-to-face interview. Researchers might use online chat for interview preparation, ask initial open-ended questions with an online questionnaire, or follow up on the initial interview via e-mail.

It is unlikely that all interview research could transition into the online environment, nor would that be desirable. Some researchers will stick to established interview modes, while others will find that new media options allow for meaningful interactions at various stages of the process. By understanding how all available alternatives work, researchers can make informed choices based on the nature of their study and the strengths and constraints of available online tools.

Taking a Position as a Researcher

A value recognized by qualitative researchers is closeness to the participant. Unlike researchers who send out surveys, the qualitative researcher makes close, immediate contact with participants—often to discuss personal views, attitudes, or perspectives. How close is too close? At what point does the degree of intimacy with the organization, group, or participant, or familiarity with the research problem, jeopardize the researcher's ability to carry out the study? When do conflict of interest and/or researcher bias taint the findings? Self-awareness about these issues is critical: Is the researcher receptive to alternative views or already set in terms of expectations for the ways participants will answer questions?

The researcher should know from the earliest design stage where he or she stands to guard against biases or conflicts of interest. Any real or potential bias resulting from insider positions should be transparent to the reader; otherwise, it could undermine the value of the study (see Chapter 11).

Researchers must be able to explain whether, or to what extent, they are working from an outside or inside position. The position of the researcher will inform not only the perspectives the researcher brings to the study but also lenses used to analyze the data. Robert Stake (1995) distinguishes etic issues as those that originate in the literature and/or from the larger research community outside the case. Stake defines emic issues as those that emerge from the actors within the case. VanDeVen (2007) describes the outside researcher as a "detached, impartial onlooker who gathers data," compared with the inside researcher, who is a "participant immersed in the actions and experiences within the system being studied" (pp. 269–270). VanDeVen describes the value found in complementarity of knowledge gained from research that uses the insider perspective to provide a concrete grounding in the research problem in a particular context or situation, together with research from an outside perspective that uses empirical evidence to build a broader understanding of the scope of the problem.

Interview research can be conducted from a full range of positions. Some methodologies are inherently oriented to an insider or outsider research role. Researchers are necessarily insiders when they conduct autoethnographies, participant observations, or action research. Some insiders contribute data in the form of reflective journal entries or field notes to complement data collected from participants. Researchers are typically outsiders when they conduct research using observations or archival or historical records analysis.

The E-Interview Research Framework (Salmons, 2012) offers two ways to think about the researcher's position. The first is with an etic/emic continuum (see Figure 3.3), and the second is by use of metaphors to examine relationships between researchers and participants (see Figure 3.4).

INSIDER (EMIC) OR OUTSIDER (ETIC)
E-RESEARCH POSITIONS

The E-Interview Research Framework posits that the position of the researcher vis-à-vis the research participants and phenomenon is important to consider in a study using online interviews and/or observations. In online research, some degree of balance between insider and outsider perspectives may be needed because at least a minimal degree of knowledge of the situation, culture, and type of experience being studied may help the researcher develop rapport and trust with the virtual research participant. Insider status may help the researcher gain access to an online environment or community. At the same time, the outsider can bring broader, objective understandings of the research problem into the study and devise thought-provoking or challenging interview questions. Whether inside, outside, or somewhere in the middle, the researcher needs to state a clear position and provide a rationale for how that position serves the study.

While the etic/outsider or emic/insider positions seem to be either/or, the distinction between them is not precise. In a discussion of an online ethnographic study, Paechter (2013) draws on Labaree's earlier work and observes the following:

> Labaree (2002) suggests that, while the mainly outsider researcher has to 'go native' in order to understand the local culture, insiders have, by corollary, to 'go observationalist', distancing themselves introspectively from phenomena. Insider positioning also necessitates the observation of oneself and one's relation to the research process; in this way, research makes outsiders of us all. (p. 75)

As this quote explains, in many situations, the researcher may vacillate between insider and outsider perspectives at different stages of the study. The researcher may have inside knowledge, access, or experience without conducting the study from an exclusively emic stance. The insider may begin with questions that emerged from experience, then generate new areas of inquiry after consulting the literature. By practicing what phenomenological researchers call *bracketing* or *epoche,* it is possible to avoid allowing insider knowledge to unduly influence the interview. Whether or not the study follows a **phenomenological approach**, researchers can intentionally clear their minds of preconceived notions and listen without prejudgment to each respective research participant's responses (Moustakas, 1994). The continuum in Figure 3.3 illustrates some of these options.

In online research, a degree of balance between etic and emic perspectives may be needed. At least some knowledge of the online situation, culture, and type of experience being studied may help the researcher develop rapport and trust with the virtual research participant. A continuum allows researchers to think about their status appropos to the study in

| Figure 3.3 | A Continuum of Etic or Emic Research Positions |

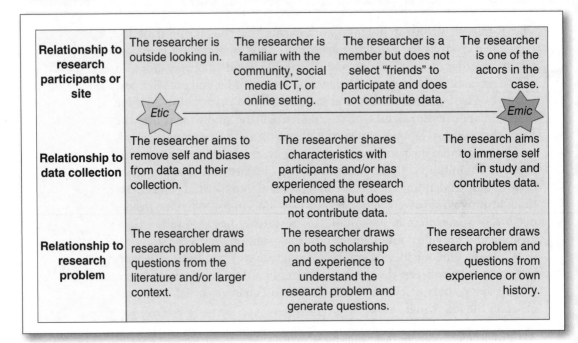

Relationship to research participants or site	The researcher is outside looking in.	The researcher is familiar with the community, social media ICT, or online setting.	The researcher is a member but does not select "friends" to participate and does not contribute data.	The researcher is one of the actors in the case.
	Etic ━━━ Emic			
Relationship to data collection	The researcher aims to remove self and biases from data and their collection.	The researcher shares characteristics with participants and/or has experienced the research phenomena but does not contribute data.		The research aims to immerse self in study and contributes data.
Relationship to research problem	The researcher draws research problem and questions from the literature and/or larger context.	The researcher draws on both scholarship and experience to understand the research problem and generate questions.		The researcher draws research problem and questions from experience or own history.

Source: Vision2Lead, Inc (2009–2014).

a way that, as Couture, Zaidi, and Maticka-Tyndale (2012) suggest, deconstructs rigid binary divisions and encourages relationships that shape, define, and challenge the research experience.

Insider status may help the researcher gain access to and trust from members of an online environment or community. At the same time, if studying a community where the researcher is a member, he or she might be recognized by others, which could lead to biases by the researcher or potential participants. Such a researcher must guard against having too much familiarity with the online setting and assuming understanding of meanings, thereby missing opportunities to probe more deeply. On the other hand, a complete outsider may need to allow extra time to learn about a setting or group before beginning to recruit or interview participants, or conduct observations. To gain entry to the group and access to potential participants, a researcher may face ethical dilemmas about whether and when to join or participate in an online group, social media, or online community for research purposes. In either case, disclosure of his or her identity as a researcher is an ethical matter that will be discussed in depth in Chapter 8.

Whether inside, outside, or somewhere in the middle, the researcher needs to consider choices carefully, clearly state a position, and provide a rationale for how that position serves the study.

Rethinking Research Metaphors: Travelers, Gardeners, or Miners?

A second way to describe the researcher's position with the E-Interview Research Framework builds on Kvale's metaphors of the researcher as a *miner* who digs for the data or a *traveler* who journeys with the participant to discover the data (Kvale & Brinkman, 2009). Most common interview practices lie between these two extremes. Given the e-interviewer's need to cultivate relationships with participants to develop trust and rapport online, I have added a new metaphor: the *gardener* (Salmons, 2010, 2012). The interviewer as gardener uses the question to plant a seed and follow-up questions to cultivate the growth of ideas and shared perceptions (see Figure 3.4). Researchers can use miner, traveler, or gardener approaches within the same study. For example, at a preliminary "mining" stage of the study, the researcher could provide background information needed to develop "seed" questions. The process of cultivation could entail "traveling with" the participant.

The etic/emic continuum meshes with this metaphorical framework. The concept of etic/emic describes where the researcher enters the study, with or without previous knowledge of the participants, setting, or research problems. As we have seen, the concept of etic/emic can also help define shifts of position during the study. The miner, gardener, or traveler metaphorical framework can be used to describe the researcher's intentioned and real relationship with the participants in the process of conducting the study.

Figure 3.4   Metaphors for the Researcher's Position

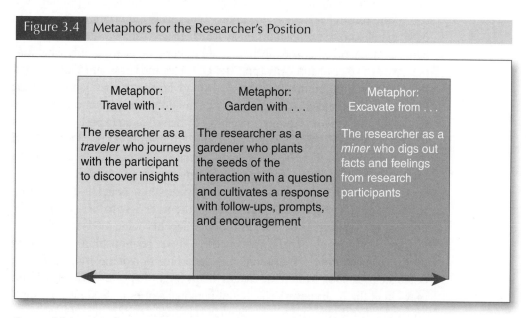

Metaphor: Travel with . . .	Metaphor: Garden with . . .	Metaphor: Excavate from . . .
The researcher as a *traveler* who journeys with the participant to discover insights	The researcher as a gardener who plants the seeds of the interaction with a question and cultivates a response with follow-ups, prompts, and encouragement	The researcher as a *miner* who digs out facts and feelings from research participants

Source: Vision2Lead, Inc (2009–2014).

While at the extreme end of the spectrum a researcher working from a purely etic position might precisely fit the mining metaphor, most researchers will look for ways to apply these metaphors in various ways as insiders or outsiders. The gardener and traveler may find that they need the access to participants and familiarity with the online milieu that comes from either having some level of emic position or collaboration with a gatekeeper who can provide this essential understanding. Again, these models offer a more nuanced set of choices than does an overly simplified etic/emic binary model. By considering these choices at the design stage, the researcher can make decisions that will fit the study, best aligning the researcher with the research purpose in the context of the ICT used for the interview medium and setting. The significance of technology choices in relation to the researcher's position is explored in more depth in Chapter 4.

Positions, Power, and Symmetry in Interviews

The researcher defines and designs the study, argues for its scientific merit, and obtains approvals from institutional review boards and other entities. Whether actualizing the miner, gardener, or traveler metaphor, the researcher is clearly in a position of power within the interview. As the one who recruits the participant and asks for a signature on the consent agreement, the researcher has undeniable responsibility for ethical and productive conduct of the interview. The question, then, is not whether the researcher is in a position of power but how this power is used, and how it is explained to the participants. Day (2012) observes that when researchers make positionality explicit, they provide context to the researcher's voice. She argues that this is important because when participants know the position from which the researcher speaks, they can better understand what is really being said rather than hearing only what they perceive as a voice of authority (pp. 70–71). Miller and Glassner (2004) suggest that the power differential can be used to advantage or may jeopardize the truthfulness of the data. On one hand, it can add confidence and motivation when "the interviewee can recognize him- or herself as an expert on a topic of interest to someone typically in a more powerful position vis-à-vis the social structure" (p. 132). On the other hand, social distances and distrust can be carried into the interview, and interviewees may purposely mislead interviewers (pp. 128, 132). Self-aware researchers consider these issues and make decisions about how to present themselves in the interview to best achieve the purpose of the study, given the kinds of participants being interviewed.

Interviewers minimize the asymmetrical power relationship by promoting a sense of collaboration in a shared task: the production of meaning (Gubrium & Holstein, 2003a). Mutual disclosure helps level the power differential; this may entail the interviewer's sharing of personal stories or feelings, or simply affirming that there is no hidden agenda (Holstein & Gubrium, 2003a).

Some researchers choose to conduct interviews online because they intend to create a less restrictive research medium. In such a medium, participants may feel better able to influence the direction of the research. Greater disclosure, mutuality, and reciprocity between the researcher and participants may emerge in a more egalitarian setting (James & Busher, 2006, 2009). However, in studies where the entire process of recruitment, selection, and interviews occurs online, the necessity of building participant confidence in the researcher and the credibility of the study cannot be ignored. The gardener metaphor is applicable here, since it is unrealistic to expect that participants will enter into a mutual, co-constructive research relationship without effort on the part of the researcher to cultivate a foundation of trust. See Chapter 4 for discussion of online interview style choices conducive to researcher–participant interactions that respect power differentials. See Chapter 8 for discussion of related ethical concerns.

Reflexivity and the Researcher's Position

Interview research is about inquiry—asking questions of participants and analyzing their answers. To build self-awareness throughout the process, the researcher may need to flip the inquiry and question his or her own ways of thinking. How do your own views about yourself, your role, and your position(s) as a researcher affect how you view the participant? How do your knowledge and opinions about the research problem (from first-hand experience or the literature) affect the ways you problemetize the research and interpret potential outcomes? Given that some or all of your communication with participants occurs online, how do you convey these attitudes and what influence do they have on the participant? These and many other questions are the basis for researchers' introspection.

Rallis and Rossman (2012) point out that inquiry is "ongoing, iterative and not necessarily linear" (p. 45). This iterative loop is described as *reflexivity*. Reflexivity enables researchers to place themselves within the study. As Bryman and Cassell (2006) define it, reflexivity is "a sensitivity to the significance of the researcher for the research process, so that the researcher is seen as implicated in the data that are generated by virtue of his or her involvement in data collection and interpretation" (p. 45). Hibbert, Coupland, and MacIntosh (2010) also point to the benefits of reflexivity:

> First, reflection suggests a mirror image which affords the opportunity to engage in an observation or examination of our ways of doing. When we experience reflection we become observers of our own practice. Reflexivity however, suggests a complexification of thinking and experience, or thinking about experience. Thus, we regard reflexivity as a process of exposing or questioning our ways of doing. (p. 48)

These writers are referring to qualitative research generally—but their points are, if anything, even truer for online researchers. Online researchers can anticipate change, and reflexivity is about change in the researcher as well as in the research activities (Hibbert et al., 2010). No matter how well developed the research design may be, changes will occur as the online study unfolds. The researcher's position may also change as familiarity with the research phenomenon and participants grows. As the researcher becomes more engaged in the study, it may become more difficult to retain an objective stance, whether in the data collection or analysis stage. Reflexivity allows for monitoring and self-correction as needed.

Reflective practice is individualized and may involve taking notes, journaling, or simply reflecting on ideas and observations at each stage of the study. A number of free note-taking software products allow for synchronization across computers and devices. LaBanca (2011) suggests using a blog for the purpose of reflective thinking and critique. The reflective blog approach allows others, such as a dissertation supervisor or research collaborators, access to one's progress and developments anytime, from anywhere (LaBanca, 2011). LaBanca listened to the viewpoints of his "auditors," which helped him stay objective and aware of his position:

> By examining the data from different perspectives, especially ones that I had not originally conceived, but valued, I was able to maximize potential for neutrality. It was just as important to receive feedback that was ultimately rejected, because it still allowed for more in-depth reflective analysis. (p. 1167)

The blog, together with comments, generated a chronological record of the study's evolution, which LaBanca reported as very valuable to his own evolution as a researcher. Blogging software is typically free and easy to use; setup usually allows the blogger the option to keep it private, with access given only to invited readers. This precaution means the researcher can maintain appropriate levels of confidentiality.

Reflexivity is not a step to ignore. Whether you set aside time for a purely personal process of reexamination of the research process and your role in it or collaborate in a reflexive process with participants or others, find the approach that works for you.

Closing Thoughts

An unanswered question for online researchers relates to the potential impact of a "cyberspace effect." Does cyberspace as the interview medium or location make people more open and willing to communicate, or does it make them more secretive and protective of privacy? Does the online environment permit or enable them to provide different kinds of responses than they might in a face-to-face interview? Is this difference advantageous or a limitation given a specific research problem. Researchers choosing to interview online will need to consider these questions in the context of their own studies, given the topics under discussion in the interview and the nature of participants' online communication experience. As well, the researcher with some degree of familiarity not only with the phenomenon but with how that phenomenon is discussed in online communities or social media may need to discern the ways associated topics are discussed online.

Optimal directions to take may be more apparent once the researcher has carefully considered all elements of the research as outlined in the E-Interview Research Framework, including considerations for selecting the best online communications technology for the study (Chapter 5), sampling (Chapter 7), and ethics (Chapter 8).

Researcher's Notebook

THE E-INTERVIEW RESEARCH FRAMEWORK: CHOOSING E-INTERVIEWS AND POSITIONS

The E-Interview Research Framework reminds us that design decisions are interrelated. Overarching questions to consider when thinking through decisions associated with the choice to collect data online and taking a position as a researcher are outlined in Tables 3.1 and 3.2.

Table 3.1	Applying the E-Interview Research Framework: Choosing Online Data Collection Method
	Choosing Online Data Collection Method
Aligning purpose and design	• Does the researcher offer a clear rationale for choosing online interviews to investigate real-world phenomena or online activities or behaviors?
Choosing online data collection method	• Does the researcher provide a rationale for decisions about why online data collection approaches are appropriate for the study?
Taking a position as a researcher	• Does the researcher explain how his or her position relates to the choice of e-data collection?
Determining e-interview or observation styles	• Does the researcher show how choices for online data collection and determination of Internet as medium, setting, and/or phenomenon relate to the selected interview/observation styles?
Selecting ICT and milieu	• Does the researcher share whether the study will investigate online behavior in or with a specific ICT or online setting? If so, does that ICT or setting lend itself to interviews and observations?

(Continued)

(Continued)

	Choosing Online Data Collection Method
	• How will the interview use text-based, audio, and/or visual communication options? • If the interview technology has capacity for visual exchange, has the researcher acknowledged the visual nature of the interview in the research design and planned for collection and analysis of visual data?
Handling sampling and recruiting	• Does the researcher explain any implications of the choice of online data collection for sampling and recruiting participants?
Addressing ethical issues	• Does the researcher offer an ethical rationale for the selection of online interviews (and, as relevant, observations)?
Collecting the data	• Does the researcher explain the rationale for design choices to participants, as appropriate?

Table 3.2	Applying the E-Interview Research Framework: Taking a Position as a Researcher

	Taking a Position as a Researcher
Aligning purpose and design	• Does the researcher reveal how his or her position furthers (or conflicts with) the purpose of the study?
Choosing online data collection method	• Does the researcher explain how his or her position relates to the choice of e-data collection?
Taking a position as a researcher	• Does the researcher reveal a position on the etic/emic continuum? • Does the researcher explain a researcher role as miner, traveler (Kvale, 2007; Kvale & Brinkman, 2009), or gardener (Salmons, 2010)?
Determining e-interview or observation styles	• Does the researcher explain how his or her position vis-à-vis the research may influence ability to carry out the selected interview style?
Selecting ICT and milieu	• Does the researcher disclose any conflicts of interest or personal preferences for a choice of ICT that might introduce bias or otherwise influence study results?
Handling sampling and recruiting	• Does the researcher disclose any conflicts of interest with the population?

	Taking a Position as a Researcher
Addressing ethical issues	• Does the researcher discuss whether he or she is a known insider in the selected research setting? If so, how might status or prior knowledge add a risk for researcher bias—and how will this risk be mitigated?
Collecting the data	• Does the researcher need to explain any positional issues to participants when conducting the interview?

STORIES OF ONLINE INQUIRY

Researchers have their own reasons for choosing to interview online and for taking the positions they do in relation to the study. However, these background steps are not usually included in published articles, where results take precedence over process. To provide some insight into such decisions, I share my own experiences with online interview research design. Two studies are referenced as exemplars for this and subsequent Researcher's Notebooks:

- A study about collaborative e-learning that aimed to explore instructional practices and organize results into a Taxonomy of Online Collaboration. Findings of the study were published in several articles and chapters (Diaz, Salmons, & Brown, 2010; Salmons, 2007, 2009).

- A study about women e-entrepreneurs that aimed to explore their uses of technology (Salmons, 2014).

When I decided in 2005 to conduct research on e-learning, it was clear that a global sample would be important to understand a global phenomenon. The need to reach an increased pool of participants without costly travel motivated me to look at online research options. My research had a global scope, but, alas, my budget was strictly local. Although cost was an important reason to choose online interviews, it was not the only or the most important reason. The second reason involved the capacity for visual methods, which will be discussed in more depth in Chapter 6.

As an experienced presenter of webinars, I was familiar with the audio and visual features of web conferencing platforms. **Voice over Internet Protocol (VoIP)** made verbal exchange with participants in many countries possible—without long-distance phone charges. The archiving feature of the web conferencing platform enabled me to save a record of all aspects of such an exchange for future viewing and transcription. Together, these features made online interviews preferable to a face-to-face discussion or even a phone conference—even without

(Continued)

(Continued)

considering cost as a factor. In addition to the interview in the web conference space, I communicated with participants via e-mail (one-to-one and through group e-mail lists).

Many of the same principles applied when I conducted a study of women entrepreneurs' technology uses (Salmons, 2014). This study included participants I identified as *real-world e-entrepreneurs* or as *digital e-entrepreneurs*. Real-world e-entrepreneurs use online communications with vendors and customers, partners and allies, and for promotions and advertising; however, products and services are physical—delivered or purchased on location. Digital e-entrepreneurs similarly use online communications but are in the business of selling electronic products and services such as online writing, teaching, training, and consulting.

The E-Interview Research Framework suggests two primary categories: e-interviews conducted to study online behaviors, trends, or phenomena, or e-interviews conducted as a way to communicate about any aspect of the lived experience. Both of these studies fit within the first category, focusing on the participants' choices, activities, and motivations for using online communications to achieve instructional or business purposes.

The E-Interview Research Framework also posits that the position of the researcher vis-à-vis the research participants and the phenomenon is important to consider in a study using online interviews. The framework offers two ways to think about the researcher's position. For both of these studies, I was largely an outsider; while I teach online and share some characteristics of the e-entrepreneurs, my own experiences were not included in the study data. By having some understanding of the research topics and worklife of participants, I was able to establish credibility and rapport with people I recruited online and never met face-to-face.

The second way to describe the interviewer's position vis-à-vis the study and participants is with Kvale's (2009) metaphors of *miner* or *traveler*—or with a new metaphor, the *gardener* (Salmons, 2012). The position of *gardener* best describes my role in relation to participants in the study of women entrepreneurs, since the process of screening participants, reviewing their blogs and websites before and after the interviews, and communicating with them throughout the study involved a great deal of nurture and cultivation. In the study of online instructors' uses of collaborative e-learning, the role of *gardener* and more of a *traveler* role were used. The stages of screening and preparing participants involved cultivating the level of trust needed for their sharing of what might be considered their own intellectual property. During the interview, I journeyed with them through a visual collaboration using shared whiteboards to map their activities using my prototype Taxonomy of Online Collaboration (Salmons, 2007).

Choices made in the design stage of these two studies drew on established qualitative and methodological foundations, but both involved a degree of experimentation. As such, I needed to stay flexible and open and take time to prepare for more than one alternative in case something did not work out as anticipated. Some of these steps are discussed in the Researcher's Notebook sections of coming chapters.

Key Concepts

- Researchers may choose to collect data online because they are interested in ICTs as a communications medium, research setting, or phenomenon.

- Online researchers need to be transparent about any relationship to the study participants, setting, or ICT that could bias study results.

- By identifying position(s), the researcher can better understand his or her role, as well as how best to leverage interactions with participants to generate robust data.

Discussions and Assignments

1. Using your library database, find two scholarly articles based on data collected through interviews. Select one example of a study based on data collected in live, face-to-face interviews and one based on data collected online.

   - First, look at the rationale given for selecting online data collection. How did the researcher describe the reasons for taking this approach? Did the researcher make a compelling case? How did the basis for selection given by the researcher align with reasons discussed in Chapter 3?

   - Second, did the researchers discuss their positions? Compare and contrast the positions taken for both studies.

2. Locate three or more scholarly resources about researcher bias in qualitative research. Write an essay about how the issues compare and contrast when the study is conducted online. For the issues you identify as unique to the online environment, recommend strategies you think e-researchers should use.

On the Web

www.sagepub.com/salmons2e
You will find related media and links to diagrams, templates, and additional readings.

4

Determining
E-Interview or
Observation Styles

In matters of style, swim with the current; in matters of principle, stand like a rock.

—Thomas Jefferson (1743–1826)

After you study Chapter 4, you will understand the following:

- Levels of interview structure and related interview styles
- Options for using online observations to complement online interviews

Research considerations discussed in Chapters 2 through 7 are interrelated and intersubjective, pointing again to the value of a circular model and a flexible, holistic approach to online research design. It is clear that the first level of thinking involves clarification of research purpose and methodology (Chapter 2). We must know what research problem the study aims to address, how, and why, to decide what kind(s) of data to collect from whom (Chapters 3 and 7). The nature of communication possible in the selected information and communications technology (ICT), characteristics of the online setting (Chapter 5), and use of visual communications or visual research methods (Chapter 6) all influence decisions about the appropriate style of interview(s) to apply and whether additional observational data will enrich the study. At the same time, decisions about the style of interview, including the degree of structure, may influence the choices about the ICT or position the researcher should take in relation to the participants and study as a whole. Chapter 4 offers the

| Figure 4.1 | E-Interview Research Framework: Determining E-Interview or Observation Style(s) |

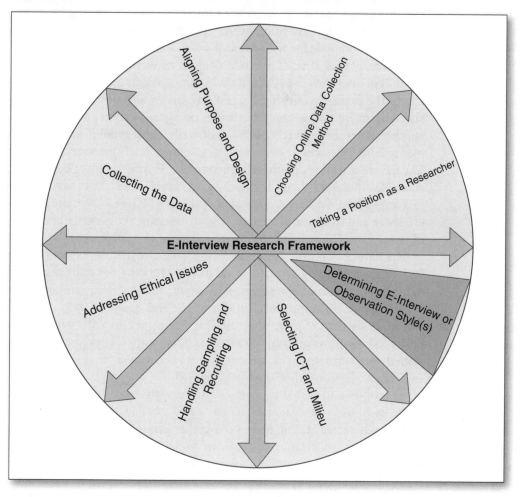

Source: Vision2Lead, Inc (2009–2014).

researcher options to contemplate in terms of the style and structure of online interviews and related observations in the context of the overall research design.

Structure and the Online Interview

At its simplest, the interview is a method researchers use to collect data. Critical differences in interview methods center on distinctions between planning and spontaneity, and on roles and expectations of the interviewer, interviewee, and their interactions during the interview. Stylistic choices are influenced by researchers' epistemic views of knowledge and whether they believe knowledge exists apart from or is created during and through the interview process. Accordingly, researchers look at the interview as a way to obtain information or answers from *respondents* or *interviewees* or to construct knowledge with *research participants*.

Structure is a pivotal methodological concern that influences the method of interview data collection. In this context, *structure* refers generally to the extent to which the questions, order, and process are planned ahead of the interview and the extent of consistency from one interview to another. Does the researcher aim to obtain the same types of answers from multiple interviewees or to make each interview a unique narrative event? The nature of online communication varies greatly depending on the ICT; some technologies lend themselves to more natural, conversational exchanges, while others require some planning. These factors are considered here and continue in Chapter 5, with assessment of visual dimensions of ICTs.

The nature of online communication varies greatly depending on the ICT. Some technologies, such as video conferencing, lend themselves to natural, conversational exchanges. Others, such as web conferencing, require some planning to set up the space and create written or visual materials used to explore the research phenomenon with participants and elicit their responses. Written exchanges may combine predetermined questions that can be cut and pasted into a chat window and informal questions that emerge from within the interview. As well, observations and visual exchanges vary greatly from technologies that allow us to use web cameras and see each other in real time, to virtual worlds where we might observe together some representation of the phenomenon under investigation, to social media sites where we can observe posts and comments while chatting with participants. Each of these options uses one or more different interview or observation style. These factors are introduced in Chapter 4 and studied more fully in Chapters 5 and 6.

Terminology for *structured, unstructured*, and especially *semistructured* interviews is not consistent in the literature. These styles are not usually applied in a rigid manner. Interviewers may choose to organize the entire interview within a similar level of structure or plan an interview with both scripted and emergent questions and interactions. In research where more than one interview is conducted, a variety of levels of structure can be used across the study. Depending on the responses offered, researchers may need to shift into a more structured approach when the interviewee is straying too far off-topic, or to a more conversational approach when it is apparent that the interviewee has important stories on points the interviewer had not thought to include in the script. To reflect these realities, structure is considered on a continuum (see Figure 4.2).

Typology of E-Interview Structures

The Typology of E-Interview Structures (Salmons, 2010, 2012) illustrates relationships between the level of structure and flexibility in online interview research (see Figure 4.2). On one end of the spectrum, **structured interviews** use predetermined questions in a planned order when interviewers query respondents. At the other end of the spectrum, few or no questions are framed in advance and conversational, **unstructured interviews** occur between researchers and participants. Between these extremes, there are many variations generally termed **semistructured interviews**: interviews with a basic structure but varying degrees of flexibility in planning and exchange.

Figure 4.2	Typology of Interview Structures

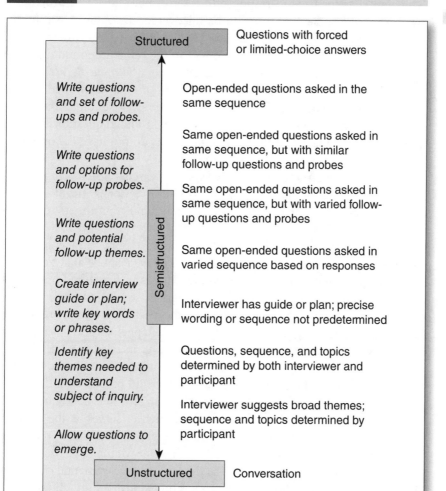

Source: Vision2Lead, Inc (2009–2014).

Figure 4.3 later in this chapter outlines a few considerations. In these interviews, the participant may co-create or co-produce knowledge with the researcher. Most common interview practices lie between these two extremes. The metaphor of the *gardener* describes these semistructured interviews, where the researcher is prepared but flexible and cultivates each unique interview relationship (see Figure 4.4 toward the end of this chapter).

STRUCTURED INTERVIEWS

Structured and *survey* interviews occupy one end of the continuum with what is essentially a live version of the questionnaire. The metaphor for interaction at this end of the continuum is excavation; the *miner* dispassionately digs for facts in response to a set of questions. "'Knowledge' is waiting in the subject's interior to be uncovered, uncontaminated by the miner" who conducts the interview (Kvale, 2007, p. 19). In structured interviews, the same questions are posed in the same order and maintain a consistent, neutral approach to questioning (Fontana & Frey, 2003; Schaeffer & Maynard, 2003; Schutt, 2006). Options may be limited to multiple choice, yes/no, or three to five alternative responses on a Likert-type scale. Structured interviews may also pose open-ended questions to elicit short narrative answers. Interview respondents do not have the option to redirect questions or elaborate on responses.

To prepare for structured interviews, the researcher articulates all questions in advance. Because the role of the interviewer is meant to be as neutral as possible, the researcher may recruit and train others to implement the interview.

Survey interviews usually ask respondents to report on facts or assess attitudes on a product, candidate, or event. The data can be analyzed using either qualitative or quantitative methods. However, structured interviews can serve other research purposes. One type of structured interview, the "laddering interview," is designed to move the discussion from a lower level of abstraction to a higher level of abstraction (Reppel, Gruber, Szmigin, & Voss, 2008). Beginning with an elicitation stage, interviewers use sorting techniques to derive interviewee preferences and develop criteria. Criteria thus derived act as the starting point for "laddering" probes, with the interviewer repeatedly asking questions about why an attribute, consequence, or value is important to the respondent. Each answer serves as the starting point for the next question. The laddering process continues until the respondent either repeats answers or is not able or willing to answer.

Structured interviews can serve as the first or developmental stage of a multistage, multimethod, or mixed-methods study. As an initial stage, structured interviews can help the researcher generate items for exploration using other methods (Gehling, Turner, & Rutherford, 2007). The structured interview may be followed with a survey in a quantitative or mixed-methods study or with observations and/or less structured interviews in a qualitative study.

SEMISTRUCTURED INTERVIEWS

Semistructured interviews endeavor to balance the organization and framework of the structured approach with the spontaneity and flexibility of the unstructured interview. The researcher prepares questions and/or discussion topics in advance and generates follow-up questions during the interview. In more structured *standardized open-ended interviews,* interviewers may ask the same open-ended questions in the same sequence but with varied follow-up questions and probes. They also may ask a consistent set of questions but vary the sequence based on responses. In more flexible *guided open-ended interviews,* researchers create themes or develop an "interview guide" of topics to discuss but do not develop precise wording or sequence in advance of the interview (Kvale, 2007).

Responsive interviewing, an approach that includes flexible interviews based on main initial questions, is based on trust, mutual respect, and relationships between interviewer and interviewee (Rubin & Rubin, 2012). Another unstructured approach recommends a three-interview series (Seidman, 2006). In Seidman's phenomenological approach, there is an overarching structure to the series, with a specific theme for each respective interview. Within the series of "Focused Life History," "Details of Experience," and "Reflection on the Meaning" interviews, a semistructured approach is used (pp. 17–19).

A metaphor for the semistructured interviewer is the *gardener.* The gardener realizes that harvest is not possible without planting the seed. At the same time, many seeds can be sown without results if contextual conditions of weather, soil, and care are not in balance. The researcher–gardener realizes that the question seeds the participant's thought process. With reflective listening and encouragement, the answer will emerge. With it, both the researcher's and the participant's understanding will grow.

UNSTRUCTURED INTERVIEWS

At the other end of the continuum, unstructured interviews are used to collect data through what is essentially a conversation between the researcher and participant. The metaphor for interaction at this end of the continuum is the "traveler on a journey to a distant country whose journey leads to a tale to be told upon returning home." The traveler has conversations with people encountered along the way, asking questions and encouraging them to tell their own stories (Kvale, 2007).

In the unstructured interview, questions emerge from the context and events occurring in the circumstance of the interview. The unstructured interview may be a planned discussion in a formal interview setting. Alternatively, it can be naturalistic, meaning it occurs onsite where the participant lives or works, in conjunction with other field or participant observations. Data collected from unstructured interviews are different for each person interviewed and may be different for the same person interviewed on multiple occasions (Patton, 2002). Some forms of unstructured interviews are described in the following.

Life Story or Oral History Interviews

Researchers interested in the "continuity and wholeness of an individual's life experience" look to narrative forms of inquiry to elicit data (Clandinin & Connelly, 2000, p. 17). Oral histories may tap into the individual's first-hand testimony to historical, community, or social events or processes, or describe "turning-point moments" in people's lives (Denzin, 1989; Smith, 2003). Some interviewers may ask a set of questions to get the story started, while others may simply ask participants to tell their stories in their own way (Clandinin & Connelly, 2000).

Postmodern Interviews

The term *postmodern* refers to a set of "orienting sensibilities" rather than a particular kind of interviewing (Holstein & Gubrium, 2003c). These sensibilities may mean blurred boundaries between interviewer and interviewee, new ways of collaborative construction of meaningful narratives in the interview that are often constructed using artistic or electronic media (Fontana, 2003; Holstein & Gubrium, 2003c, p. 5). An important postmodern sensibility points to the **active interview,** a term that signifies the importance of a mutual exchange and highly interactive interview. (Note: the active interview does not refer to "action" research.) Meaning is not simply elicited by interviewers' questioning; it is actively and communicatively assembled in the interview encounter. "Respondents . . . are constructors of knowledge in collaboration with interviewers" (Holstein & Gubrium, 2003a).

Two types of active interviews that can be described as postmodern are **co-constructed narratives** and **creative interviews.**

Co-Constructed Narratives

Researchers and interviewees may share stories in collaborative interviews through co-constructed narratives, which means that the narratives are jointly created. The narrative process is called *mediated* when the researcher monitors the exchange between relational partners and *unmediated* when a researcher and interviewee, or two researchers, exchange and study their own stories (Ellis & Berger, 2003).

Creative Interviews

Jack Douglas's (1984) book *Creative Interviewing* introduced a naturalistic, life-story approach to interviews. These unstructured interviews occur on location in situational, everyday settings of people in society (Douglas, 1984; Fontana & Frey, 2003). For example, a researcher might observe someone at work and ask him in an informal but disciplined exchange to explain what he is doing, why he did it, and what he has to think about to do the work (DeVault & McCoy, 2002).

Postmodern researchers "travel with" their participants. They object to the image of interviewees as "passive vessels of answers" for interview questions posed by a neutral interviewer (Gubrium & Holstein, 2003a). Postmodern researchers see interviewees as participants in, rather than subjects of, research (Fontana, 2003; Holstein & Gubrium, 2003a, 2003c). Looking at interviews as generative processes happening in the interactions between researcher and participant "transforms the subject behind the respondent from a repository of information and opinions or a wellspring of emotions into a productive source of knowledge" (Gubrium & Holstein, 2003a, p. 32). The interviewer uses active listening to create a sense of equality and interdependence with the participant (Gubrium & Holstein, 2003a). The *what* (interview purpose and guiding issues) and the *how* (respectful questioning) are fully meshed in the **postmodern interview.** Issues guiding the interview questions and interviewees' responses emerge in the interview (Ellis & Berger, 2003; Gubrium & Holstein, 2003a).

Structure and Technology

In online interviews, decisions about the degree of structure may also relate to decisions about the technology and online setting for the interviews and/or observations (for more on this, see Chapter 5). There are no firm rules about what ICT aligns with what level of structure. Like many topics in qualitative research, the answer starts with "it depends . . ." Some considerations for each interview type are addressed next.

STRUCTURED INTERVIEWS

- What technology will allow the researcher either to read verbatim the questions and response options or to cut and paste prepared questions in text? Which will be preferable to participants? What will make it easy for participants to see or hear the questions and respond quickly? In a fully structured interview, is there a reason to conduct it synchronously (given the need to coordinate schedules to do so) or can you securely e-mail or post the questions for asynchronous response?

- Will the structured interview be accompanied by some data collection via observation? If so, will the researcher look for the same kinds of nonverbal cues during the interview and the same kinds of posts, records, or activities for each participant? Will the same ICT be used for the interviews and for observations?

SEMISTRUCTURED INTERVIEWS

- What technology allows the researcher to deliver the main questions so participants can easily see or hear them? What technology allows for timely delivery of follow-up and probing questions?

- To what extent are synchronous spoken or written exchanges used for all or some of the interview? Are both researcher and participant frequent text-chat communicators who are able to think and type quickly enough to make a less-structured interview work smoothly? Or might the researcher find that trying to think of questions or follow-ups and then type them is too slow a process.

- If visuals will be used to prompt discussion, will they be used in the same way across all interviews (more structured) or will different images or visual exchanges be used in different ways for each respective interview? (For more on visual interviews, see Chapter 6.)

- If a virtual world or game is used as a setting, will time be needed to navigate to different settings or show various features, possibly creating a gap between question and response? Would this type of interview be best conducted as a semi- or unstructured interview?

- Will the semistructured interview be accompanied by some data collection via observation? Will the same ICT be used for the interviews and for observations? To what extent will observations be consistent from one participant to the next? What kinds of nonverbal cues will the researcher look for during the interview, or will the researcher look for emergent cues? What kinds of posts, records, or activities will the researcher observe to learn about each participant? Or will the researcher follow up on particular responses by looking for related posts and materials after the interview?

UNSTRUCTURED INTERVIEWS

- Can you use an ICT that allows for natural dialogue, such as video or web conferencing, so the conversation can easily flow and change course? If you want to conduct an asynchronous, unstructured interview, how will you retain focus on the research purpose between communications?

- Will the semistructured interview be accompanied by some data collection via observation? Will the same ICT be used for the interviews and for observations? Will the researcher develop observation approaches based on each interview? What will guide such observations?

Motivations for Online Interviews and the Typology of E-Interview Structures

Interview structure and technology choices also relate to the motivation for choosing online interviews for data collection. As discussed in Chapter 3, technology can serve the purpose of communications medium, research setting, or the phenomenon at the center of the research problem. The researcher who chooses to conduct interviews online to discuss lived experiences more generally can determine what kind of interview style best accommodates participants' schedules, comfort levels, and access to an ICT. The researcher who chooses to conduct interviews online to discuss online behaviors, activities, or experiences needs to factor in the features, characteristics, and limitations of participants and the online community, social media site, or other online research setting (see Figure 4.3).

The Researcher's Position and the Typology of E-Interview Structures

Representative points on the Typology of E-Interview Structures continuum relate to the interviewers position, as discussed in Chapter 3. The three metaphors—miner, traveler (Kvale, 2006, 2007), and gardener (Salmons, 2010, 2012)—can be associated with the roles researchers take when conducting different types of interviews. On one end of the continuum, the researcher is characterized as a *miner* who digs out facts and feelings from research subjects. These interviews may be designed with limited response options: yes/no or multiple-choice questions. In these tightly scripted interviews, research subjects have

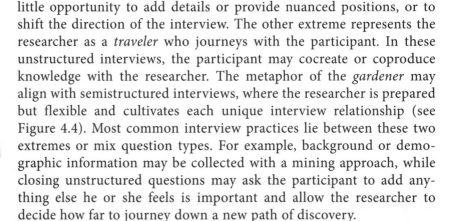

Figure 4.3 Medium, Setting, or Phenomenon, ICT and Interview Style

Online interviews: Medium or setting to investigate real-world, offline experiences			Online interviews: Medium or setting to investigate online experiences or phenomena		
What tools will enable interviewees to participate comfortably in an online interview?			**What tools correspond to online phenomena being studied?**		
What tools and media does interviewee use? What is the ICT literacy level?	What type of online communication (text, audio, visual) will allow collection of most relevant data?	What level(s) of interview structure fit the research purpose, participants, and ICT?	Is it important to use the same style and type for all interviews?	To what extent can interview experience mirror interactions being studied?	Does the online setting have communication norms or parameters, use of avatars or other features?

Source: Vision2Lead, Inc (2014).

little opportunity to add details or provide nuanced positions, or to shift the direction of the interview. The other extreme represents the researcher as a *traveler* who journeys with the participant. In these unstructured interviews, the participant may cocreate or coproduce knowledge with the researcher. The metaphor of the *gardener* may align with semistructured interviews, where the researcher is prepared but flexible and cultivates each unique interview relationship (see Figure 4.4). Most common interview practices lie between these two extremes or mix question types. For example, background or demographic information may be collected with a mining approach, while closing unstructured questions may ask the participant to add anything else he or she feels is important and allow the researcher to decide how far to journey down a new path of discovery.

The role, position, and power dynamic of the researcher are related to the structure as well. (For more on positions, roles, and power, see Chapter 3.) Anyone could conduct the structured interview, and perhaps a research assistant would be preferable since the interviewer needs to remain neutral for this interview type. In semistructured and unstructured interviews, however, the researcher must respond to the participant and make decisions in the moment about whether to allow the participant to go off in a new direction or to bring the participant back to the researcher's agenda.

Figure 4.4   Typology With Interview Metaphors

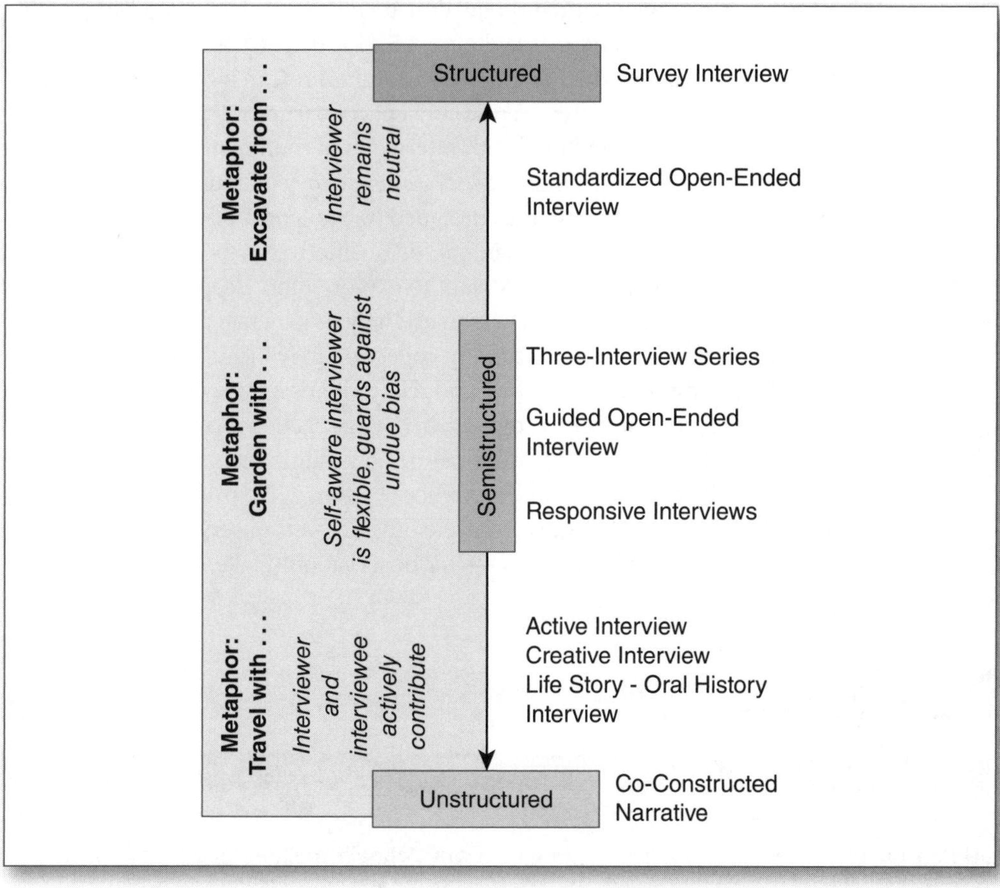

Source: Vision2Lead, Inc (2014).

Interviews in Qualitative, Mixed-Methods, and Multimethod Studies

The in-depth interview is a method researchers use to collect data for qualitative or mixed-methods studies. *Qualitative research* "aims to produce rounded and contextual understandings on the basis of rich, nuanced and detailed data" (Mason, 2002, p. 3). *Mixed methods* is an umbrella term covering a variety of combinations of qualitative and quantitative methods. Online interviews may be a part of a study or an entire qualitative study that also includes other data collected online or face-to-face. Or online interviews may be used to gain a deeper understanding of the experiences that underlie other numerical data or statistical analysis.

Qualitative researchers have long collected data by recording their observations of interview participants in field notes and visually with photography or film. Types of qualitative data collection are not so neatly distinguished online; there are a lot of overlaps (see Figure 4.5). Participant observers take part in the activity being studied or choose to conduct research on their own activities. The Internet has extended the concepts of participant and outsider observations that can be combined with interviews in multimethod studies. Online interviews may include some observations or review of user-posted material from the participant, or studies designed to draw data primarily from observations, use of user-posted material, or qualitative analysis of big data may reveal patterns that researchers want to explore more deeply with interviews. Interviews allow such researchers to ask why or generate alternative explanations for seeming trends. Document collection may include review of reports, records, correspondence, diaries, and related items. Observations may include fieldwork descriptions of activities, behaviors, actions, conversations, interpersonal interactions, organizational or community processes, or any other aspect of observable human experience (Patton, 2002, p. 4). While observers view the subject of the study from the outside—*etic* observation—participant observers adopt an inside view—*emic* observation (Stake, 1995).

| Figure 4.5 | Multimethod Online Qualitative Studies |

Data Collection for Qualitative Research	Online Data Collection
Interviews	**E-Interviews**
Data Collection:	**Data Collection:** Questions posed using synchronous or asynchronous ICTs.
Data: Researcher collects in-depth responses to questions or prompts in person.	**Data:** Text, graphics or visuals, recorded audio or vidio.
Observations	**E-Observations**
Data Collection:	**Data Collection:**
Researcher is participant or outside observer of live events, cultures, etc. exemplifying research focus or phenomenon.	Participant or outside observer of public/private live or recorded online events or discussions.
Data: Field notes, recordings.	**Data:** Field notes, copied text/images, artifacts, recordings.
Documents	**E-Documents**
Data Collection:	**Data Collection:**
Researcher finds and reviews reports, records, journals, correspondence, news items, etc.	Researcher finds and reviews public or private documents, records and posts.
Data: Field notes and excerpts.	**Data:** Field notes, screen shots, copied text/images.

Source: Vision2Lead, Inc (2010–2014).

Researchers can mix online interviews and online observations in numerous ways. A synchronous interview–observation mix is one of those ways. It is possible to record interviews conducted in video or web conference settings. This approach is most comparable to the traditional face-to-face interview. Using a webcam, the researcher can see the participant and the participant's immediate environment. The participant can share artifacts by bringing them into the camera's range. Since the interview is recorded, the interviewer can focus on questions during the interview, then analyze nonverbal cues and other visual elements such as attire when viewing the archive. A semi- or unstructured interview will work in this example, and to complement the "interview guide" the researcher may construct an "observation guide"; that is, the researcher may identify in advance particular elements to watch for during the exchange.

Interviews could follow observations or vice versa. Whichever comes first can use an unstructured style to allow for a broad view of the topic as the basis for more structured interview questions or observation criteria. Or a more structured style of interview and precise observation can become the basis for a wider-ranging, unstructured second stage of the study.

One approach could involve mixing asynchronous observations with synchronous or asynchronous interviews. The researcher may use the Internet to do some background research on the participant, his or her company, school, interests, or other details. This research can be a formal part of the study and thus included in the informed consent agreement, or it can be a more informal scan of publicly available information (see Chapter 8). In such studies, findings from the observations may become the basis for semistructured interview questions. Alternatively, the participant may discuss online involvement or experiences in the interview that the researcher wants to view to gain a better understanding. In such a case, the interview may precede the observations.

The key to integration of methods is to establish a credible rationale for what you are trying to do. In other words, you need to determine and be able to articulate the framework for your inquiry. Where we make the distinctions will impact issues of consent, open versus covert data collection, and of course the research design. (See Chapter 8 for more on consent and ethical ramifications of these decisions.)

Closing Thoughts

This chapter offers an overview of an important aspect of online research design: the alignment of interview style and approach with the purpose of the study. In an online setting, naturally, the affordances and limitations of the selected ICT are always a critical factor in decision making. While some essential questions are discussed in Chapter 4, the issues of interview and observation style are interwoven with the other dimensions described in the E-Interview Research Framework and in coming chapters.

Researcher's Notebook

THE E-INTERVIEW RESEARCH FRAMEWORK:
DETERMINING STYLES FOR ONLINE INTERVIEWS

The E-Interview Research Framework is based on the premise that research design should be approached holistically. Key questions related to decisions about online interview style are outlined in Table 4.1.

Table 4.1	Applying the E-Interview Research Framework: Determining E-Interview or Observation Styles
	Determining E-Interview or Observation Styles
Aligning purpose and design	• Does the researcher explain how the style of interview (and, if used, observation) aligns with the research purpose? • How will data collected from e-interviews relate to theories? Does the researcher want to explore, prove, or generate theory? Will the selected interview style(s) enable the researcher to make the intended theoretical contribution?
Choosing online data collection method	• Does the researcher show how determination of Internet as medium, setting, and/or phenomenon relates to the selected interview/observation styles?
Taking a position as a researcher	• Does the researcher explain how his or her position vis-à-vis the research may influence ability to carry out the selected interview style?
Determining e-interview or observation styles	• Does the researcher plan to use *structured, semistructured, unstructured*, or a combination of styles for the interview(s)? • Does the researcher plan to complement interviews with consistent observational approaches or with approaches unique to each participant?
Selecting ICT and milieu	• How does the researcher align ICT functions, features, and/or limitations with the selected e-interview style(s)? • What communications options with the selected ICT might influence the style or structure of the interview? • Where will the interaction fall on the *time–response continuum*? • Does the researcher use the same or different ICT for the interview and observation(s)?

	Determining E-Interview or Observation Styles
Handling sampling and recruiting	• Are there any concerns about whether participants are willing and able to participate in the selected style of interview? If so, are concerns addressed or is flexibility built in to address variations in participants? • Does the researcher explain any issues that would make the intended style problematic for the population? • What does the researcher need to explain to potential participants during the recruitment stage?
Addressing ethical issues	• Does the researcher identify any potential ethical issues related to the data collection style?
Collecting the data	• Does the researcher need to explain any aspects of the data collection style to participants? • Does the researcher have the experience needed to conduct interviews as planned—including ability to devise follow-ups, probes, or unstructured questions?

STORIES OF ONLINE INQUIRY

As noted in the Researcher's Notebook in Chapter 2, most research problems can be studied many different ways. In this Researcher's Notebook entry, I explore and sketch out the different ways each interview and related observation style could be adopted. Interviews—whether online or not—may be designed so the entire exchange falls within a similar degree of structure, or a variety of questioning styles can be used. A general topic, "career change after a job loss," will be used for the purpose of this exercise. Examples will be keyed to Figure 4.6.

For an online interview, in addition to serving the purpose of the study, the main considerations are about whether preparation is needed in the specific ICT being used for the interview. These issues are addressed in the Chapter 5 Researcher's Notebook.

1. *Structured.* The topic of "career change after a job loss" could be explored with yes/no or multiple-choice questions in a structured interview:

   • Did your career change involve going from a professional to a nonprofessional job, yes or no?

   • Does your new career use your education and experience, yes or no?

(Continued)

(Continued)

- Did you make more money or less money after your career change?
- Which did you prefer, your previous career or your current career?
- Which career was better for work–life balance?

Figure 4.6 Examples Using the Typology of Interview Structures

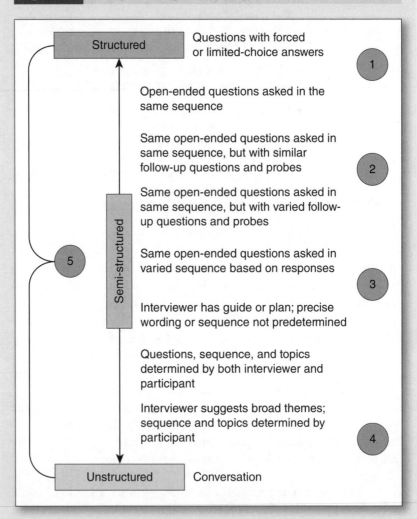

Source: Vision2Lead, Inc (2009–2014).

Simple, quick structured questions can be used as a one-time exchange, or the researcher can establish a regular daily or weekly check-in with the participant. Structured interview questions could provide the foundation for subsequent stages of the study, either for more open-ended questioning in another interview or for data collection with observations.

2. *Semistructured.*

- How do you perceive this career change?
- Do you feel you are going up or down the career ladder? Why?
  - ○ Are you happy about the direction you are going?
  - ○ Why is [*response*] important to you?
  - ○ How do others respond to this change?
- Discuss how you are using your past experience and education and/or learning new skills.
- Share your thoughts and feelings about work–life balance before and after the change.
  - ○ How has your spouse/partner/immediate family responded to this change?
  - ○ What new interests have you developed since the change?

3. *Unstructured.*

- Tell me about your career change and what it means for your work and your personal life.

4. *Mixed.*

- Do you feel you are going up or down the career ladder? Why?
- Are you using past experience or developing new skills in your current work?
- Tell me about how you define career success and how your ideas about career and success have changed in the past 10 years.
- What do you hope to achieve in your new work life and/or your personal life?

A mixed-structure interview could begin with some overarching questions to steer the participants toward answers relevant to the research purpose and also some unstructured, broadly open-ended questions that allow the participants to take the responses in whatever direction seems important to them.

Key Concepts

- Researchers and theorists define *interview* in ways that create implications for interviewers' and interviewees' roles, and for communication and questioning styles. These styles range from unstructured to highly structured. Many researchers choose semistructured approaches that allow for consistency between interviews, as well as flexibility to follow up based on responses.

- Just as interviews can be more or less planned given the level(s) of structure used, observations may take many forms. When used to complement online interviews, observations may use the same or different technologies and may be structured to collect similar or different data from or about each participant.

- When conducted online, choices for interview style are inextricably linked to choices for the communications technology.

Discussions and Assignments

1. Choose a topic of interest and develop at least three different interview plans using varied styles and levels of structure. Choose one plan and explain how it will be implemented. Provide a rationale to support why this plan is appropriate to the purpose of the study.

2. Conduct a practice online interview. Address the topic using questions from at least two different approaches. Discuss how, as a researcher, you experienced these styles. Ask your practice partner for his or her perspective on the experience of different styles. Based on the practice interview and debrief, provide guidelines for researchers using your preferred style(s).

3. Conduct two practice interviews, one using text-only chat and one using verbal exchange. Ask the same questions in both interviews. Compare and contrast the kinds of data and the quantity and quality of data collected. In a debriefing discussion, ask the participant which interview type he or she preferred and why.

On the Web

www.sagepub.com/salmons2e
You will find media pieces, examples, links, and references to additional resources on interview and online interview methods.

Selecting Information and Communications Technologies and Research Setting Milieu

5

Every expansive era in the history of mankind has coincided with the operation of factors . . . to eliminate distance between peoples and classes previously hemmed off from one another. . . . It remains for the most part to secure the intellectual and emotional significance of this physical annihilation of space.

—John Dewey (1916)

After you study Chapter 5, you will be able to do the following:

- Understand theoretical and practical ways to describe online communications
- Compare and contrast characteristics of online communication tools
- Align synchronous, near-synchronous, or asynchronous communication options with interview and research purpose

| Figure 5.1 | E-Interview Research Framework: Selecting ICT and Milieu |

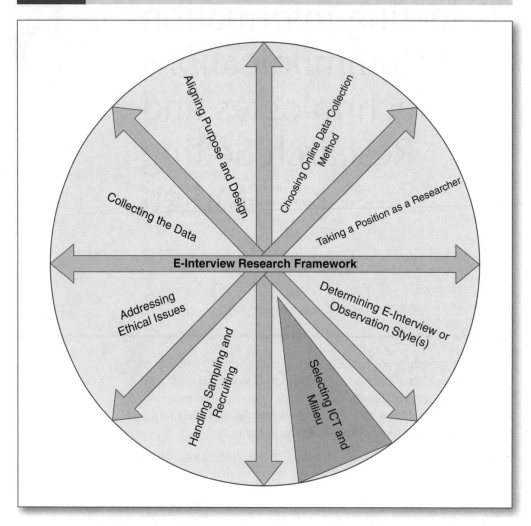

Source: Vision2Lead, Inc (2009–2014).

Technology Equals Change

The moment you write about (or worse, buy) any kind of software or hardware, a new option is bound to appear that is smaller, lighter, and faster. The directions of new technology development represent movement toward increased mobility and convergence of multiple technologies into integrated features and **interactivity**. These directions combine with trends toward greater interactivity, more access generally, and increased access to **broadband**, Wi-Fi, and global positioning systems (GPS). Some features—such as the ability to listen to MP3 files on one's cell phone or maneuver with touch screens instead of buttons—are not of great consequence for online interviewers. But in general, the fact that more people can access faster, richer media from any place at any time is advantageous for their potential research participation.

Programmers, inventers, and technology entrepreneurs who create low-cost, widely accessible communications tools usually don't have scholarly research in mind, yet their efforts benefit researchers. Even so, as we learn new ways to build trusting, authentic dialogue with research participants, we still grapple with the "intellectual and emotional significance of this physical annihilation of space." John Dewey (1916), educator and philosopher, pointed to the advent of the industrial revolution (p. 85). Exchanging messages and building relationships are *not* the same thing. Chapter 5 explores information and communications technologies (ICTs) and their potential for tapping the intellectual and emotional significance of participants' experiences through online interviews and related observations.

Forces for Change

THE INTERNET: THE MEDIUM WARMS

The word *Internet* simply does not mean the same thing today as it did even a decade ago. As a result, many criticisms of electronic tools as inadequate for the nuanced, sometimes emotion-filled communication intrinsic to research interviews must be reexamined. Early comparisons of behavior and communication focused on what was lost in the migration from in-person to online interactions. Some critics expressed concern that text-based e-mail messages and static websites disallowed development of intimacy, **immediacy**, or a sense of presence. In 1998, one participant described an asynchronous, text-based online discussion:

> It is a cold medium. Unlike face-to-face communication you get no instant feedback. You don't know how people responded to your comments; they just go out into silence. This feels isolating and unnerving. It is not warm and supportive. (Wegerif, 1998, p. 38)

Early online experiences could be characterized as transactional. They consisted primarily of users' accessing websites and reading materials posted online. **Forums**, bulletin boards, newsgroups, and e-mail lists enabled text-based exchange between computer users. But like the globe, the Internet is "warming" with many ways to convey immediate and supportive (or even confrontational) feedback. The many forms of Internet communication mean contrasts between online and face-to-face communications are less stark. Indeed, direct comparisons become harder to make as the online reality becomes more pervasive and interwoven with other aspects of life. In contrast to the earlier linear forms of information search and retrieval, contemporary online behavior is more flexible and reciprocal.

The notion of *cyberspace* grew out of the term *cyborg* and a post-human association of the person to the Internet and the computer as a machine. As the Internet has gone from being a place out there that we log into from our desktops to personalized mobile devices we carry in our pockets, these concepts and the dualistic notion of distinctions between "online" and "offline" have become outdated. Hayles (2006) says the notion of the cyborg "is not networked enough to encompass the emergent possibilities associated with the Internet and the world-wide web and other phenomena of the contemporary digital era," and "given the complexities of these [networked] dynamics, the individual person—or for that matter, the individual cyborg—is no longer the appropriate unit of analysis" (Abstract, p. 160). This social, networked process is called the "cognisphere" (p. 160). Elwell (2013) describes self-identity in this meshed real–physical space as the "transmediated self" (p. 11) that is developed narratively with audience response and ongoing interactions.

Meek (2012) suggests a continuum that allows for both the disembodied sense of cyberspace and "cyberplace." Cyberplace is a concept Meek uses to describe an embodied engagement with place, a "spatial hybridity of technologically mediated social life" where interactions are explicitly embodied in space, time, or events (p. 1430). By situating the networked person in a specific time and place, the possibilities for enacting and understanding social and political action in a digital world become apparent.

In this ubiquitous and multilayered online world, the concept of "presence" is itself evolving:

> Presence is not simply the opposite of absence. Technologies of communication are not just substitutes for face-to-face interaction, but constitute a new resource for constructing a kind of connected presence even when people are physically distant. In the regime of "connected" presence, participants multiply encounters and contacts using every kind of mediation and artifacts available to them: relationships thus become seamless webs of quasi-continuous exchanges. The boundaries between absence and presence get blurred and subtle experiences of togetherness may develop. (Licoppea & Smoredab, 2005, p. 321)

In the physical environment, "presence" is an either/or situation—you are either present or not. Online, people feel present in different ways. While scholars have discussed these concepts in many terms, for our purposes the following definitions will be used:

- *Environmental presence:* The extent to which the online or virtual environment itself recognizes and reacts to the person. This type of presence refers to the ability to create and return to an online identity in an environment that recognizes patterns of interest and behavior.

- *Personal presence:* The extent to which the person feels physically present in the environment.

- *Social presence:* The "subjective feeling of being connected and together with others during computer mediated communication" (Sung & Mayer, 2012, p. 1739) to achieve meaningful interactions, establish and maintain relations, and create productive social systems in online environments (Garrison, Anderson, & Archer, 2004). Sung and Mayer observe that "the degree of online social presence is based on the characteristics of the medium and the user's perception. These are associated with two components of online social presence, which are intimacy and immediacy" (p. 1739).

- *Cognitive presence:* The extent to which the person feels the potential to participate in critical thinking and community of inquiry (Baños et al., 2008; Garrison et al., 2004; Heeter, 2003; Kehrwald, 2008; Suler, 2003).

Recent evidence shows that people feel deeply present with others online. Familiarity with Internet-based interactions using varied communications technologies in daily professional, social, and family life enhances their comfort in the medium and strengthens the connections they make online. These developments open the door for online researchers to build on participants' positive associations with online communication and establish the rapport necessary to collect data through one-to-one or group interviews.

TECHNOLOGY CONVERGENCE: "TECHNOLOGIES ARE CRASHING TOGETHER"

Not long ago, communications media were separate, and their services, deliveries, uses, and means of access were distinct. Television broadcasting, voice telephony, and online computer services were individually received on different devices: televisions, radios, telephones, and computers. Broadcasts were received at a given time. **Convergence** describes flow of content across multiple media platforms where signals, regardless of type (i.e., voice, quality audio, video, data), are merged and can be accessed through various devices, at times convenient to the user (Dwyer, 2010; Knemeyer, 2004; Seybold, 2008).

The term *convergence* is used here to acknowledge that the ways one communicates are not dictated by the device used to access the Internet. Convergence offers a user the flexibility to make choices about which features to use for which communication purpose. Where communication by telephone was once assumed to use voice, we now have the option of **text messaging, instant messaging, and chat**; sending digital photographs; or even using video conferencing features on smartphones. Where communication by text message was assumed to be written, we can now share files or plug in a headset and use Voice over Internet Protocol (VoIP) to add audio. If convergence makes connectivity more broadly available, it also allows for more mobile connectivity. The full range of laptops, notebooks, netbooks, tablet computers, smartphones, mobile phones, **wireless** Internet connections, public kiosks, and Internet cafés has changed where and how people access the Internet. Communications can occur anywhere and can be linked with specific geographic information using GPS technologies and/or maps. Computer-mediated communication (CMC) is embedded into the fabric of the world around us and is an adjunct to everyday interaction. Anytime, anywhere, Internet and telephone communications are becoming more widely accepted by individuals and intrinsic to knowledge sharing across organizations.

INTERACTIVITY AND COLLABORATION

The Internet is continually expanding our ability not only to communicate but to create open or private spaces where we can meaningfully interact and collaborate. With next-generation technologies, individuals do more than access materials others have posted; they post comments, pictures, and media, and generate material that known or unknown people may view. They have many more choices about how to communicate with colleagues and family members and new ways to develop relationships with communities of users they will never meet in person. Users participate in online social contexts, and in the process they change the technologies they use and create new means of exchange.

Relationships and information are now intertwined. As Hargrove predicted in 2001, "The so-called Information Revolution is, in reality, a Relationships Revolution" (p. 113). Readers and customers can relate directly with the authors or companies who are purveyors of information. We are seeing a change in the flow of information, with individuals both consuming *and* creating content. When users experience the creative, generative aspects of online communication, they become more comfortable with tools and approaches that may be used in online research.

COMMUNICATION RICHNESS

Media richness theory (MRT) provides one way to analyze CMC. MRT distinguishes between *lean* and *rich* media based on the degree to which it is possible to give and receive immediate feedback, personalize the message, and use multiple cues and communication channels (Daft & Lengel, 1986). Daft and Lengel argued that richness in communication is assessed by the degree to which the medium allows people to provide and receive immediate feedback, check interpretations, and understand multiple cues via body language, tone of voice, and message content. One construct of MRT defined by Daft and Lengel is "task equivocality," which means that the greater the risk for ambiguity or multiple interpretations, the richer the communication medium to use.

Others believe it is important to assess richness in terms of the potential for creating immediacy and, as noted earlier, a sense of presence. Using Daft and Lengel's theory, others have posited that "rich" media results in greater socioemotional communication, bridges the physical or psychological distance between individuals, and fosters affiliation (Erickson & Herring, 2005; Kahai & Cooper, 2003; Mehrabian, 1971; O'Sullivan, Hunt, & Lippert, 2004).

Critics of MRT have pointed out that it is more important to emphasize understanding between parties than to evaluate channel capacity (Otondo, Scotter, Allen, & Palvia, 2008). They question the assumption that decreasing richness, as Daft and Lengel defined it, means less ability to process information and build understanding (Ross, 2001, p. 76). To address shortcomings and update the theory to encompass contemporary Internet communications and extend MRT, Dennis, Fuller, and Valacich (2008) proposed media synchronicity theory (MST). Dennis et al. first redefined the concept of *the task* as "the *set of communication processes* needed to generate shared understanding" (p. 576). They also further refined the concept of richness by offering a definition for *synchronicity* that describes a high level of mutual focus and attention in communication. Dennis et al. observed that not simply the choice of medium but also

> the *manner* in which individuals use media influences their communication performance (the development of shared understanding). Generally speaking, convergence processes benefit from the use of media that facilitate *synchronicity*, the ability to support individuals working together at the same time with a shared pattern of coordinated behavior. (p. 576)

In other words, the medium is not what dictates whether shared understandings can be achieved; it is the way the medium is used. An ICT may have the potential for rich communication and immediate give-and-take but be used in ways that allow users to multitask without giving the communication partner full and undivided attention.

Both MRT and MST can help the researcher think about how to match the communication task or need for shared understanding to the available communications medium. The essential point here is not to support or refute a particular theory or to offer a preferential position on "rich" or "lean" media. These differentiations are offered as a way to describe the nature of communication in various ICTs so the best choice for data collection can be made. In an unlikely application of Wallis Simpson's observation, "You can't be too rich or too thin," we can say here that the degree of richness or leanness does not matter; what matters is the appropriateness of the technology to the style of interview, population of participants, and purpose of the study, and the understanding of expectations for focused communication by the researcher and participant.

Nonverbal Communications and Online Interviews

Another way to assess online communication is to examine the degree to which nonverbal cues are conveyed. Online researchers grasp meaning from varied verbal and nonverbal cues. To do so, they must reexamine the ways such messages are defined and interpreted.

Nonverbal communication affects any interview process. Ong (1990) observes that "'words, words, words' mean nothing unless built into a nonverbal context, which always controls meanings of words" (p. 1). Interviewees reveal depth of expression and display cultural and social norms through nonverbal behavior (Fontana & Frey, 2003; Kalman, Ravid, Raban, & Rafaeli, 2006).

Four modes of nonverbal communication are described in the following:

- *Chronemics* refers to the use of pacing and timing of speech, and the length of silence before a response in conversation.

- *Paralinguistic* communication, or paralanguage, describes variations in volume, pitch, and quality of voice.

- *Kinesic* communication includes facial expressions, eye contact or gaze, body movements, and postures.

- *Proxemic* communication describes the use of interpersonal space to communicate attitudes (Gordon, 1980; Guerrero, DeVito, & Hecht, 1999; Kalman et al., 2006).

The social information processing (SIP) theory argues that "when most nonverbal cues are unavailable, as is the case in text-based CMC, users adapt their language, style, and other cues to such purposes" (Walther, Loh, & Granka, 2005, p. 37). When participants communicate with text-only chat or e-mail, the timing of response, silence, or nonresponse provides researchers with chronemic nonverbal data. When people chat or text message in real time, the length of time between post and response provides pacing and turn-taking in the conversation. Conversations can overlap, with many participants effectively "speaking" at once, as often happens in online chats. As Jacobsen (1999) describes it, "cyberdiscursivity" is a dynamic rhetoric allowing for mutual, reciprocal "textual creation/recreation" (p. 9). Network latency and multitasking by participants introduce effects that are different from face-to-face contexts and can lead to misinterpretation of temporal cues. The interviewer may believe the participant is struggling with a slow response, when in fact he or she has been distracted by an incoming e-mail.

In synchronous chat or asynchronous e-mail, interviewees control when they choose to respond (Mann & Stewart, 2000). Pauses can occur in face-to-face interviews, of course, but in an e-mail interview the delay in interaction between researcher and subject can range from seconds to hours to days. In planning the interview with participants, the researcher usually wants to accommodate the participant by allowing him or her some degree of freedom to determine pace of response. The way participants exercise such freedoms may or may not offer further insight. Slower responses may indicate more powerful reflection on the deeper meanings of the inquiry (Bampton & Cowton, 2002; James & Busher, 2006). On the other hand, quick replies may indicate lack of adequate consideration by the interviewee.

If the gap between questions and answers is too long, responses and follow-up probes can lead to discontinuous responses, and the thread of the interview is lost (James & Busher, 2006; Kitto & Barnett, 2007; Mann & Stewart, 2000). The researcher may be left to wonder why the interviewee has not responded. The interviewee may simply be busy or need more time to devise an answer. However, it also is possible that there is a problem with some aspect of the question and the respondent is reluctant to ask for clarification (Bampton & Cowton, 2002; Kitto & Barnett, 2007). When an interview takes too long and loses focus, enthusiasm can wane for the interviewee. Similarly, if the researcher is too slow to respond, participants may doubt the researcher's commitment and engagement in the research (James & Busher, 2006).

Uncertainty regarding the meaning of chronemic cues in the e-mail interview may be addressed by creating some protocols for timing and follow-up and for the anticipated length of the interview. The researcher must strike an appropriate balance between allowing interviewees time to respond as they wish and maintaining the momentum of the dialogue (Bampton & Cowton, 2002).

While text-based exchanges can foster the trust and rapport necessary to collect data, verbal interchange in real time provides additional nonverbal as well as verbal data. The rich media interview brings researcher and participants together in real time in a virtual space, allowing for increased immediacy and presence. In interviews conducted with web-based applications combined with audio through VoIP or telephone, researchers listen to interviewees and collect data on chronemic and paralanguage aspects of their responses. Researchers using **video conferencing or video calls** can use some level of kinesic communication, such as facial expressions and gestures, although eye contact may be more difficult to attain. When a shared whiteboard or immersive space is used, haptic movements become part of the kinesic communication process. Proxemic communication, interpreted as physical distance between communicators, is not applicable or must be reinterpreted for online contexts.

A further issue of nonverbal cues and online interviews involves determining when an interview is nearing its end. If the interview participant fails to respond, it may be a signal that he or she wants to withdraw from the study but does not want to tell the interviewer (Hunt & McHale, 2007). In a face-to-face interview, the interviewer can usually sense when time is running out and adjust his or her approach to the discussion accordingly, ensuring that certain issues are tackled as a matter of priority. It is difficult to sense when an online interviewee is ready to conclude the interview unless he or she states so explicitly (Bampton & Cowton, 2002). In addition, the interviewer has less control over the interviewee's deciding to terminate the interview. An online interviewee can end the interview at the press of a button, whereas an interviewee in a face-to-face interview has to physically leave or request that the interviewer leave (Chen & Hinton, 1999; James & Busher, 2006). The online interviewer has fewer options for recovering a difficult interaction (such as apologizing for an inappropriate question, requesting that the interviewee remain, or retracting a line of questioning) before the interviewee simply logs out (James & Busher, 2006).

Scholarly research guidelines require that an interview be complete for the data from the interview to be used without conditions. When the interviewee fails to complete the interview, the researcher must decide whether to use the partial information collected or discard the data (Hunt & McHale, 2007). Careful design (see Chapters 3 and 4), participant selection (see Chapter 5), preparation (see Chapter 6), and alignment of ICT with interview approach (see Chapters 2 and 7) can optimize the potential for successfully engaging the participant through all stages of data collection.

Synchronous, Near-Synchronous, and Asynchronous Communication

This chapter has so far discussed a number of dimensions of online communication. Yet another distinguishing factor is the timing of message and response. Online interaction is typically categorized according to the ability to send, receive, and respond to messages at the same time—that is, **synchronous communication**—or at different times—that is, **asynchronous communication.** The medium may be new, but none of the many modes of electronic communication is wholly unique to the online environment. Whether face-to-face or online, communication typically mixes verbal and nonverbal, written and symbolic visual modes. In person, synchronous real-time communication occurs when people meet or talk on the telephone.

Online, synchronous communications can include written, verbal, and/or visual exchange. By attaching a headset and logging onto a free online service, people can use VoIP instead of the telephone, making it possible to have free conversations with anyone in the world with similar access to a computer. By adding a web camera, researchers and participants can use desktop video conferencing and see each other while they converse. Researchers can adopt platforms designed for online meetings for interview purposes, using shared whiteboards and other tools that allow them to see materials and artifacts in addition to talking with and seeing each other. Or they can interact in immersive 3-D virtual environments such as **Second Life** or games where they are represented by avatars they design.

Asynchronous communications, which do not constrain people to participate at the same time, occur when people correspond by letter or read and write print publications. Online asynchronous communications occur when people correspond by e-mail or write posts and respond to others in discussion **forums**, social media sites, **wikis**, or blogs.

Each ICT has its own set of opportunities and limitations. Online, asynchronous communication entails two types of displacement: time and space. Synchronous communication entails one type of displacement: space (Bampton & Cowton, 2002). Synchronous modes bring people one step closer together, but many people find that the reflective pause between message and response in asynchronous communications leads to deeper consideration of the matter at hand.

The terms *synchronous* and *asynchronous* have until recently represented an either/or principle: communication either at the same time or at a different time. Now we have additional refinements, including the concept from Dennis et al. (2008) introduced earlier—that is, *synchronicity*—and a concept we will call *near-synchronous* conversations (Salmons, 2012). Synchronicity occurs when communications partners are devoting full attention to the dialogue—no multitasking or other simultaneous conversations. *Synchronous*, then, describes a more basic definition of communication with a technology that allows for real-time message and response. In near-synchronous communication, one party may post, text, or send a comment, update, or question to the receiving party with the expectation that the other party will respond the next time he or she is online. Near-synchronous communications may take the form of an extended conversation. The term *asynchronous* still remains a descriptor for communications involving the expectation of a time gap between message and response.

These communication options are presented in Figure 5.2 as a *time–response continuum*. This model offers a way to categorize the level of immediacy and timing of the response in a way that offers more subtle gradations than the prior synchronous/asynchronous dichotomy.

The choice between time–response modes—or the choice to blend them—is significant. Because the online environment offers many modes of communication, researchers can match the characteristics of the media to specific design requirements of their inquiry. Researchers base their choices on requirements of the research design for robust communication

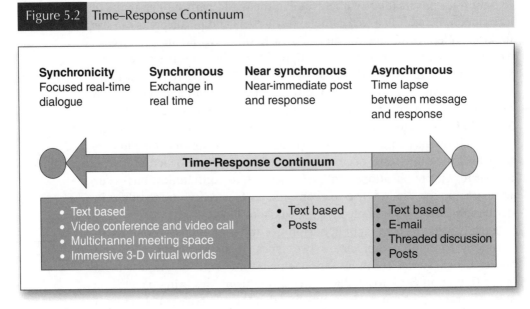

Figure 5.2   Time–Response Continuum

Source: Salmons (2012).

that allows interviewers to ask questions and interpret immediate responses, or written modes that allow interviewees to take time to think about the question and respond.

Tools and Features for Online Interview Research

 Almost any communications tool can be adapted for research interviews. One way of categorizing the options is by determining the options for exchange. Some tools use text only, while others allow for audio or voice, video, or visual exchanges. In Table 5.1, some features of online communication are outlined. These types of ICTs may live on the open, public World Wide Web or in social media or closed, proprietary online environments. Multiple features are often combined on one social media site, software, or platform.

For the purpose of this book, these communications tools are organized into broad categories, shown in Figure 5.3.

Aligning Features With Research Purposes

Researchers using interviews for data collection need several exchanges with research participants in addition to the actual interview. Every stage should be seen as an opportunity to build trust with and learn about the research participant. A mix of synchronous, near-synchronous, and asynchronous methods may allow for flexibility, variety, and convenience throughout the

Table 5.1	ICT Features for Preparation, Interviews, or Follow-Up With Participants
Text-Based Communication	**Multiple Channels for Communication**
Blog: A blog is a personal online journal where entries are posted chronologically. Microblogs allow for very short entries. Blogs can be text only or include links, images, or media. Viewing may be public or limited to specified group of subscribers or friends. Researchers can create blogs to share information about the study with participants or other stakeholders. Researchers can also collect data from participants' blogs. *E-mail:* Researchers can send and receive questions and answers. *Forum:* A forum (also known as a bulletin board or threaded discussion) is a public or private site where posts and responses are organized in sequential order. Researchers can post and respond to questions and answers in a forum in an online community or on a site restricted to participants. *Text message or chat:* Researchers can post and respond to questions and answers. *Wiki:* Multiple authors add, remove, and edit content on a wiki website. It can include a blog, forum, or a space for text chat, used as described above.	*GPS or geographic information systems:* Researchers identify locations of interview-related events or map location-related data. *Podcast or vodcast:* Researchers ask and answer questions by exchanging recorded audio or video files. *Shared applications:* Researchers and participants view and discuss documents, media, or examples by logging in together and using web-based software applications, research tools, or forms. Participants can generate responses by writing, drawing, or diagramming ideas on a whiteboard or in shared documents. *Video:* Researchers and/or participants post, view, and respond to video clips. *Video conferencing or video call:* Researchers and participants see each other while conversing. *Visual exchange:* Researchers and/or participants post, view, and respond to photographs, charts and diagrams, and visual maps. *Virtual world:* Researchers and/or participants ask and respond to questions through the physical form and identity of an avatar, experience immersive events or phenomena, and/or view examples or demonstrations. *VoIP:* Researchers and participants ask and answer questions using live audio.

Figure 5.3	Types of Online Communication

Text Based	**Video Conference**
• Communicate through typed words, limited use of images through emoticons or exchange of pictures. • Connect on phone, mobile device, or computer.	• Communicate through audio and video. • Features may include text messaging and/or file sharing. • Connect in studio, computer, or mobile device.
Communication Types for Online Interviews	
Multichannel Web Conference	**Virtual Environment**
• Communicate through audio, video, text, and/or shared applications. • Connect by computer or mobile device.	• Communicate through audio or text, and visual exchange. • Connect by computer or mobile device.

stages of the study. Researchers make choices based on the nature of the study and the options available to the researcher and participant.

The interview research relationship is initiated with the initial contact, in the sampling and selection of the research participants. (See Chapter 7 for more about sampling and recruiting participants.) Depending on the nature of the study, asynchronous tools such as e-mail lists or posts on blogs or websites may be useful for communicating announcements for a study and inviting participation. Posted information such as background on the research, information about the researcher(s), and links to institutions or foundations that sponsor, support, or provide supervision for the study can provide the credibility potential participants need. Online questionnaires can be used as a preliminary step to determine whether the potential participant meets sampling criteria. Researchers and participants can discuss details using synchronous tools such as chat, VoIP calls (especially in multinational studies where telephone calls are costly), or desktop video conferencing.

Once the researcher and participant have agreed to proceed with the study, informed consent and preparation are next. (See Chapter 8 for more about ethical research and informed consent.) After participants agree to participate, every interaction affords an opportunity to collect data or develop understanding of the environment and context of the participants' experiences. Participants need to fully understand the purpose of the study and the researcher's expectations; researchers need to communicate fully and in clear terms and must be certain participants understand and agree. Background information on the study can be posted on a private, password-protected website or blog where participants can review materials at their leisure. Synchronous tools can be used to ensure that all questions or concerns have been addressed.

The actual interview (in some cases, several interviews) is often the main formal data collection stage. As noted, some researchers may also choose to conduct a portion of or the entire interview through e-mail. Synchronous tools allow for varied types of rich exchange. Data collection using these tools will be explored in detail in coming chapters of this book. (See Chapters 9 and 10 for more about preparing for and conducting interviews with text-based communications, video conferencing or video calls and web conferencing meeting spaces, and in virtual environments.)

After the interview, the researcher may choose to design in a follow-up stage, where participants have a chance to review what they have said, elaborate, or correct responses. Asynchronous tools can be used to send documents through e-mail or to discuss any unresolved issues.

Researchers who understand and can use a variety of ICTs are prepared to match communication to particular stages of the research, needs of the participants, and requirements of the design.

CHOOSING, FINDING, OR CREATING A CONDUCIVE MEETING SPACE

Every researcher needs a safe, neutral location conducive to the interview. An ideal location will be comfortable for the interviewee, with minimal distractions or interference. Few obstacles should prevent the preferred type of interviewee from reaching the location—obstacles such as lack of transportation or access for people with disabilities. The setting should not itself become a factor in the interviewee's response because of negative associations or feelings of intimidation. To address these considerations, some researchers have chosen to conduct interviews in the field or in settings familiar to the interviewee.

Similar considerations exist when researchers select an online interview setting. Productive, generative interviews require a meeting place where participants feel safe and at ease and where researchers and participants can focus on the inquiry. It is important to remember that selecting ICTs is about more than simply deciding what tools will be used to transfer messages back and forth between researcher and participant. Technology choices influence the characteristics and feeling of the online space that serves as the research setting.

Some questions researchers should consider when making this selection include the following:

- Do people in the target interview demographic generally have access to the type of technology to be used, or will a particular choice of technology exclude many potential participants?

- Will the interviewee feel comfortable, or will additional preparation time be needed to familiarize the interviewee with the setup? Can the researcher be reasonably sure that distractions (noise, family members, others in the office) can be kept to a minimum? (For more on this topic, see Chapter 9.)

- Are interviewees receptive to—or distracted by—creatively presented online environments? Most ICTs take advantage of the graphical nature of the World Wide Web, making it possible for the researcher to customize pages or environments used in the interview to create a comfortable, appropriate setting that meets participants' needs. A thoughtful consideration of these elements may involve decisions about inclusion or exclusion of animated graphics, background images, fonts, or colors. (See Chapter 6 for more about visual stimuli in interviews.)

- If the setting involves an online community or social media site, are there codes of conduct or norms that allow for or restrict the presence of researchers? Is there a community manager or host who needs to give permission? (Related ethical issues are explored in Chapter 8.)

- Can you protect—and delete—data saved in recorded interviews? (Related ethical issues will be explored in Chapter 8.)

Closing Thoughts

This chapter surveyed some of the technology trends and tools of relevance to researchers who want to conduct online interviews. The process of designing and carrying out a study entails a complex set of steps and tasks, so any one tool is not likely to be adequate. In considering which tools make sense for the study, researchers need to consider the access and ease of use for participants and appropriateness for the given tasks. Another question to consider is this: What kind(s) of data do you want to collect? Will verbal, text, or visual data best help you answer the research questions?

In addition, researchers need to reflect on their own time and skills. Are you more comfortable with a scheduled synchronous interview, or would you prefer a more flexible series of near-synchronous exchanges? What does "rich media" mean to you? What strengths and skills can you apply to your work as a researcher? Which ICTs are you able to use comfortably to converse? Do you have the time to learn new tools and techniques or to set up new blogs, wikis, or websites?

Coming chapters will build on Chapter 5 and explore each step in the design and conduct of interview research, which may provide additional insight into these decisions.

Researcher's Notebook

*THE E-INTERVIEW RESEARCH FRAMEWORK:
SELECTING ICTS AND MILIEU*

The E-Interview Research Framework is based on the premise that choices made in every aspect of design influence others. Nowhere is this truer than in the selection of the technology used to collect data. Key questions related to decisions about the selection of ICT and online interview style are outlined in Table 5.2.

Table 5.2	Applying the E-Interview Research Framework: Selecting ICT and Milieu
	Selecting ICT and Milieu
Aligning purpose and design	• Does the researcher relate the approach for e-interviews and related data collection to the purpose of the study? • How will the features of ICT achieve the purpose of the study?
Choosing online data collection method	• Does the researcher share whether the study will investigate online behavior in or with a specific ICT or online setting? If so, does that ICT or setting lend itself to interviews and observations? • How will the interview use text-based, audio, and/or visual communication options? • If the interview technology has capacity for visual exchange, has the researcher acknowledged the visual nature of the interview in the research design and planned for collection and analysis of visual data?
Taking a position as a researcher	• Does the researcher disclose any conflicts of interest or personal preferences for a choice of ICT that might introduce bias or otherwise influence study results?
Determining e-interview or observation styles	• How does the researcher align ICT functions, features, and/or limitations with the selected e-interview style(s)?

(Continued)

(Continued)

	Selecting ICT and Milieu
	• What communications options with the selected ICT might influence the style or structure of the interview? • Where will the interaction fall on the time–response continuum?
Selecting ICT and milieu	• Does the researcher explain what ICT and milieu will be used, why, and how?
Handling sampling and recruiting	• Does the researcher describe any issues related to the population's preferences for, access to, and skills to use the selected ICT? • Does the population prefer to communicate synchronously or asynchronously?
Addressing ethical issues	• Does the researcher identify and address any specific ethical issues (e.g., privacy, protected areas, use of avatars, need for community agreement) present in the selected milieu? • Does the researcher specify minimum requirements regarding hardware, software, or technical skills in the recruitment materials and agreement? • What user-generated data (e.g., use of video or images, avatars, profile info) should be included in an agreement? • Will the interview setting be in a public or private online milieu? • Do codes of conduct for participating in the selected milieu limit permissible types of exchange? • Is permission needed to access profiles or posted documents or images?
Collecting the data	• Does the researcher have the skills needed to manage the ICT during the interview? • Does the researcher have a contingency plan in case technical difficulties occur?

STORIES OF ONLINE INQUIRY

Chapter 4 offered examples for interview questions using a variety of levels of structure. In this Researcher's Notebook, those same questions are explored in the context of technology options.

1. *Structured.* This structured interview could be conducted online using text chat since responses are short and quick to type. Questions, prepared in advance, can be cut and pasted into the chat box. This type of exchange could be conducted using text messaging on a mobile device or in a chat area on a social media platform.

2. *Semistructured.* Semistructured interviews make use of some prepared questions and some questions that emerge during the interview. These interviews can be conducted with technologies that use written or verbal exchanges. Keep in mind that to use an all-written, synchronous interview approach, it will be necessary to be alert to important points in the participant's response and to craft and type the follow-up questions—all without losing the participant's attention. A web conferencing or video conferencing platform is ideal, particularly if visual methods are also to be used (see Chapter 6).

3. *Unstructured.* As noted earlier, an in-depth interview requires careful, active listening on the part of the researcher, who must be able to articulate the follow-ups or probing questions in a timely fashion. Doing this entirely in writing requires fast thinking and typing! Since questions are not articulated in advance, a verbal exchange will best serve the conversational style of an unstructured interview. This kind of interview might be conducted using video conferencing or a multistage e-mail exchange.

4. *Mixed.* An interview that includes structured (prepared) questioning and unstructured (spontaneous) questioning should be conducted with a technology that allows for varied styles of dialogue. This kind of interview might be conducted using video conferencing or web conferencing.

Key Concepts

- Technologies change continuously. Forces for change include convergence of features, increased **mobile access**, and more ways to interact.

- Researchers can use synchronous and asynchronous communications to take care of the tasks associated with planning and carrying out a study. Researchers can choose the most appropriate tools to communicate with research participants through the sampling, preparing for the study, conducting the interview, and following up on the study.

Discussions and Assignments

1. Which ICTs can you demonstrate or teach others to use? Offer peer learning opportunities to improve one another's skills.

2. Which ICTs do you want to learn how to use? Select a technology tool you have not used before. Working with a classmate, try a new communications tool. Ask your peer questions, and record or take notes. Discuss your perceptions of this tool's potential for research interviews. (Note: Many software tools offer a free or trial version you can use for this project.)

3. What factors make you feel safe and willing to reveal personal or sensitive thoughts or feelings in online communications?

   • The style or features of the technology?

   • The culture or expectations of the online community or social media site?

   • The personality, style, or credibility of the person with whom you communicate?

   • The ground rules or agreements you state before the interaction?

4. Discuss steps or actions you can take to help others trust you when you communicate online.

5. What strengths and skills can you apply to your work as an online researcher? What skills do you need to develop?

On the Web

www.sagepub.com/salmons2e
You will find media pieces and links to articles and materials related to emerging ICTs suitable for interviews.

Visual Research and the Online Qualitative Interview

6

After studying Chapter 6, you will be able to do the following:

- Define and explain the meaning of visual literacy

- Offer an overview of visual research methods

- Align the online visual research method with research purpose using the Typology of Online Visual Interview Methods

The process of deciding on and planning to use an information and communications technology (ICT) includes determining whether and how to use visual interview approaches. Communication between researcher and participant in interviews occurs primarily through words—written or spoken. Sometimes, whether due to the nature of the research phenomenon or the characteristics of the participants (age, verbal literacy, learning style), words alone may not be adequate. Visual research methods, whether used online or off, can enrich the otherwise word-intensive process of data collection through in-depth interviews or documents. Digital cameras, web cameras, camera applications or mobile devices, and compact video cameras offer simple, accessible ways to take photographs or videos. Gestural and stylus-oriented graphics programs allow for images to be drawn. Global positioning system (GPS) programs allow for documentation of locations, and geographic information systems (GIS) and other mapping software programs can be used to generate maps. Any of these visual elements can be readily shared among researchers and participants online.

This chapter discusses the use of visual communication to augment verbal and textual exchanges during online interviews. The chapter also surveys visual dimensions of observations and the collection of visual artifacts.

Seeing the Interview: Visual Questions, Visual Answers

Visual research has long been essential to inquiries in fields such as sociology, ethnography, and anthropology. The specialized disciplines of visual sociology and visual anthropology are grounded in the idea that valid scientific insight in society can be acquired by observing, analyzing, and theorizing its visual manifestations: behavior of people and material products of culture (Pauwels, 2011, p. 3). Visual research methodologies, according to Banks (2007), have traditionally encompassed two main strands. The first strand points to ways researchers use visual images to capture observations in the field or graphically describe field data. Photography (still or moving images) or graphics (drawings, diagrams, or maps) have commonly been used to document research phenomena.

The second classic approach to visual research revolves around collecting and studying images created by research participants or others in the participants' culture. This approach is used when researchers want to understand the significance or function of artifacts, or artistic or creative expressions.

Several additional types of visual methods appropriate for interview research have emerged, including visual elicitation and image collaboration.

Visual elicitation refers to interviews that use visuals to elicit responses and stimulate discussion about participants' experiences of the research phenomenon. The general term *visual elicitation* is used here to encompass the introduction of any kind of visual material into the interview, including photographs, videos, drawings, artwork, diagrams, or graphics. Visual representations of some aspect of the research phenomenon can be generated by the researcher, by the participant, or obtained from other sources.

Visual elicitation approaches use "artefacts employed during interviews where the subject matter defies the use of a strictly verbal approach" (Crilly, Blackwell, & Clarkson, 2006, p. 341). Goldstein (2007) points out that fruitful dialogue can take place based on the viewer's response to the content, perception of intent, and context of the image. Stanczak (2007b) describes an interview process in this way:

> In conjunction with or as an alternative to conversational questions, participants are asked open-ended questions about a photograph. Prompting a participant with "tell me about this photograph," for example, shifts the locus of meaning away from empirically objective representations of objects or interactions. Instead, images gain significance through the way that participants engage and interpret them. (pp. 10–11)

Rose (2012) points out that such interviews "can prompt talk about different things, in different ways. Things are talked about in these sorts of interviews that don't get discussed in talk-only interviews" (p. 305). By using these approaches, the image becomes a common frame of reference for both parties—researcher and participant. By sharing photographs or video, researchers and participants can visit other time periods or spaces that would be difficult for them to enter physically (Näykki & Järvelä, 2008). When the subject matter is of a sensitive nature, interviewee and interviewer can both turn to the visual image "as a kind of neutral third party" (Banks, 2007, p. 65).

Participants who generate the visual material discussed in the interview have another opportunity to reflect on and experience the research phenomenon by re-creating or reimagining it, and then by explaining the image to the researcher during the interview (Rose, 2012). Drawing or creating diagrams allows participants to use visual and spatial thinking and explore possible solutions to problems (Buckley & Waring, 2013).

Finally, an in-interview visual research approach is the *collaborative image*, where the researcher and the subjects work together to represent the phenomena of interest by creating new images or adding to preexisting images (Banks, 2007, p. 7). For example, Thygesen, Pedersen, Kragstrup, Wagner, and Mogensen (2011) asked participants to draw the emotional changes of their most salient emotion(s) over time on a grid, which was developed in advance of the interview.

Pink (2013) suggests that rather than simply "eliciting" or drawing out responses to the image or media, the researcher and participant can discuss images in ways that "create a 'bridge' between their different experiences of reality. Photographs [graphics or media] can become reference points through which [researchers and participants] represent aspects of their realities to each other" (p. 84). Using the image as a "bridge" will help avoid the danger Crilly and colleagues (2006) point to: Presenting interviewees with a single graphic or photographic image could constrain their thinking. Interviewees may be inclined to suggest only modifications to the diagram or image, rather than offering new conceptualizations. In other words, simply presenting an image to elicit responses can constrain the more creative and collaborative part of the process. By using a variety of collaborative and participant-generated visual approaches, the researcher can build understandings of concepts, feelings, and relationships not sufficiently explained verbally.

Multimodal Communication in a Multilingual World

ICT advances have made it possible to communicate in more ways, more immediately, more cheaply, using more kinds of tools and devices. In related or parallel developments, an increasingly global economy and global culture have emerged. In this multilingual world, communication is not limited to words; it also occurs through still and moving pictures, drawn or captured images, icons, and emoticons. Gergle, Kraut, and Fussell (2004) observe that "using visual information to infer what another person knows facilitates efficient communication and reduces the ambiguity otherwise associated with particular linguistic expressions" (p. 492). Kress (2003) suggests that this shift from words to pictures is interrelated with a shift from print to digital:

> There is, on one hand, the broad move from the centuries-long dominance of writing to the new dominance of the image and, on the other hand, the move from the dominance of the medium of the book to the dominance of the medium of the screen. (p. 1)

Kress points out that even when the screen contains text, it is inherently visual as a result of the layout of the online page and use of colors, fonts, and other elements. Kress calls this type of communication *multimodality*.

With the use of digital media, the number of modes available for meaning making multiply. "Most—we would say all—representations are multimodal. . . . Modes have differing 'affordances,' different potentials for making meaning" (Kress & Selander, 2012, p. 267).

Kress and others argue that understanding and decoding these multimodal messages requires new literacies (Koltay, 2011; Kress, 2005; Kress & Selander, 2012; Sutherland-Smith, 2002). The term **visual literacy**, coined by John Debes (1968), can be defined as the ability to decode and interpret (make meaning from) visual messages and also to encode and compose meaningful visual communications. It includes the ability to visualize internally, communicate visually, and read and interpret images (Bamford, 2003). In addition, visual literacy "encompasses the ability to be an informed critic of visual information, able to ethically judge accuracy, validity, and worth" (Metros, 2008, p. 103). Words and images are easily meshed electronically; thus, visual literacy in an online world intersects with ICT or information literacy, defined as follows: using digital technology, communications tools, and/or networks to access, manage, integrate, evaluate, and create information to function in a knowledge society (Educational Testing Services, 2006, p. 2).

As online pioneer Howard Rheingold (2012) puts it, digital literacy is an active process:

> Participatory culture, in which citizens feel and exercise the agency of being co-creators of their culture and not just passive consumers of culture created by others, depends on widespread literacies of participation. You can't participate without knowing how. . . . I use the word "literacies" to encompass the social element as well as the individual ability to encode and decode in a medium. (p. 53)

Developing 21st century literacies (information, digital, and visual) is needed so the 21st century literate individual can critically evaluate diverse types of information, including visual and textual, and integrate elements in new ways to create and communicate complex messages using technology tools.

VISUAL LITERACY AND SPATIAL INTELLIGENCE

Howard Gardner's (1983) theory of multiple intelligences also aligns with Kress's thinking about multimodal communication and with related ideas about new literacies. Gardner suggests that intelligence comes in many flavors—including linguistic, interpersonal, and spatial. While people with linguistic intelligence think in words and people with interpersonal intelligence gain understanding by discussing concepts with others, people with spatial intelligence "see" and understand meaning through interaction with images and patterns:

> Central to spatial intelligence are the capacities to perceive the visual world accurately, to perform transformations and modifications upon one's initial perceptions, and to be able to re-create aspects of one's visual experience, even in the absence of relevant physical stimuli. (Gardner, 1983, p. 183)

Using Gardner's and Kress's terminologies, it is possible to describe an integrated "intelligence" made up of linguistic, interpersonal, and spatial abilities used by people who relate to one another using multimodal communications. They have the necessary levels of literacy needed to access, consume, create, communicate, and evaluate messages that integrate written and spoken words, images, and sounds.

How are these matters relevant to interviewers? Online researchers have unique opportunities to use a full range of multimodal communications to engage and understand participants by connecting to their diverse intelligence styles and literacies. Researchers may observe participants during the interview, as well as in other online events and activities. Documents or posts may include user-generated visual images or media. The potential approaches for online research are described here in a conceptual framework called the Typology of Online Visual Interview Methods.

Typology of Online Visual Interview Methods

New communication technologies enable researchers to extend previously used methods for creating or gathering visual records of their work and using images to facilitate dialogue. Four main types of visually oriented interactions are available to researchers and participants online. For one, they can *transmit* visual images. Researchers and participants can send each other image or media files, links to images posted on a server or website, or images captured in the moment. In addition to sharing images, they can *view* visual representations of phenomena together. Researchers can view photos, graphics, artifacts, or media during the interview. Researchers and participants can also immerse themselves in a virtual environment to *navigate* through visually rich games, software applications, or virtual environments. Finally, they can *generate* visual images. Shared tools or whiteboards allow researchers and/or participants to create drawings, diagrams or visual maps, snapshots, or videos.

Researchers can make strategic use of these four types of visual exchanges to accomplish various data collection activities. One way to think about using visual exchange in research is to distinguish it as either stimulus or response. When researchers ask questions or introduce themes, they hope to stimulate a fruitful response from the participants. While interviews generally use a verbal stimulus to produce a verbal response, visual research methods allow for a wider range of possibilities. For example, the participant can answer a verbal question by drawing a diagram or sharing a photograph. Likewise, a visual representation of the concepts in question can be answered with a visual, text, and/or verbal response.

Visual methods introduced earlier are adapted for online research and categorized here as visual elicitation, visual communication, and visual collaboration. Researchers and participants may use *visual communication* techniques to convey the stimulus or represent the response. Visual communication describes the use of images to communicate abstract concepts, relationships between concepts or data, or examples of research phenomena.

Visual elicitation refers specifically to the process of using visual stimulus to draw out a verbal or visual response. The scenery or events in an immersive virtual environment navigated by researcher and participant, the images or media viewed together, or the graphic generated during the interview may stimulate response.

Visual collaboration refers to a collaborative approach either to stimulate new thinking or to create responses in relation to visual representations of the research phenomenon. Researchers and participants together can create, edit, or embellish images during the interview. "A collaborative method assumes that the researcher and participant are consciously working together to produce visual images and specific types of knowledge through technological procedures and discussions" (Pink, 2007, p. 53). (See Table 6.1 for a summary of the Typology of Online Visual Interview Methods.)

Table 6.1	Typology of Online Visual Interview Methods
Possible Researcher Actions	**Possible Interactions With Research Participants**
Transmit visual images. Image or media files, links to images posted on a server or website, or images captured in the moment are sent to the other party during the interview.	*Visual communication* describes the use of images to communicate abstract concepts, relationships between concepts or data, or examples of research phenomena.
View visual representation of phenomena together. Researchers can view photos, graphics, artifacts, or media during the interview.	*Visual elicitation* refers specifically to the process of using visual stimulus to draw out a verbal or visual response. The scenery or events in an immersive virtual environment navigated by researcher and participant, the images or media viewed together, or the graphic generated during the interview may stimulate response.
Navigate in a visual virtual environment. Observe and experience websites, software applications, or 3-D virtual environments.	*Visual collaboration* refers to a collaborative approach either to stimulate new thinking or to create responses in relation to visual representations of the research phenomenon. Researchers and participants together can create, edit, or embellish images during the interview.
Generate visual images. Access shared tools that allow researchers and/or participants to create drawings, diagrams or visual maps, snapshots, or videos.	

These principles align with the interview structure continuum discussed throughout this book. As mapped out in Figure 6.1, researchers can variously use visual elicitation, communication, and/or collaboration in structured, semistructured, or unstructured interviews. As outlined in Figure 6.2, visual communication options exist in most ICTs.

Figure 6.1 Types of Online Interviews and Visual Exchange

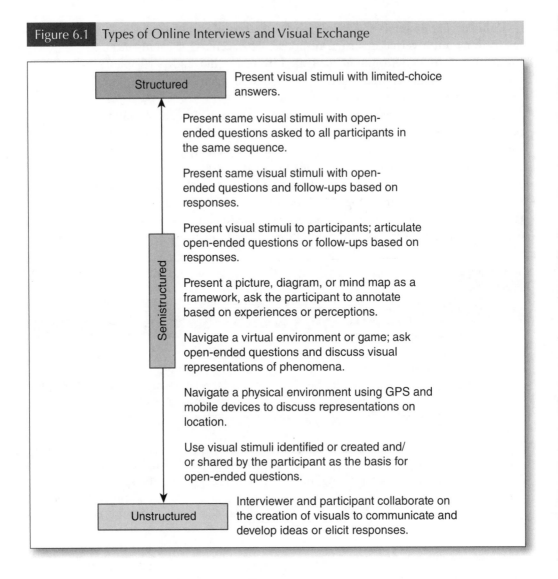

Visual Methods in Online Interviews

Visual research methods for communication, elicitation, and collaboration can variously augment verbal communication in online interviews. Visual communication can complement verbal communication to stimulate answers or show responses to the research phenomenon.

TEXT-BASED INTERVIEWS

Interviews via text generally apply fewer visual research techniques than do interviews with other technologies.

Figure 6.2	Types of Visual Communication

Text Based	Video Conference, Video Chat or Call
• Use visual communication. • Transmit images or files. • Post and link to visuals. • Use emoticons, colors, fonts to add visual elements to text.	• Use visual communication and/or elicitation. • Transmit and view visual images. • Observe interviewee and setting.

Visual Communication Types for Online Interviews	
Multichannel Web Conference Meeting	**Virtual Environment**
• Use visual communication, elicitation, and/or collaboration. • Transmit, view, and/or generate visual images. • Navigate online environments.	• Use visual communication and/or elicitation. • Navigate through visually rich virtual worlds, games, or simulations.

What was known as *text chat* when the medium allowed only for exchanges using the written word has evolved into multimedia messaging services with the ability to share images and audio (Lillie, 2012). Researchers and participants can communicate visually through textual elements such as colored text in different fonts. They can also use a form of shorthand by replacing words with emoticons (Laflen & Fiorenza, 2012) or emoji (Baron & Ling, 2011; Ueda & Nojima, 2011; Wortham, 2013), digital images that convey emotions through a symbolic shorthand.

> **Research tip:** In general, novice researchers should choose a style with at least some structure and preparation, since managing the visual interview requires focus and it may be hard to devise meaningful questions on the fly.

Text chat is primarily a synchronous communication form. It can also be used in a near-synchronous way, with researchers posting questions, image files, or links to which participants can respond at their next log-in.

In an asynchronous e-mail exchange, images can be sent back and forth or posted on the researcher's website, and links provided. Using a forum, the images can be posted and a threaded discussion can proceed with main and follow-up questions. Participants might be asked to keep a photo or video diary over a period of time, using the camera feature to record events, and then asked to transmit the file(s) to the researcher.

> **Research tip:** Steps for preparation discussed in Chapter 9 should be observed.

Researchers and participants can transmit images before, during, or after the text-based interview. These images—while they may or may not be visible within the text chat—can be used to elicit responses and stimulate discussion about their significance (see Figure 6.3 for an example).

Figure 6.3 Text Interview With Visual Elements

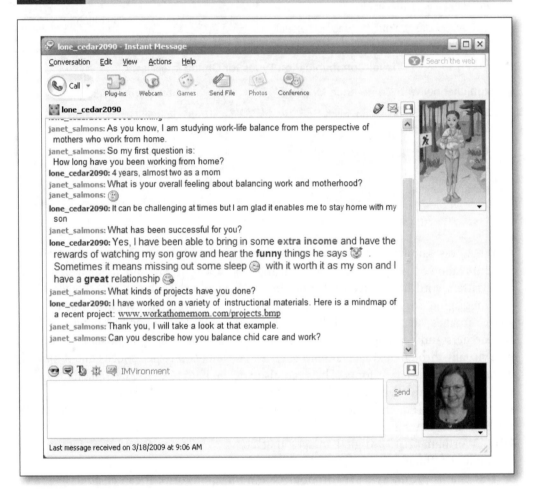

VIDEO CONFERENCE, VIDEO CALL, OR VIDEO CHAT

Interviews via video conferencing can make use of two interactive visual research dimensions. When both researcher and participant use web cameras, live images of interviewer and interviewee are transmitted. In this way, the researcher has the opportunity to observe the participant and the setting of the interview. Additionally, artifacts or items of interest can be shown on camera for researcher or participant to view. These images may serve communication or elicitation purposes in the interview (see Figure 6.4).

| Figure 6.4 | Sharing an Image to Elicit a Response in a Desktop Video Call Interview |

MULTICHANNEL WEB CONFERENCE MEETING SPACES

Interviews in web conferencing spaces can be used with any visual research and ICT type. Researchers and participants can transmit images, view visuals together, navigate virtual environments, and generate images individually or collaboratively. They can weave together visual communication, elicitation, and collaboration to complement and enhance the verbal exchange of the interview.

Ahead of the interview, images can be loaded and organized for sequential viewing in tandem with interview questions. Images also can be uploaded during the interview.

Photographs, diagrams, or media can be viewed together and discussed. Video clips created by the researcher or participant, or publicly available media that show examples of the research phenomenon in action can also be viewed together and discussed. Using web tour features, the researcher and participant can navigate to other websites, shared software applications, or even immersive games or virtual environments.

Using the shared whiteboard or shared application tools, researchers and participants can generate charts or illustrations. Collaborative diagramming can be used to show ideas or represent experiences in nonlinear ways (see Figure 6.5). Uploaded images such as photographs or graphics can be individually or collaboratively manipulated by using the drawing tools to label elements or arrange them on the whiteboard to show relationships between people, places, objects, and/or concepts.

| Figure 6.5 | Creating a Diagram to Illustrate Points in the Interview Response |

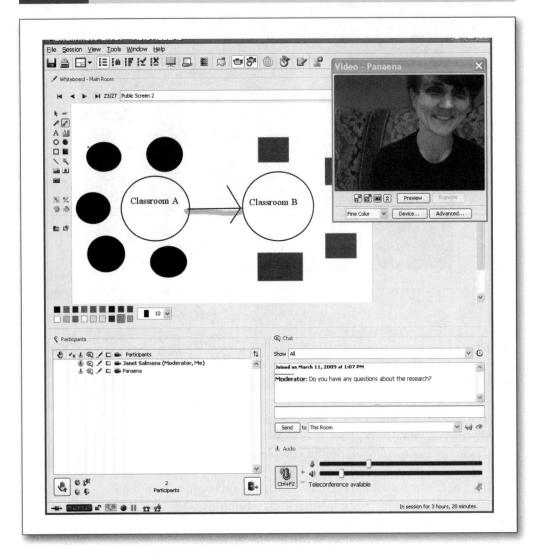

Research Tip: Choice of communication media also influences style to some extent. You need to think about what technology tools your participants will have and be comfortable with: audio, text, or both?

IMMERSIVE VIRTUAL ENVIRONMENTS

Interviews in virtual environments such as Second Life can use varied interactive approaches to transmit, view, and navigate visual stimuli in real time.

The researcher and participant communicate through audio, text chat, or written notecards. They can transmit virtual objects or artifacts into the virtual inventory of the other. Through avatars they can communicate visually by using gestures or physical expressions. They can navigate through the virtual environment, which can offer a variety of visual stimuli. The researcher can construct simulations or design environments that have specific elements to represent some aspect of the research phenomenon.

As noted earlier in the book, every researcher needs a safe, neutral location conducive to the interview. A preferred location will be comfortable for and accessible to the interviewee, with minimal distractions or interference. When choosing a virtual setting, the researcher faces many of the same issues as does the interviewer who must decide whether to meet in an agency office, community location, or participant's home.

> **Research Tip:** If the interview will use text for verbal exchange, see preparation and considerations for text-based interviews described in Chapter 9.

> **Research Tip:** If the interview in a virtual world will use audio, consider the setting. If eavesdropping is possible, consider using external audio (telephone or Skype call). Also, consider using a digital recording device to capture audio.

In some cases a neutral location, without stimuli of relevance to the meanings exchanged in the interview, will be the best choice. Researchers may decide to create their own virtual office or meeting space that allows for private, permission-only access by selected participants. A private space can deter eavesdropping or accidental interruptions. Many academic institutions, libraries, and nonprofit organizations have virtual spaces in Second Life available for educational use. Such settings have fewer distractions. These settings do not communicate personal expressions of interviewer or participant or reveal potentially private information about the avatar.

Alternatively, the interview setting may offer visual representation of phenomena and thus elicit response in the interview. Together, researchers and participants can navigate the virtual environment to observe, participate in, simulate, or experience some aspect of the subject of inquiry.

In some cases the participant's environment, which visually communicates choices in design, mood, purpose, and/or creativity, can be an appropriate setting. If observations of such settings are part of the research data, the consent agreement should reflect that intention.

> **Ethics Tip:** The ethical dilemma (discussed in more detail in Chapter 8) is in the degree of observation you may use to complement the interview. Typically, researchers take stock of attire, surroundings, and so on if they conduct the interview *in situ*. Or you may want to observe and discuss phenomena with participants. How do you handle observation activities in different kinds of immersive virtual settings? What aspects of observation should be discussed with participants and spelled out in the consent agreement?

Using Visual Methods to Enrich Online Interview Data

Visual research methods for communication, elicitation, and collaboration using technologies allow researchers to transmit or view images or media, navigate online environments, or generate images together. Online visual methods offer researchers and participants the chance to visit and discuss virtual environments, as well as enabling them to explore the participant's world. Digital and web cameras enlarge the possibilities for communication elicitation based on photography or video, because images can easily be taken and shared. Readily available drawing and graphics software make it possible to easily create charts, graphs, maps, or diagrams that convey complex information and relationships between concepts.

The Typology of Online Visual Interview Methods, along with a continuum of visual approaches in structured, semistructured, or unstructured interviews (refer back to Figure 6.1), shows a range of design and planning options for using visuals to enhance the online interview. In structured interviews, the same visual stimuli can be presented to all with limited response options offered to the participants. Questions such as the following might be used: "Does this image represent your experience? Yes or no?" or "To what degree does this image represent your experience? A lot, somewhat, or not at all?" Such questions could be followed up with the same secondary questions or open-ended questions based on participants' responses.

In semistructured interviews, the same or varied visual stimuli can be presented to participants, with the same or varied questions and follow-ups. For example, "How does this image represent your experience? Compare and contrast your experience with this representation. How do you feel about this experience? Was it important to you? If so, how? What different images would you choose to represent your own experience?" If the interview is being conducted in a web conferencing space or uses shared applications, the participant could be asked to annotate the image or create new images.

In semistructured interviews where the researcher and participant navigate a real or virtual environment, the environment can be selected by the researcher and used with every participant, varied by participant, or chosen by participant. Researchers and participants can go online together in a virtual world or game to discuss specific features or to simulate some kind of experience. Mobile devices allow interviews to occur in various geographic places; participants can report from various settings and document the specific location using GPS. Such interviews may use a more or less structured questioning but would create the most value by using a flexible approach that allows for discussion of participants' varied experiences.

In less structured or unstructured interviews, participants can be asked to share or create their own photographs or media, drawings or graphics to depict their experiences of the research phenomenon. Researchers can ask open-ended questions to solicit participants' thoughts and feelings about the images.

These visual approaches can add richness to the interview exchange and appeal to individuals with the kinds of spatial–visual intelligences Gardner (1983) identified. The integration of any or all of these approaches should be congruent with the stated purpose of the study.

Issues in Online Visual Research

PERCEPTUAL ISSUES

Images are not value free. Whether generated by people associated with the study or not, they were created from someone's subjective perspective, and that perspective enters the research discourse. Goldstein and Stanczak discuss these issues as they pertain to photography:

> When looking at a photograph, it is useful to first consider all of the technical choices made by the photographer. All of these results in the content of the image: what's in the frame (or, more accurately, what's before us, since the frame itself may be an important part of the image). However, the more interesting question is often why the photographer made these choices. Were they conscious or unconscious? What did he or she intend that we notice, and why? Do we see something that was perhaps unintended? If we decide that certain intent is present, does it work effectively, or could other choices have been more effective? What makes these questions interesting is that they often have more than one answer, or no answer at all. (Goldstein, 2007, p. 75)

> Eyewitness accounts and photo or video recordings may provide evidence not available in any other form, but they can also introduce judgments that depart from the facts of a matter. Material artifacts are similarly useful and problematic, not because artifacts make judgments but because the variations, arrangements, and modifications that make artifacts meaningful to researchers can reflect both naive and manipulative human agency. (Stanczak, 2007a, p. 27)

Comparable choices are made for graphics, including what to include or omit, how to present, what colors to use, and where to draw visual attention. One reason visuals are valuable in interviews is because they do not present or evoke one "right" answer. Stanczak (2007b) observes that

> reflexive epistemologies of visual research hold that the meaning of the images resides most significantly in the ways that participants interpret those images, rather than as some inherent property of the images themselves. (pp. 10–11)

In a qualitative interview, the researcher focuses not on the image per se but on the participants' explanations of the images. The researcher—and,

Ethics Tip: If you are using found photographs, artwork, graphics, or media, keep copyright and intellectual property in mind. Make sure you have permission to use the image, not only within the interview but in research reports or publications.

Ethics Tip: Follow the consent agreement, and make sure the participant is aware of video or still photography.

Ethics Tip: Always observe copyright laws and respect others' intellectual property.

Ethics Tip: If you plan to incorporate participant-generated drawings, photographs, or media, make sure you include permissions to use these images in the informed consent form. Make sure you have permission to use the image in research reports or publications.

Ethics Tip: If you plan to incorporate participant-generated photographs or media, keep in mind that other people who may appear in those images are not consenting participants. Photographs taken in protected environments (e.g., laboratories, workplaces, hospitals) may include proprietary or confidential information. Avoid using such photographs in research reports or publications without permission.

to some extent, the participant—needs to demonstrate visual literacy skills to decode and interpret visual images. It is important to evaluate, acknowledge, and discuss perspectives, choices, and potential biases represented in images associated with the study. According to Pauwels's (2011) "Integrated Conceptual Framework for Visual Social Research," reports of the visual aspects of a study need to be related to, and compared and contrasted with, responses to verbal questions or data from documents or observations. In addition to discussion of methodologies and design choices, the researcher should provide an explanation of the broader context (cultural, historical) in which the visual product needs to be considered (Pauwels, 2011).

ETHICAL ISSUES

Issues of public versus private settings and related need for informed consent should be handled with the same care as any data collection (see Chapter 8). Covert research is unacceptable; "covert research implies the researcher videoing and photographing the behaviour of [research participants] in a secretive rather than collaborative way, for example, using a hidden camera" (Pink, 2007, p. 53). Images should be treated as private data, with appropriate permissions articulated within the consent agreement (Banks, 2007). Permission to publish or disseminate images also must be part of informed consent. Ownership of images created for or during the interview should be spelled out. If images belonging to research participants (e.g., family photographs) are used in the interview, permissions to use them should be discussed and stated in informed consent or a separate agreement. If images are *not* the intellectual property of the researcher or participant, copyright regulations must be observed.

Closing Thoughts

Much of the early literature about online interviews described exchanges using bare-bones text communications. The evolution of ICTs—with the advent of myriad Internet-connected handheld devices with cameras, as well as computers with built-in web cameras and varied drawing and diagramming software—has changed online communications. These changes provide researchers with many options for visual research previously limited to well-funded studies with budgets for film or video cameras, technicians, and graphic artists. At the same time, the changes toward more visual communication styles—and greater orientation to the screen versus the page—mean research participants may be more comfortable expressing themselves with pictures. Drawing relevant practices from visual ethnography, sociology, and/or anthropology, contemporary researchers can design studies that build new understandings from verbal, text, and visual data collected in online interviews.

Researcher's Notebook

STORIES OF ONLINE INQUIRY

The Typology of Online Visual Interview Methods, along with a continuum of visual approaches in structured, semistructured, or unstructured interviews (see Figure 6.6), shows a range of design and planning options for using visuals to enhance the online interview. Visuals used in these interviews using elicitation, navigation, or collaboration may draw on researcher-generated, found, or participant-generated images, media, artifacts, graphics, or drawings.

Some visual interview options are discussed, using a general research question as their basis: "What are workers' preferences for types of office and work arrangements?" Below, examples from structured to unstructured approaches are presented and keyed to the continuum in Figure 6.6. You can adapt and apply these ideas to fit your own research questions.

STRUCTURED VISUAL ONLINE INTERVIEWS

In a structured interview, the researcher could present visual stimuli and offer a limited range of options to the participant, such as in the following exchange:

View these three photographs: (a) a worker in a private office, (b) a worker in an office cubicle, and (c) a worker in a home office.

(Continued)

(Continued)

- Which most closely resembles your place of work: a, b, or c?

- Which would you prefer as a place to work: a, b, or c?

- Does your company offer employees the choice to telecommute from a home office: yes or no?

This type of interview could be conducted using a variety of ICTs. Images could be sent by e-mail ahead of the interview or posted on a website that the participant accesses during the interview. In a web conferencing space, the images could be shown to participants, and

| Figure 6.6 | Examples of Visual Interview Approaches With Different Levels of Structure |

Structured

Present visual stimuli with limited-choice answers. ①

Present same visual stimuli with open-ended questions asked to all participants in the same sequence. ②

Present same visual stimuli with open-ended questions and follow-ups based on responses.

Semistructured

Present visual stimuli to participants; articulate varied open-ended questions or follow-ups based on responses. ③

Present a picture, diagram, or mind map as a framework; ask the participant to annotate based on experiences or perceptions. ④

Navigate a virtual environment or game; ask open-ended questions and discuss visual representations of phenomena. ⑤

Navigate a physical environment using GPS and/or mobile devices to discuss representations on location. ⑥

Use visual stimuli identified or created and/or shared by the participant as the basis for open-ended questions. ⑦

Unstructured

Interviewer and participant collaborate on the creation of visuals to communicate and develop ideas or elicit responses. ⑧

Source: Vision2Lead, Inc (2009–2014).

questions and answers conveyed by voice or text. The questions and answers could also be conveyed by text chat, Voice over Internet Protocol (VoIP) audio, or telephone.

SEMISTRUCTURED AND UNSTRUCTURED VISUAL ONLINE INTERVIEWS

Within the range of semistructured interview options, the interviewer could use images in various ways as stimuli to elicit responses to open-ended main and follow-up questions. The same or different visual stimuli could be used with consistent or varied questions across the interviews. Here are three different examples:

1. View these three photographs: (a) a worker in a private office, (b) a worker in an office cubicle, and (c) a worker in a home office.

   - How does your place of work compare to or contrast with one of these offices?

   - Which would you prefer for a writing project?
     - Why? Tell me more.
     - What about this space makes it conducive to writing?
     - How would you feel if you had to complete a writing project in one of the other spaces? How would you adapt?

   - Which would you prefer for a team project?
     - Why? Tell me more.
     - How would you determine what the other team members prefer?
     - How would you adapt to other members' work preferences?

2. Another semistructured approach is described in this example:

   - I am going to show you five pictures of different kinds of offices. Pick the one that most resembles your current office. Now pick the one that comes closest to your ideal place to work.

   - Depending on the participant's choices, questions and follow-ups may vary.

   - Tell me about your current office. What do you like or dislike? What about the space allows you to be focused? On time? Creative? Productive? A good team member? Does your current office enable or obstruct work–life balance?

   - Now tell me about the ideal office. What about this office makes it desirable? What kinds of work activities could be successfully achieved in this space? Why? Which would motivate you to do your best at work?

(Continued)

(Continued)

3. This semistructured approach is used for visual collaboration, to generate visual depictions of the participant's response:

   • Here is a blueprint for an office space and icons for items found in a typical office. Use the whiteboard tools to generate a design for the kind of space that would allow for both creative individual and team work. Place furniture, computers, plants, artwork, or other office fixtures. Use colors as you wish.

   • Tell me about your choices and why they would enable you to be productive and happy while you completed different kinds of work.

4. Semistructured interviews may use visual stimuli identified by the participant when navigating a physical or virtual environment. Questions can emerge based on the participant's explanation of the image or setting.

   • In this semistructured approach, researcher and participant navigate a virtual environment to stimulate discussion of the research phenomenon. The environment in this example was created by the researcher as a simulation for the purpose of the study. The researcher and participant will both need to be able to create an avatar, log in, and function in the selected virtual world.

   • Today we are going to navigate through three different model offices created in a virtual environment for the purpose of this study. In each office, tell me what you like or dislike. What about the space allows you to be thoughtful? Creative? A good team member? In each space, tell me what you would change to make it an office you would prefer. Why?

   • Today we are going to use the video conference features on a mobile device. It is up to you to navigate through the various places where you work and to show me the spaces and discuss what makes each one conducive to individual or team-oriented activities.

5. Researchers can develop a multistage process and in a preparation stage invite participants to collect images or take photographs. These can be sent to the researcher prior to the interview.

   • Prior to the interview, take pictures of all the places you work this week, including your own office, others' offices, conference rooms, web meeting spaces, coffee shops, your home, airplanes, and so on. Explain your pictures, and tell me what you like or dislike about working in each respective space. What kind(s) of work activities are best suited to each space?

6. In an unstructured, collaborative interview, the researcher and participant may generate images as the interview unfolds.

- Use the whiteboard to sketch out the blueprint for your ideal office. Explain your choices. Now I am going to suggest different kinds of work activities. Arrange or rearrange your space to make it most conducive to each assignment. Now I am going to add elements to your design. Explain whether these elements would enable you to work more or less effectively.

The preceding examples use diverse ICTs. In Examples 1 and 2, the participant simply needs to view the images. Again, images could be sent by e-mail ahead of the interview or posted on a website for the participant to access during the interview. In Example 3, a shared whiteboard in a web conference meeting or shared application could be used. In Example 4, a virtual world is selected and simulated environments created in advance of the interview. In Example 5, the participant's smartphone or tablet could be used, or the researcher could provide the device. Depending on the sample population and nature of the study, a research assistant could accompany the participant on location while the researcher logs into a video conferencing environment where the interview is conducted and recorded. For Example 6, a web conference meeting or shared application could be used to generate drawings or graphics.

In any of these interviews, questions and answers could be conveyed by text chat, VoIP audio, or telephone.

Key Concepts

- Narratives and pictures go together, and the online interviewer can likewise tell a more comprehensive story by more fully understanding the interviewee's experiences and perspectives with the help of images.

- Text-based, video conferencing, online meeting space, or immersive environment technologies offer different ways to accomplish visual research purposes, including visual ideation, visual elicitation, visual communication, and visual collaboration.

Discussions and Assignments

1. Review an article or report of a study based on verbal interview data. Develop an alternative data collection plan using online visual interview methods. Use at least two visual research method types (i.e., visual ideation, visual elicitation, visual communication, visual collaboration) and two synchronous approaches (i.e., view, transmit, navigate, generate). Provide a rationale for your choices.

2. Create a planning checklist for visual interview preparation. Exchange with peer learners to compare, contrast, and refine your checklists.

3. Think of a time when someone successfully used visual approaches to communicate with you. Describe the experience, and identify why the message got through to you by visual means.

4. What does "visual literacy" mean to you? How visually literate are you? What can you do to become more visually literate?

5. Do you think in words or pictures? Which form of Howard Gardner's intelligences is strongest for you, and how does it impact your inclinations and abilities as a researcher?

6. Conduct a practice online interview with a peer using visual research methods.
   - Using the same interview questions, experiment with different combinations: verbal stimulus/verbal response, verbal stimulus/visual response, visual stimulus/verbal response, and visual stimulus/visual response.
   - Compare and contrast the ways you communicated and the kinds of results you obtained.
   - Based on your experience, what kinds of questions elicit the richest responses?

On the Web

www.sagepub.com/salmons2e
You will find links to media pieces articles and resources about visual research methods and the technologies that enable researchers to use them online.

Handling Sampling and Recruiting

7

Selecting Participants for Online Interviews

The ideal interview subject does not exist—different persons are suitable for different types of interviews.

—Steiner Kvale and Svend Brinkman (2009)

After you study Chapter 7, you will be able to do the following:

- Describe sampling issues in qualitative research
- Compare and contrast sampling types
- Relate sampling types to a design for online interview research
- Apply recommendations for online sampling plans and recruitment

A Critical Decision: Whom to Interview?

Every researcher must make a variety of conceptual and practical decisions about how to conduct the proposed study. Every researcher must consider ways theoretical stances and principles influence approaches to data collection and analysis. Because all aspects of the research design are interrelated, each design decision a researcher makes has implications for the entire study. Ripple effects of each decision impact other areas of the research design and may have subtle or radical effects on the outcomes of

| Figure 7.1 | E-Interview Research Framework: Handling Sampling and Recruiting |

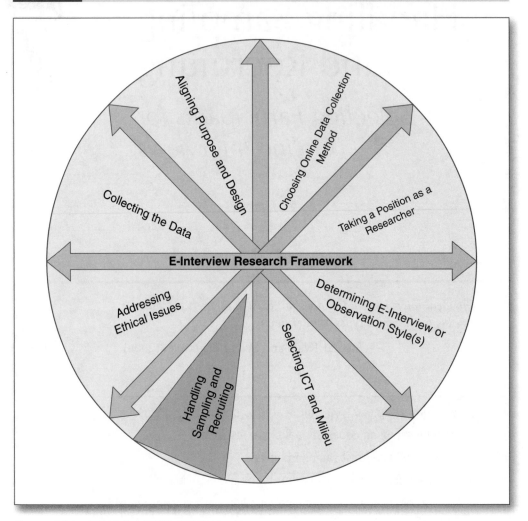

Source: Vision2Lead, Inc (2009–2014).

the study. Researchers must assess and balance risks and opportunities, and determine what is to be gained or lost with each choice.

Nowhere are researchers' choices more critical than in determining how they will identify and select the individuals who will contribute relevant thoughts and experiences as research participants. Interview researchers depend on interviewees to generate high-quality data. As noted in Chapter 4, the interviewee's role is to respond honestly to an interviewer's questions or to participate in discussion with the researcher. Interviewees' responses ideally offer insight into perceptions, understandings, or experiences of personal, social, or organizational dimensions of the subject of the study. Once a researcher decides on the purpose of the study (see

Chapter 2), the role of the interviewer (Chapter 3), and the style of interview (Chapter 4), including the technology to be used for the interview (see Chapters 5 and 6), it is possible to clarify the expectations for interviewees and the characteristics they will need to possess to participate. Gaining participants' consent, preparing for the interview, and conducting the interview are described in Chapters 8, 9, and 10, respectfully.

How does a researcher find the right people who have the ability, experience, and willingness to serve as research participants? In addition to the issues every researcher must consider, the online researcher also must think about potential consequences of the interview technology and virtual milieu for the conduct of the study and the nature of its results. Online sampling for online research is a new area without established conventions. General approaches to sampling for qualitative research can be adapted to structure and organize the process; however, new approaches are needed when researchers use the Internet to locate and recruit participants.

This chapter provides an overview of key issues in qualitative research sampling in general and a discussion of significant issues in sampling specific to online interview research. The chapter recommends ways the online researcher can creatively address common expectations reviewers of a research proposal may hold for online sampling and in the process strengthen the research design.

Sampling in Qualitative Research

If research interviews are "conversations with a purpose," then sampling is the systematic process for determining who can serve the purpose of the study. The qualitative research interview is conducted to describe a particular experience and/or context in-depth, with as much nuance and complexity as possible. The researcher needs to locate individuals who can and will provide honest, robust information about themselves and/or the phenomenon of interest and fully participate in an interview and related communication about the study.

The term **sampling** originated in quantitative research methodology where researchers look for participants who are a "sample" of a larger population. In what is sometimes called **probability sampling,** members of the research population are chosen at random and have a known probability of selection. Quantitative methods use standardized measures so the varying experiences of participants in the sample can be fit into a limited number of predetermined response categories to which numbers are assigned (Patton, 2002). With a quantitative approach, it is possible to "measure the reactions of a great many people to a limited set of questions, thus facilitating comparison and statistical aggregation of the data" (p. 14). Quantitative researchers are concerned with minimizing bias in the group; so the sample represents groups in their proportion to the population at large, thereby producing a statistically representative sample (Koerber & McMichael, 2008). This enables the researcher to test hypotheses and make generalizations from a small population to the whole population (Wilmot, 2008, p. 3).

Qualitative research typically uses a nonprobability basis sampling. Probability sampling is inappropriate for qualitative interview research, or for research that integrates qualitative interviews into a larger mixed-methods study. Qualitative studies tend to entail a deeper, more detailed exploration with a smaller number of research participants. The goals do not include producing a statistically representative sample or drawing statistical inference. Qualitative researchers have other goals and means for ensuring rigorous sampling appropriate to the study, including triangulation and cross-checking, discussed later in this chapter.

Qualitative researchers often use what is broadly defined as **purposive or purposeful sampling** when selecting people to interview because the sample is intentionally selected according to the needs of the study (Coyne, 1997). Mason (2002) suggests that there are two kinds of purposes the sample should satisfy: the empirical purpose, which is to provide data needed to address the research questions, and the theoretical purpose, which is to generate ideas that advance your understanding of, prove, or develop a theory.

To align with empirical purposes, the researcher seeks participants because they typify a circumstance or hold a characteristic that may have salience to the subject matter of the study (Ritchie & Lewis, 2003, p. 82) and because they are experienced, are knowledgeable, and offer diverse perspectives (Rubin & Rubin, 2012). To align with theoretical purposes, the researcher seeks participants on the basis of how their characteristics or experiences relate to theoretical positions and the explanation or account the researcher is developing (Mason, 2002). According to Miles and Huberman (1994, p. 29), the researcher wants to see different instances of theoretical principles, at different moments, in different places, with different people, so the qualitative researchers' concern is with the *conditions* under which the construct or theory operates, not with the generalization of the findings to other settings. In grounded theory studies, the theoretical purposes for sampling take priority. In grounded theory, the data provide the basis for describing the theory, whereas in other studies, the theory provides the basis for explaining the data. When grounded theory researchers see a new phenomenon in the data, they purposely look for new research participants who can confirm it or raise relevant questions about it (Charmaz, 2006; Koerber & McMichael, 2008).

Sampling decisions may be motivated by different goals and purposes—empirical and theoretical—sometimes in the same study. These decisions should be articulated in a systematic and well-defined sampling plan (Lee & Lings, 2008, p. 213). The sample plan lays out the approach(es) to be used and explains how they align with the research purpose and questions, epistemology, and methodology. Interrelated questions the researcher considers to develop the sample plan may include the following:

Criteria

- What rationale supports the inclusion/exclusion criteria for study participation?
- What criteria are essential for all participants to meet? Are there criteria that only some participants should meet? How much detail on the sample criteria will be developed in advance of the study? How flexible can the researcher be about defining the inclusion/exclusion criteria?
- To what degree do the research methodology and design permit the researcher to introduce new criteria that might emerge during the study? What criteria may be added for additional rounds of interview or stages of the study?
- Based on these criteria, what type or combination of types of sampling will I use?

Population

- What is the target population?
- How many people need to be sampled? Should the sampling strategy take a planned or iterative approach to determining sample size and selecting participants before or during the study?
- How much diversity is needed to represent the variations known to exist within this population (Koerber & McMichael, 2008)?
- What is it about this population that interests me (Mason, 2002)?
- Am I interested in people as individuals, groups, or collectives (Mason, 2002)?
- How should I classify people for the purpose of the study (Ritchie, Lewis, & Elam, 2003)?
  - By characteristics such as age, sex, class, ethnicity, occupation, social class?
  - By specific life experiences, feelings, perceptions, behaviors?
  - With time parameters such as era of the experience or life stage of the experience?
- Who should be excluded from the sample?
- "What relationship do I want to establish, or do I assume exists, between the sample or selection I am making, and a wider population" (Mason, 2002, p. 123)?

Logistics

- What, besides agreement to informed consent, is required of participants?
- What is the time commitment? How long will the interview be?
- In addition to the actual interview, what are other expectations for preparation and follow-up (see Chapter 9)?
- What is the budget?
- What is the time frame for recruiting participants?

The online researcher begins the process of developing a sample plan by reflecting on these questions, in concert with consideration of issues that relate specifically to sampling for data collection through online interviews.

Types of Sampling

The online interview researcher first selects the sampling type that aligns with the purpose and methodology, and then customizes it to the online milieu of the study. Researchers have found many ways to meet the specific research purposes they have identified. A number of approaches are presented in Table 7.1.

Size of Sample

How many research participants are appropriate given the research design and type of sampling selected for the study? Sampling procedures for qualitative research do not follow standardized guidelines, and guidelines for sample size are no exception. There is little agreement in the field about what constitutes an appropriate number of participants, with "it depends" typically preceding the fuzzy answers given. One perspective asks researchers to consider data needs in the context of the research purpose and methodology: "The adequacy of the sample is not determined solely on the basis of the number of participants but the appropriateness of the data" (O'Reilly & Parker, 2012, p. 6). Another points to the sufficiency of the criteria used to select appropriate participants: "With a purposive non-random sample the number of people interviewed is less important than the criteria used to select them" (Wilmot, 2008, p. 4). Yet another view suggests that researchers interview "as many subjects as necessary to find out what [they] need to know" (Kvale, 2007, p. 43).

Table 7.1	Qualitative Approaches to Sampling	
Type	**Description of Approach**	**Advantages**
Combination or mixed purposeful	More than one sampling approach is used to address different aspects of the research design or purpose.	Triangulation, flexibility, meets multiple interests and needs (Patton, 2002).
Convenience	The researcher selects participants who are readily available and easy to contact.	Saves time, money, and effort but has the lowest credibility; yields information-poor cases (Patton, 2002).
Criterion	Participants are chosen because they meet a predetermined set of criteria (Patton, 2002).	Useful for quality assurance (Miles & Huberman, 1994); enables the researcher to explore and understand central themes of the study (Ritchie et al., 2003).
Critical case	The researcher selects cases seen as "critical" to an understanding of the subject of inquiry (Patton, 2002; Ritchie et al., 2003).	Permits logical generalization and maximum application of information to other cases; what's true of the critical cases is likely true of all other cases (Patton, 2002).
Deviant or extreme	Participants are chosen because they are unusual or uniquely manifest the phenomenon (Miles & Huberman, 1994; Ritchie & Lewis, 2003).	Researchers can learn from highly unusual manifestations of the phenomenon of interest, such as outstanding success/notable failures, those who are top of the class/dropouts, exotic events, or crises (Patton, 2002).
Emergent	Participants are chosen as opportunities arise during the study (Patton, 2002).	Useful in fieldwork or when there can be no a priori specification of the sample; cannot be drawn in advance (Lincoln & Guba, 1985, p. 201).
Heterogeneous	This method deliberately includes participants who have widely different experiences of the phenomenon of interest (Ritchie & Lewis, 2003).	(See *maximum variation*.)
Homogeneous	Participants are chosen to give a detailed picture of a particular phenomenon or experience they have in common (Patton, 2002; Ritchie et al., 2003).	Focuses the study on common characteristics, reduces variation, and simplifies analysis (Miles & Huberman, 1994).

(Continued)

Table 7.1 (Continued)		
Type	**Description of Approach**	**Advantages**
Intensity	The researcher selects participants who manifest the phenomenon intensely but not extremely (Patton, 2002).	Although similar to deviant or extreme sampling, intensity sampling allows the researcher to focus on participants that strongly manifest or have deeply experienced the phenomenon of interest rather than participants who are unusual (Ritchie & Lewis, 2003).
Maximum variation	The researcher purposefully picks a wide range of variation on dimensions of interest, documents unique or diverse variations that have emerged in adapting to different conditions, and identifies important common patterns that cut across variations (Patton, 2002).	Researcher can document unique or diverse variations and identify important common patterns in the data (Creswell, 1998; Patton, 2002).
Nominated	Potential participants are recommended by other participants or by knowledgeable experts (Roper & Shapira, 2000).	Researcher's choices can be confirmed by input or recommendations from a third party.
Opportunistic	The researcher takes advantage of opportunities that arise to find participants (Ritchie & Lewis, 2003).	(See *convenience* and *emergent* sampling.)
Politically important	Participants are chosen because they connect with politically sensitive issues in the study (Miles & Huberman, 1994).	Attracts desired attention or avoids undesired attention to politically sensitive studies or findings (Miles & Huberman, 1994).
Snowball, chain, or respondent-driven sampling	The researcher identifies people who know other people who would make good interview subjects (Patton, 2002).	Snowball sampling can be used to access hard-to-reach populations or "individuals and groups often 'hidden' because openly identifying with specific factions or lifestyles can result in discrimination" (Browne, 2005, p. 47). In respondent-driven sampling, peer networks are tapped through participant–participant referrals (Hughes, 2012b).

Type	Description of Approach	Advantages
Stratified purposive	This is a hybrid approach used to select participants in subgroups.	Illustrates characteristics of particular subgroups of interest; facilitates comparisons.
Theoretical sampling	"Theoretical sampling is the process of data collection whereby the researcher simultaneously collects, codes and analyzes the data in order to decide what data to collect next. Deciding where to sample next according to the emerging codes and categories is theoretical sampling" (Coyne, 1997, p. 625).	Grounded theory researchers conduct interviews with an initial sample of participants selected using criterion sampling. In analysis of this initial set of data, they identify categories of experience or perspectives. To gain insight into these categories, they select additional research participants on the basis of how participants' characteristics or experiences help them explicate the data (Charmaz, 2006).
Theory-based sampling	This involves finding manifestations of a theoretical construct of interest so as to elaborate and examine the construct (Patton, 2002).	To get to the theoretical construct, "we need to see different instances of it, at different moments, in different places, with different people. The prime concern is with the conditions under which the construct or theory operates, not with the generalization of the findings to other settings" (Miles & Huberman, 1994, p. 29).
Total population	The researcher studies an entire population of people who share a particular characteristic or experience.	Appropriate for studies of a publicly experienced phenomenon, event, or crisis, or situations where a small group constitutes the "total" population.
Typical case sampling	This method illustrates or highlights what is typical, normal, or average (Creswell, 1998; Miles & Huberman, 1994).	What is "typical" must be known in advance. This is useful in mixed-methods studies where participants are selected based on responses to a survey (Patton, 2002; Ritchie & Lewis, 2003).
Volunteer	The researcher studies people who volunteer to be a part of the research.	Useful when the researcher is studying a common experience or phenomenon.

Although the literature does not offer a straightforward protocol for determining the number of participants, key questions will help the researcher think through the most appropriate sample size:

- *Heterogeneity or homogeneity of the population:* If the population is diverse in nature, a larger sample will be needed; the more homogeneous the sample population, the smaller the sample can be.

- *Number of selection criteria:* The more different criteria, the larger the sample (Ritchie et al., 2003).

- *Multiple samples within one study:* If it is necessary to have more than one sample within a study for reasons of comparison or control, then a larger sample will be needed (Ritchie et al., 2003).

- *Interview length:* The intensity, and therefore the length, of the qualitative interview will also impact the design of the qualitative sampling strategy and the decision of sample size. Longer interviews may provide more data than shorter interviews. Depending on the nature of the study, a larger number of shorter interviews or a smaller number of longer interviews may be conducted (Wilmot, 2008, p. 4).

- *Emerging factors in data:* Unexpected generalizations may lead the researcher to seek out new research participants who can add to or contradict the data (Silverman & Marvasti, 2008). Researchers using snowball, chain, or nominated sampling expect this to occur. Researchers using other sampling strategies need to decide whether or not they are open to an increase of sample size while the study is in progress or whether they prefer to make a note of the emerging factors for consideration in a follow-up or future study.

- *Saturation or redundancy:* **Saturation or redundancy** occurs when the researcher begins to hear the same or similar responses from interviewees. "If the purpose is to maximize information, the sampling is terminated when no new information is coming from the new sampled units; thus redundancy is the primary criterion" (Lincoln & Guba, 1985, p. 202).

Like the storied Goldilocks, the interview researcher needs a sample size that is not too big—in other words, so big "that it is difficult to extract thick, rich data" (Onwuegbuzie & Leech, 2007, p. 6). At the same time, the sample should not be too small, thus taking the risk of missing key constituencies or lacking enough diversity to show important influences. The researcher will need to consider how many interactions to have with each participant. In a study that entails more than one interview, or involves multiple types of data collection such as questionnaires and observations as well as interviews, a relatively small sample is appropriate. On the other hand, if the data collection from each participant occurs through a single interview, then more participants may be needed to generate a rich body of data. The researcher can look at other similar studies to find both examples and support for decisions about sample size. The researcher must weigh all factors and determine what size is just right for the proposed study.

Sample Frames

Fundamental to the sampling strategy is the choice of a **sample frame**, which refers to a list or grouping of people from which the sample is selected.

There are two broad types of frames:

- *Existing sample frames:* Existing frames usually consist of records previously constructed for administrative purposes. They could include membership lists for organizations or associations or lists of students or program participants (Ritchie & Lewis, 2003; Wilmot, 2008). In mixed-methods studies where a quantitative research instrument is administered as the first step, the survey sample can be used as a frame from which interview participants are selected for the qualitative stage of the study.

- *Constructed or generated sample frames:* Where an existing frame or list is not available, researchers may have to create their own. In some cases, researchers can construct a frame from partially adequate or incomplete existing frames. Another way to construct a frame is by working through organizations that provide services to or represent a population of potential participants. Researchers can generate sample frames by approaching people in a particular organization, location, setting, or meeting. This method is best used to identify people who are willing to consider taking part in the study, seeking their permission to contact them privately to discuss the study in detail (Ritchie & Lewis, 2003).

Fortunate researchers find an existing frame and can move directly into creating a sampling plan and recruiting participants. More often, researchers encounter issues in the selection and use of a sampling frame that may require significant time and attention. The researcher may discover that information about the population relevant to the study is inadequate. Available information may be out of date or simply incomplete (Mason, 2002). The researcher may find that not all representatives of the target population are included in the available lists. Sections of society missing from the frame may have different characteristics and indeed different behaviors, opinions, and attitudes than do those covered by the frame (Wilmot, 2008). In such situations, the researcher may need to augment or build on the existing frame to develop an appropriate pool of potential participants.

Sampling and Recruiting for Online Interview Research

The integrity and authority for any study results depend on the quality of the data. Obtaining the best data means finding the best research participants for the study. The credibility of the research participants is, quite simply, essential to the credibility of the study. Lincoln and Guba (1985, p. 290) point specifically to the need to establish confidence in the "truth value" of the research participants in the context of the inquiry.

Reviewers unfamiliar with online research—whether they are review board or committee members, or peers—may scrutinize online sampling plans more closely to assess the "truth value" of the online research participants. Chapter 8 points to common areas for concern: age and identity of the research participants and whether they voluntarily consent to share information and participate in the study. Although the ability to generalize results from the sample to the general population is less relevant in qualitative than in quantitative research, reviewers may want to know whether the target population has adequate access and technology literacy needed for a worthwhile sample. Are Internet access and the skills needed to engage in online communications common throughout the target population or limited? Does a known limitation in access and/or information and communications technology (ICT) skills within the target population correlate to factors being studied in such a way that they might skew the results of the study?

A challenge the researcher will confront is this: No generally accepted standards, approaches, or guidelines exist for sampling research participants for online interview research. A typology of sampling approaches and a set of recommended practices are presented here to guide those who are designing studies with online interview data collection.

DESIGN DECISIONS INFLUENCE
SAMPLING AND RECRUITING

Whether to *interview* online or whether to *sample and recruit* online are two different decisions. A researcher could use online sampling and recruiting for interviews conducted in person or could use face-to-face approaches for sampling but conduct the interviews online. The research purpose, rationale for deciding to interview online, geographic scope of the study, and researcher's access to the target population are determining factors for the decision to use online or other sampling approaches.

One important distinction influences where and how to recruit participants: whether the digital environment serves as a means for exchange or part of the subject of inquiry. As noted in Chapter 3, researchers who conduct online interviews to collect data fall into two broad categories:

- Those who choose to conduct interviews online to study online or technology-mediated behaviors, culture, practices, attitudes, or experiences

- Those who choose to conduct interviews online to study phenomena that occur in the face-to-face world

More and more activities in the fields of business and sales, education and training, government and civil society, culture and entertainment, and personal and family life that once occurred face-to-face and locally can now occur online, without regard to geographic location. Researchers whose purpose is to study online behaviors may find an online research method the logical choice because they can be assured that participants have access and are comfortable communicating electronically. In these studies, the Internet community, social media site, game, or project is the research site and may be important to understanding the research problem. For such studies, online sampling and recruiting is appropriate.

Other researchers choose online interview methods to study behaviors or phenomena that occur face-to-face because such methods allow for flexibility of timing and location for the interview, or because they permit the use of shared applications or visual methods (see Chapter 6). For these researchers, the online environment is the meeting venue and is not part of the research phenomenon or subject of inquiry. These researchers may take either an online or more conventional approach to the sampling strategy.

For example, consider a hypothetical study designed to improve understanding of community college instructors' attitudes toward methods of instruction for at-risk learners:

- *Researcher A* is interested in the attitudes of instructors who teach in face-to-face classrooms but chooses to conduct interviews online to work around teachers' erratic schedules. Researcher A might use as a sampling frame a local community college and, after getting the school's permission, visit a faculty meeting or post notices to recruit participants. Alternatively, this researcher could use an online sampling plan or a hybrid approach to sampling, including both online and face-to-face strategies to recruit participants.

- *Researcher B* wants to compare attitudes of instructors who teach in face-to-face classrooms of urban, suburban, and rural community colleges in different parts of the United States. Researcher B chooses to interview online to gain access to perspectives from geographically diverse communities without the need for extensive travel. Researcher B needs to use an online recruiting strategy to locate dispersed participants who meet the sampling criteria.

- *Researcher C* is interested in the online, e-learning experiences of community college instructors. Researcher C may use online sampling strategies similar to those of Researcher B, but Researcher C has a greater interest in the digital culture(s) and context of the interactions with potential interviewees. For Researcher C, a preliminary scan of online teachers' communities and types of e-mail lists or newsletters they share may inform not only approaches to sampling and recruiting but also the questions and themes of the interview itself. This researcher may decide to gain the permission of an association or other online group not only to recruit its members for the study but also to use its online community as the setting for observations and interviews.

The following examples show how a similar pattern of choices might apply across different disciplines:

- In business research, Researcher A is interested in experiences of business owners in the local community but chooses online interviews that allow flexibility and ease of recording; Researcher B is interested in experiences of business owners in different markets and chooses online interviews to broaden access to participants; and Researcher C is interested in experiences of business owners who sell products and services online through e-commerce, so is interested in the digital milieu where the business operates.

- In social sector research, Researcher A is interested in the experiences of leaders in agencies that serve the local community; Researcher B is interested in experiences of leaders in agencies in locations beyond reach for face-to-face interviews; and Researcher C is interested in experiences of leaders whose agencies provide services online.

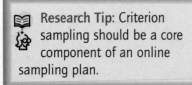

Research Tip: Criterion sampling should be a core component of an online sampling plan.

Research Tip: Mesh criterion sampling with other approaches as needed to devise explicit sampling plans.

The empirical purpose of these studies is similar, yet the sampling strategies they could use and the way they will describe those strategies in the sampling plan may vary greatly.

All the sampling plans will need to answer the questions listed earlier in this chapter. In addition, researchers should address the following questions to determine what sampling approach is appropriate:

- How will the researcher assess whether the target population has access to the technology the researchers intends to use, and the capability and willingness to use it as a research participant?

- How can the researcher locate credible research participants? How will the researcher verify the identity and age (or other relevant criteria) of research participants recruited online?

- How will the researcher present a credible and trustworthy identity that will motivate potential participants to volunteer?

- How will online recruitment be carried out? What opportunities and constraints are present in the setting where the researcher intends to reach out to potential participants? What permissions are needed to post recruitment messages to specific groups?

- What are the practical steps, and how long will they take?

No two researchers will answer such questions in the same way. Still, some common principles for online sampling can be identified. Some of these principles are not unique to online research; however, these principles are applied differently in practice in large part because the researcher needs to counter potential communication gaps or breakdowns that are more prevalent in online communication. Considerations for each question and recommendations are offered here.

SAMPLING APPROACHES APPROPRIATE FOR ONLINE INTERVIEW RESEARCH

If research interviews are "conversations with a purpose," then the first step is to clearly determine the specific purpose for each research participant. What indicators will signal the researcher that a potential research participant can help build understanding of the phenomenon or question at the heart of the study? These indicators should be defined and articulated as criteria for sample selection. Precision and clarity are important in any project involving online communication.

Criterion sampling is based on the researcher's identification of specific characteristics that serve as the basis for selection of research participants. The researcher sets some parameters or priorities for the kind of participant who, by participating in an online interview, can contribute data needed to answer the research questions. Clear delineations of the inclusion criteria will be a boon to recruiting, especially when researchers need to explain to a moderator why permission should be granted to

Table 7.2	Sampling Approaches: Define Criteria to Describe Scope and Focus of Sample
Type	**Kinds of Criteria**
Convenience	Define specific factors that would make the participant someone "convenient" to interview online, such as same time zone or member of a group familiar to researcher. The potential risk with convenience sampling is that participants may be known to the researcher or the researcher may have conflicts of interest with the participants. The rationale for using this approach will need to provide sound reasons for why drawbacks associated with convenience sampling are outweighed by factors associated with the research problem and purpose. See Chapter 3 about the position of the researcher and ways to avoid bias.
Critical case	Define "critical" in the context of the study, and articulate criteria for being included in the sample. What descriptors can be used to explain distinctive attributes of the case? What parameters can be drawn so it is clear what cases will be excluded?
Deviant or extreme	Identify which characteristics are within the norm, and state criteria defining what qualifies as "extreme." If "deviant," "heterogeneous," or "maximum variation" will be determined based on the variety within the sampling group, how will you recruit a wide range of potential participants from which to select diverse examples? How can you communicate your interest in a wide range of experiences?
Emergent	Identify the known characteristics desired in the sample population, and where possible, identify the kinds of characteristics the researcher may hope to find.
Heterogeneous	Identify range of diversity desired for specific characteristics in the target sample population—for example, different experiences of the same phenomenon, different educational levels, or different cultural backgrounds.
Homogeneous	Identify and clearly state the characteristics that members of the target sample population should have in common—for example, a certain number of years of experience in the profession, level of education, or demographic factors such as age range.
Intensity	Identify which characteristics are within the norm, and state criteria defining what qualifies as "intense."

Type	Kinds of Criteria
Maximum variation	Identify range of variation desired for specific characteristics in the target sample population, and articulate the maximum acceptable in the interview sample. For example, state the maximum age range of sample.
Politically important	Define "political" in the context of the study, and differentiate between "important" and "unimportant." On this basis, articulate criteria for sample appropriate for the study.
Snowball or chain	Identify criteria for initial participants, then state criteria to be communicated to those interviewees who might be able to recommend other people appropriate for the study.
Theoretical sampling	Identify criteria for initial interviewees; based on theoretical constructs that emerge from the first round of interviews, state criteria participants will need to exemplify to be included in study. In "theoretical" or "theory-based" approaches, be sure to translate theoretical concepts into language the potential participants will understand. Avoid jargon when stating criteria.
Theory-based sampling	State criteria describing what participants will need to manifest in relationship to the theoretical construct of interest to be included in study.
Total population	Determine the characteristic or experience that defines the population.
Typical case sampling	Define "typical" in the context of the study; on this basis, articulate criteria for sample appropriate for the study.
Volunteer	Determine criteria volunteers will need to meet to participate in the study.

promote a study to an online community or e-mail list. Any terms specific to the study should be defined as a part of the criteria-setting process. If as a researcher you are unclear about what you want, it will be challenging to build the relationships needed to gain entrée to an existing sample frame. By stating criteria, the researcher also creates additional factors that can be independently verified by other sources besides the research participant's own statements.

Criteria can be refined by using other types of sampling to align further with the purpose and research questions guiding the study. For example, when the researcher is looking for a variety of perspectives using a deviant, heterogeneous, or maximum-variation sample, it may still be important to identify criteria all participants must meet, such as minimum age. See Table 7.2 for suggested ways to think through and select the best approach for the study at hand.

Sampling and recruiting decisions should be spelled out in the sample plan and reviewed by the **institutional review board (IRB), research ethics board,** or others who may be overseeing the research. Otherwise, the researcher may find that other interactions outside the approved study are needed or that potentially illegitimate data were collected. Either case may precipitate a return to the review process for **IRB approval** of additional interactions with the interviewees and/or a revision of the consent agreement to allow inclusion of all data (Garg, 2008).

COMMUNICATING WITH POTENTIAL PARTICIPANTS

When communicating the study's purpose to potential participants, clear, succinct messages may mean the difference between whether or not they will click on a website button or respond to a text or e-mail recruitment notice. Clearly defined study purpose and participation criteria are also valuable when seeking assistance from others who might refer, suggest, or introduce potential participants, or promote a call for participation to their respective networks. Keep in mind that the ways you describe the research design and sample for an academic audience may be stylistically quite different from the ways you will communicate to potential participants. Translate any jargon or "academese" into plain language understandable to your target audience.

In addition to clear inclusion/exclusion criteria, it is important to spell out what the researcher expects from participants. Will the participant be asked to discuss potentially sensitive information or not? If hot-button issues such as financial information or marital/relationship/family information are not going to be discussed, then emphasize those exclusions in the initial recruitment messages through the screening process.

> **Research Tip:** Clarify your expectations for research participants. Translate "academese" into straightforward statements. Define any specialized terms.

The time required for one or more interviews and the period for multiple interactions through the course of the study should be defined as closely as possible in advance. Some interview types may necessitate participant preparation in advance of the interview (see Chapter 9), multiple interviews, and/or follow-up during data analysis to substantiate the researcher's understanding of participant statements (see Chapter 10).

> **Ethics Tip:** Be open and disclose unknown factors that could result in changes in expectations, scheduling, and so on that could affect the research participant.

In online research, a participant may drop out by simply closing the interview window or deleting the e-mail. In this digital milieu, the researcher should specify expectations from the beginning of the relationship to ensure persistence. When you consider the Typology of E-Interview Structures in the context of sampling (see Figure 7.2), it is apparent that the requirements and level of commitment for participation may vary greatly depending on the type of interview. It makes sense that the more the researcher views the interview as a knowledge-generating interaction, the more time he or she will need to build trust, relationships, and understanding of the study's purpose.

Figure 7.2   Structure and Time Frame

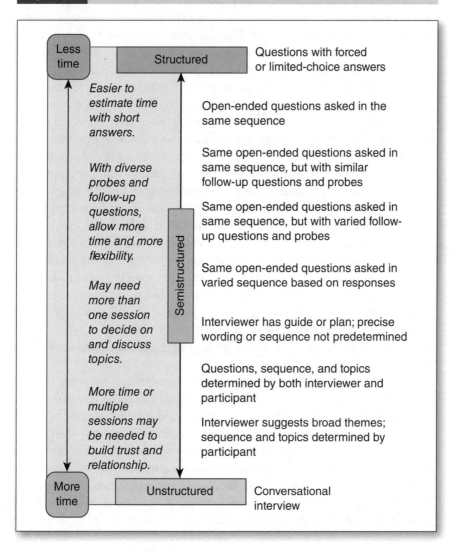

Source: Vision2Lead, Inc (2014).

> **Research Tip:** Identify means of communication for each stage of the study. Do not assume that the ICTs the researcher wants to use are best for sample populations. Change if possible—or offer a practice session—if the participant objects to using a particular ICT.

Beyond specifying expectations for the time and nature of potential research participants' commitment to the study, online researchers also need to specify technology access and skills involved in research participation. What combination of online communication tools does the researcher intend to use for preparation, interview, and any follow-up communication? Will routine communication such as arranging times to meet for the interview or discussing the purpose of the study be carried out through e-mail, text messaging, or telephone? Will the synchronous interview require a microphone, a web camera, or other specialized hardware or software? What can the researcher provide? Does the researcher need to seek funds to subsidize participants' acquisition of technology? Can the researcher arrange for interviewees to participate from a computer lab or another setting?

Participant access is a fundamental question that influences any research design. Researchers who intend to interview people in person are concerned with geographic access to the desired meeting place and access for people with disabilities or other restrictions. Researchers consider possible effects of the setting on interview responses—will participants be intimidated or influenced by the room arrangement or by associations with the institution, power, or authority reflected in the meeting space? Online interviewers must ask similar questions when selecting the data collection methods and tools. Will potential participants who fit the sample demographic have access to the online tools the researcher intends to use? Will they feel comfortable responding to questions in the selected online meeting space? Will it be necessary to schedule a pre-interview online meeting to introduce the ICT or specific features to the participants? Or will it be necessary to arrange for someone else to assist the participant? For example, might an adult child or senior center volunteer assist the elderly participant? If so, should that assistant sign some kind of consent form or agreement to ensure confidentiality of the participant's responses?

ICT literacy, technology adoption, and census studies mapping rates of Internet access by people in various demographic categories and geographic areas provide researchers with useful background information on the target sample population. In addition, the researcher can look for signs of an online presence for the target population. Are there websites on topics of interest to this population? Are online communities or social networking sites by and for them up-to-date and active? This kind of broad exploration may help the researcher answer the general questions; specific questions will need to be posed to individuals as part of the initial discussion of needs and requirements for participation in the study. Based on the hypothetical example presented earlier, Researchers A and B are more concerned with questions of access and

ICT literacy than is Researcher C, who is exploring Internet-related behaviors, transactions, events, or cultures and can assume that participants are comfortable with various forms of online communication.

 Research Tip: Determine where online the target population can best be reached.

ENSURING THAT PARTICIPANTS ARE CREDIBLE

Once the researcher has developed a clear and specific set of criteria and identified the ICT-related issues, the next step is to devise a way to locate people who fit the study's purpose and requirements. Strategies to verify potential research participants' identities and ensure that they authentically meet the study criteria are important to any online sampling plan but critical when the researcher intends to recruit in public online environments. Researchers who have access to private, members-only online spaces have less concern for identity and consenting age of potential participants and can proceed in a similar style to that used by any researcher. Once again, the Public–Private Internet Continuum illustrates the differentiation and points to the fact that the issues are not black and white (see Figure 7.3). Researchers will have to use their own judgment, based on the nature of the study, the target population, and the norms and culture of the online environment where they hope to find information-rich cases for research participation.

Two approaches are suggested here as the basis for locating credible research participants online: *nomination* and *existing sample frames*. The first relies on verification of identity by another person who knows the potential participant; the second relies on verification by membership in a group, organization, or reliable administrative list. These approaches succeed when the researcher is very specific about desired characteristics—another reason why criterion-based sampling has added value online.

Ethics Tip: Err on the safe side if you have any reason to doubt the age or the identity of a potential participant, and seek additional verifiable evidence before selecting the individual to participate in the study.

Participants Are Nominated by Trustworthy Third Party

Can someone else recommend potential participants who meet sampling criteria? In the act of nomination, the identity of the potential participant is verified. A nomination from a known person or organization deflects the question, "How do you know the participant is who he or she says?" The use of this approach does add another step for the researcher, who must explain the study and ask for assistance from others who can make the nomination. Online, nomination could be accomplished with an

Figure 7.3 Public–Private Environments: Considerations for Sampling

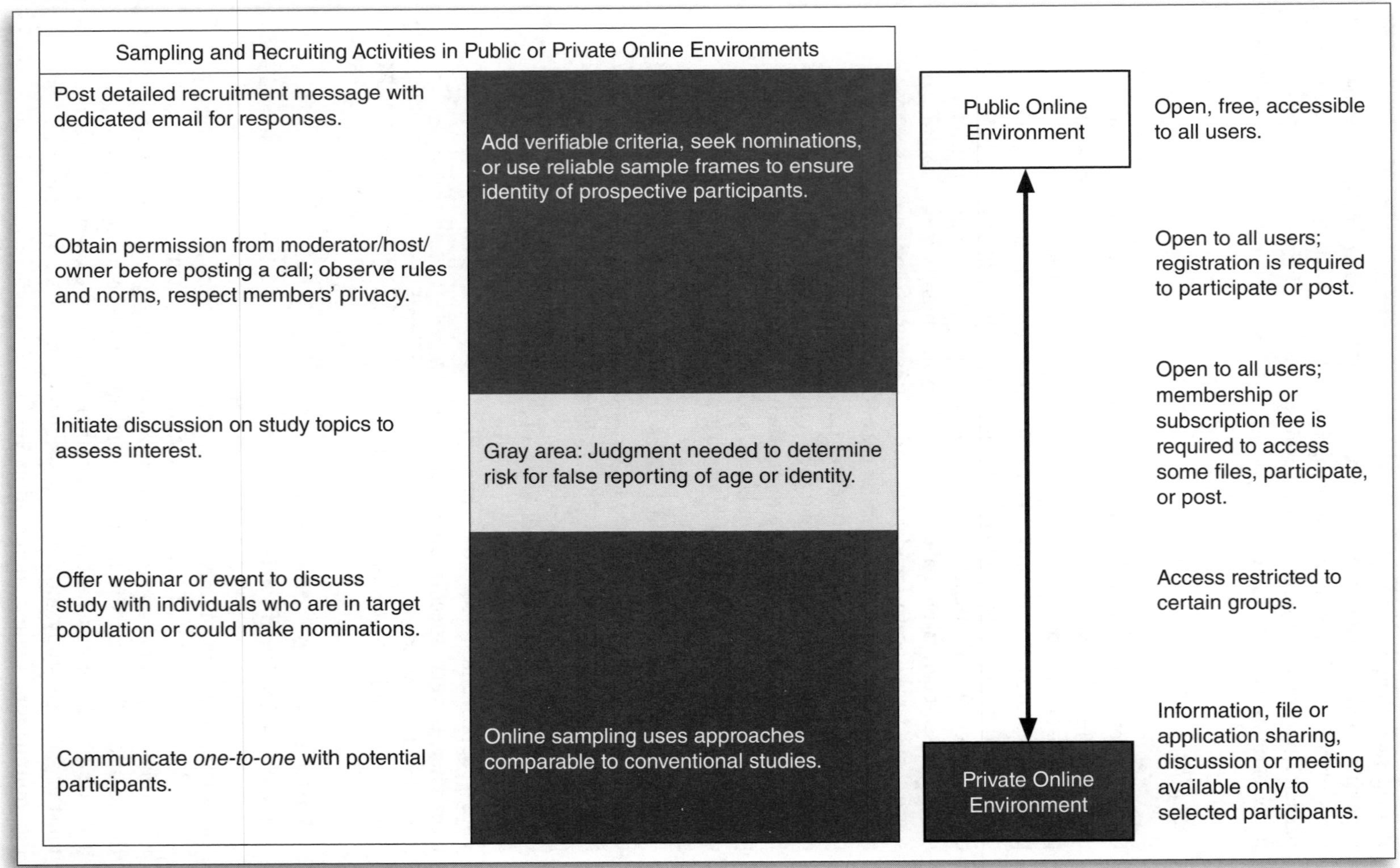

Sampling and Recruiting Activities in Public or Private Online Environments

	Public Online Environment	Private Online Environment
Post detailed recruitment message with dedicated email for responses.		
Obtain permission from moderator/host/owner before posting a call; observe rules and norms, respect members' privacy.	Add verifiable criteria, seek nominations, or use reliable sample frames to ensure identity of prospective participants.	
Initiate discussion on study topics to assess interest.	Gray area: Judgment needed to determine risk for false reporting of age or identity.	
Offer webinar or event to discuss study with individuals who are in target population or could make nominations.		
Communicate one-to-one with potential participants.	Online sampling uses approaches comparable to conventional studies.	

Public Online Environment

Open, free, accessible to all users.

Open to all users; registration is required to participate or post.

Open to all users; membership or subscription fee is required to access some files, participate, or post.

Access restricted to certain groups.

Private Online Environment

Information, file or application sharing, discussion or meeting available only to selected participants.

e-mail request to colleagues, program direc-
tors, or others in a position to know individuals who meet the sample criteria.

Nomination can be meshed with a snowball or chain approach. Research participants whose identities and credibility have
been established may be asked to nominate
others who share characteristics or experiences. A crucial element of
successful nomination by research participants is trust. Streeton, Cooke,
and Campbeii (2004) note the importance of trust when recruiting
participants:

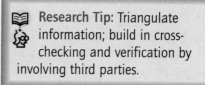

Research Tip: Triangulate
information; build in cross-
checking and verification by
involving third parties.

> Trust and networking, and the role of the professional relationship, have an
> impact on the nature, strength, and numbers of further nominations in this
> type of recruitment and retention. Researchers rely on the truth and fidelity
> of information received from their contacts, and perhaps more importantly,
> contacts must feel they can trust the fidelity of the researchers. (p. 45)

In the sample plan, the researcher should explain the nomination strategy and specify the individuals or organizations the researcher will count
on to nominate potential interviewees.

Participants Are Pulled From
Existing Sample Frames

Fundamental to any sampling strategy is the choice of sample frame, the
list or grouping of people from which the sample is selected. As discussed
earlier in this chapter, some researchers construct sample frames while
others rely on existing frames. Constructing a sample frame online is possible but adds more layers of information or identity the researcher must
verify. Thus, constructing a new sample frame online may be too time-
consuming to be practical.

Existing sample frames can serve the online researcher because they
are aggregate pools of individuals who have verified their identities (and
perhaps even credit card numbers) to qualify as members. With the advent
of online communities and social networking websites, and the movement
of professional associations and clubs to the Internet, many potential
sample frames exist online. In some cases faculty, employee, or membership lists may be posted on a website or published in a directory. What
groups or affiliations would attract and engage the target sample population, and what appropriate means can be utilized to communicate the
study's call for participation?

By using nomination or existing frames, researchers avoid a time-
consuming recruitment process of filtering out potential participants who

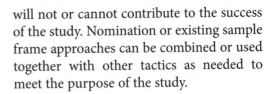

Research Tip: Create a recruitment statement so all posts or requests use consistent language to describe the study and convey the same message to potential participants.

Ethics Tip: Keep ethics and privacy issues in mind when communicating online.

will not or cannot contribute to the success of the study. Nomination or existing sample frame approaches can be combined or used together with other tactics as needed to meet the purpose of the study.

Ensuring Research Participants That *Researchers* Are Credible

As noted in earlier chapters, we live in an interview society, a society where nearly every purchase is followed by a request for participation in a follow-up questionnaire. Our telephones buzz with a stream of polling requests. At the same time, people who participate online in social media and other communities are increasingly wary about their privacy. They wonder, Who wants my information and why? How will this information be used? Why should I spend my precious time giving you my information? These conditions may lead to reluctance to participate in research studies. While as researchers we are concerned with the credibility of participants, potential participants are equally concerned with our credibility. A thoughtfully crafted web presence is one way to address this issue by introducing ourselves and our research interests in a way that builds positive impressions with potential participants.

The researcher's web presence can take numerous forms; two are described broadly here as (a) statements and images posted on others' sites, blogs, friendship walls, or communities or (b) statements and images posted on the researcher's own site, blog, or social media page.

The first step is to create a statement that introduces the researcher. Think from the position of a potential participant: What would inspire someone to trust me as a researcher, and what would generate interest in my work? This statement should include the researcher's academic and professional credentials and affiliations. Student researchers may want to identify their academic institutions and (with permission) their professor or dissertation supervisor. However, the simple statement "I am a doctoral student conducting research for a dissertation" is not usually adequate to appeal to potential participants. The introduction should point to the new knowledge the study aims to contribute to build a sense of importance for study participation.

To build this sense of importance, a very specific recruitment message should be used to better reach the target population. The researcher can fruitfully use this message to appeal to potential participants who meet inclusion criteria or ask for nominations of research participants.

The statement should explain the researcher's approaches and expectations on the matters discussed in this chapter. A succinct but comprehensive statement may include these elements:

- *Purpose of the study:* Summarize the research questions, reasons for conducting the study, and the researcher's goals for the results should be outlined. Is the researcher conducting dissertation or thesis research? If so, note the institution. Such academic purposes assure potential participants of some level of faculty oversight of the study. Is the researcher assessing needs for programs or services? Creating the basis for a larger survey research project? How will the researcher disseminate the findings? What aspects of the researcher's goals will draw in potential participants and motivate them to contribute?

- *Ethics and privacy:* Offer assurances about ethical conduct of the study, confidentiality, protection of privacy, and private data storage. Indicate appropriate ethics, institutional, or other review board approvals granted for the study. If the study anticipates an international sample, indicate how you will address multiple sets of requirements.

- *Criteria:* State key sampling criteria, including characteristics, scope, and focus of the desired sample.

- *Expectations:* List the time frame for the study, time commitment, and technology tools needed for participation. All steps of the study should be spelled out, particularly when the researcher wants more than one interview, the opportunity to send follow-up questions by e-mail, review of the interview transcript after the interview, or additional data collection steps such as a questionnaire or observation of the participant's interactions in an online community.

- *Screening and selection process:* Provide sample size information, and explain how the researcher will choose participants.

- *Incentive for participation:* Discuss reasons target population members should participate. Appeal to their sense of altruism and point out that they will be creating new solutions to a problem, improving understanding of an issue, or adding to the body of knowledge on a topic. Mention any other incentives for completion of all data collection steps, such as a gift card or perhaps an executive summary of findings or invitation to a webinar on the findings.

One benefit of such a statement is consistency of language and message so that all potential nominators or research participants begin from the same common understanding of the researcher's identity and the nature of the study. In the case of a heterogeneous or extreme case sample, the researcher may refine some elements of the statement to appeal to diverse audiences.

Researchers can create a space where the researcher's introduction, statement about

> **Ethics Tip:** Keep in mind that when interviewing people internationally, different principles or regulations may be in place. For example, when data is transferred from a European Union (EU) to a non-EU country, data must be adequately protected under EU regulations.

the study, and recruitment message can be posted online: a website, blog, or virtual space. Free blog or website services are ideal for this purpose. In addition to text-based descriptions of the call for participation, the researcher can create a video clip or audio version of the recruitment message. These personal touches can help increase interest and build presence with site visitors. Links to the researcher's academic institution or other publications can convey integrity and authenticity of the study. Be sure to provide means for contact, such as a link to an e-mail or messaging address, preferably one associated with the educational institution to reinforce academic credibility. Avoid using the researcher's physical address or phone number, which could lead to privacy violations for the researcher.

Once crafted, the statement can become the basis for communication with potential participants or those who can help with recruitment. When a brief, restricted-length post is needed on a social media site, e-mail list, or online community, the short message can include a link to the full statement.

GETTING OUT THE RECRUITMENT MESSAGE

Locating the right people and recruiting them to participate in a study is a challenge for any researcher. Central to the challenge for online researchers is the avoidance of sending or receiving unwanted messages, commonly known as spam. If the researcher posts a recruitment message or advertisement on a public website, networking community, or e-mail list, a deluge of unwanted responses may result. On the other hand, if the researcher sends unsolicited e-mail requests to potential participants, the message may be perceived as spam. Ethical issues related to types of online communication are discussed in Chapter 8.

Keep in mind that online posts will reach a very general audience. Where can you find potential participants who meet specific sampling criteria? The researcher can share a recruitment statement or link to the researcher's recruitment site through e-mail discussion lists. If relevant to the topics of the list, the researcher can initiate a discussion about the nature and importance of the study. Similarly, the researcher can interact with others in a social networking space. A researcher may seek help from an online community with shared interests, such as a professional association, to characterize the subjects of a study and to find participants. The potential for interacting informally with members of the target population means researchers can gain insights that may help in determining sampling and recruitment strategies best suited to the study. A best practice is to approach the moderator of the list or discussion group directly to get permission for the recruitment posting, and respect any norms or guidelines.

Another way to find participants is by using the networking possibilities of the digital milieu: The researcher can offer a **webinar** or host an online event or discussion on issues related to the study. By doing so, the researcher creates an opportunity to interact with individuals who are interested in the subject of inquiry and to attract potential participants or people who can nominate participants.

Closing Thoughts

Decisions about the type or combination of types of sampling, sample size, and recruitment are essential steps in the research design, proposal development, and planning process. Although researchers using observation or documents for data collection also must make hard decisions about sampling, interview researchers have a more delicate task since they are choosing people with whom they will communicate personally. Interview researchers will have before them a human being—not simply an information-rich data source. If the sampling was successful, trust and rapport will develop so the researcher gains the information needed to answer the research questions, in an interchange characterized by mutual respect. Sampling is a complex and sensitive process for any interview researcher, regardless of experience or research design. The online researcher has some additional considerations—and some additional options.

Researcher's Notebook

THE E-INTERVIEW RESEARCH FRAMEWORK: HANDLING SAMPLING AND RECRUITING

The E-Interview Research Framework points to the importance of keeping the entire study in mind with each decision. This is certainly critical when it comes to sampling and recruiting since interview researchers will not get far without interview participants! Key questions related to decisions about sampling and recruiting in the context of the overall study are outlined in Table 7.3.

STORIES OF ONLINE INQUIRY

This Researcher's Notebook again focuses on the two studies discussed in Chapter 3. Both studies used data collected from online interviews conducted in web conferencing spaces. These studies used different strategies for sampling and recruiting.

(Continued)

(Continued)

Table 7.3	Applying the E-Interview Research Framework: Handling Sampling and Recruiting
	Handling Sampling and Recruiting
Aligning purpose and design	• Does the researcher show how sampling approaches are appropriate given the purpose of the study and e-research approach?
Choosing online data collection method	• Does the researcher explain any implications of the choice of online data collection for sampling and recruiting participants?
Taking a position as a researcher	• Does the researcher disclose any conflicts of interest with the population?
Determining e-interview or observation styles	• Are there any concerns about whether participants are willing and able to participate in the selected style of interview? • Does the researcher explain any issues that would make the intended style problematic for the population? • What does the researcher need to explain to potential participants during the recruitment stage?
Selecting ICT and milieu	• Does the researcher describe any issues related to the population's preferences for, access to, and skills to use the selected ICT? • Does the population prefer to communicate synchronously or asynchronously?
Handling sampling and recruiting	• Does the researcher specify the sampling and recruiting approach and provide a rationale for its suitability to the study?
Addressing ethical issues	• Does the researcher have a plan to locate credible research participants? • How will the researcher verify the identity and age (or other relevant criteria) of research participants recruited online? • Does the researcher outline what will be included in the consent agreement to encompass all aspects of the interview(s) and/or observations?
Collecting the data	• Does the researcher state what will be discussed with participants during recruiting and screening processes?

The research design for my online interview research on collaborative e-learning was best served by a small, purposeful sample of information-rich cases; thus, a criterion-based approach was used. Although it sounds paradoxical, I used aspects of both homogeneous and hetero-geneous sampling. Common, homogeneous characteristics included online teaching experience at the college level, within comparable subject areas of leadership and management. All were expected to have used a minimum of two different instructional techniques in support of collaborative e-learning.

In looking for research participants, I sought heterogeneity in regard to their online teaching experience and looked for as many different instructional approaches as possible to enhance the richness of the data. I also wanted as global a representation as possible; indeed, global access was a big reason for selecting online interview methodology.

While snowball or emergent sampling would have worked given the type of study, I feared they might introduce too many unknowns into the process and thus sound alarms for the institutional review board. Instead, I relied on several existing sample frames. In the year prior to the study, I participated in numerous online conferences, belonged to professional e-mail lists, and took an online class. "Teaching and Learning in Virtual Learning Environments" was cosponsored by five European universities for educators worldwide. Course, meeting, and attendee lists served as fertile sample frames for the study. By participat-ing in these events and meetings and observing other participants, I was able to identify active contributors. The presentations, writings, and/or comments of these contributors were reviewed. Those with interests and experience relevant to the study were contacted to introduce the study and discuss possible participation. The recruitment message was sent primarily in the context of one-to-one e-mails and in one members-only e-mail list. Research participants' identity information could be readily triangulated with information from other sources; there were no ques-tions about whether the interviewees were who they said they were.

For the second exemplar, given the exploratory nature of the study, I wanted a maximum-variation sample of research participants who were in different lines of business. Stratified purposive sampling was used to achieve maximum variation. A stratified approach allows the researcher to identify subgroups that facilitate comparisons (Miles & Huberman, 1994). Main subgroups were defined as follows:

- *Real-world e-entrepreneurs* who use the Internet to market or carry out other business activities for operations that occur in the physical world

(Continued)

(Continued)

- *Digital e-entrepreneurs* who use the Internet to market or carry out other business activities for operations that occur online

Given the nature of the study, I could assume that potential participants were active online and members of social media sites, making online recruitment a sensible choice. Much had changed between recruitment described in the first exemplar, which took place in 2004, and this recruitment in 2012.

For the first step, I created a space on my website for the study and posted a detailed description about the study and what I wanted to achieve. Limitations were explained as well: I wanted to assure potential participants that I was not interested in proprietary or financial information. An interested participant could look at my site and see my other work and publications. A link to this site was embedded in short posts to Twitter, Facebook, and LinkedIn. Messages sent to e-mail lists also included the link for anyone interested in more information.

An additional strategy involved direct invitations. I searched sites such as Kickstarter, an online crowdsourcing mechanism for entrepreneurs seeking funding, and selected successfully funded businesses that met my study criteria. I wrote to select individuals using the Kickstarter messaging system to introduce myself and ask if they would participate in an online interview. Again, I shared the link to the research site. It might seem as though a cold-calling approach would be lost in the piles of incoming messages, but the response was very good and two participants were recruited.

In summary, online recruitment takes time and flexibility, creativity and persistence. The approaches described here offer a few successful ways to begin.

Key Concepts

- Before the researcher seeks out people to interview, a sampling plan is needed.

- Qualitative researchers use nonprobability sampling. Although a combination of sampling approaches can be used in online research, developing specific criteria will help the researcher locate and verify potential interviewees. Thus, criterion-based sampling is recommended as a component of the online sampling plan.

- Online interviewers may recruit participants through online or offline approaches. Nomination and existing sample frames offer ready verification of the identities of participants recruited online.

Discussions and Assignments

1. In assignments for previous chapters, you located articles describing interview studies. Look at those articles again.

   - What kind of sampling did each use? Look at the tables in this chapter and identify the approach. Do you feel the researcher made the best choice? Why or why not? What would you recommend?

   - Did any of the studies discuss online recruitment of participants? What other recruitment strategies would you suggest?

2. Discuss issues of identity in online culture. Do you believe people are more or less honest about their identities online? Support your answer with specific examples.

3. Create a researcher blog with an introduction and recruitment message. Share the link with at least three colleagues, peers, or fellow classmates.

   - What feedback do they offer that can help you develop a credible presence as an online researcher?

   - What suggestions do they have for making the recruitment message more appealing?

On the Web

www.sagepub.com/salmons2e
You will find a media piece, examples, models, and templates for creating plans for sampling and recruiting study participants.

8

Addressing Ethical Issues in Online Interview Research

> *I have always thought that one man of tolerable abilities may work great changes, and accomplish great affairs among mankind, if he first forms a good plan, and . . . makes the execution of that same plan his sole study and business.*
>
> —Benjamin Franklin (1757/2004)

After you study Chapter 8, you will understand the following:

- A general overview of ethical components of research design
- An exploration of ethical issues important to researchers proposing to collect data through online interviews
- Practical steps for designing studies acceptable to institutional review boards or other decision makers

Ethical Research Design and Online Interviews

A *research design* is a comprehensive strategic plan for a study. It describes all elements of the study coherently and argues for scholarly and scientific merit. The research design shows how all of the major parts of the research project work together to accomplish the study's purpose and address the research questions. As noted in Chapter 2, epistemological and theoretical perspectives influence and support the choices made in the research

Figure 8.1 E-Interview Research Framework: Addressing Ethical Issues

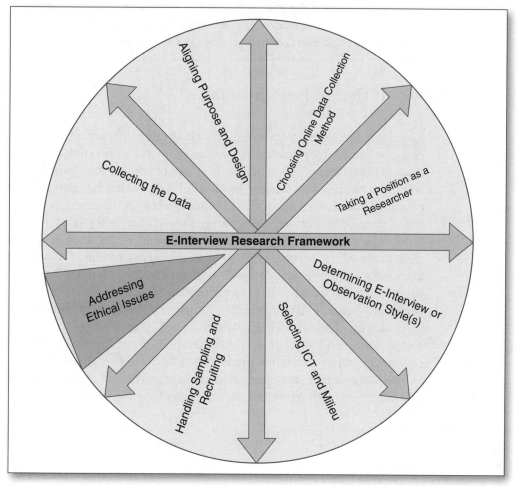

Source: Vision2Lead, Inc (2009–2014).

design. Research design is a complex process and covering it comprehensively is beyond the scope of this book. The focus here is on ethical questions researchers should consider from the design stage and throughout the conduct of the online interview study.

When an organization or business presents a strategic plan that diverges from past practices, strong supporting evidence and proof are needed to validate the soundness of the intentions and new direction. Similarly, when a researcher presents a study design that departs from established approaches, additional care may be needed to substantiate the proposal. Institutional review boards (IRBs), research ethics boards, ethics committees, or other review bodies representing potential interviewees or research fellowship staff may be uninformed or misinformed about online data collection. They may have particular concerns about ethical practices in online research.

Aspects of research design related to online interview methods are discussed in depth throughout this book. This chapter focuses on design issues and ethical dilemmas particular to studies built around data collected from online interviews. Recommendations are offered to help online researchers design and conduct credible and ethical studies.

Ethical Research Design Fundamentals

A study that relies on interviews for data collection depends on the willing participation of interviewees. A qualitative multimethod study may also include observations of participants, or use of content they post online. Any time **human subjects** are involved, the researcher has a moral and ethical responsibility toward them. Ethical practice is the researcher's central responsibility from the design stage through the final report.

No research involving human subjects should occur without a clear expectation of its benefit, whether it is the advancement of a body of knowledge, new understanding of human experience, or a direct benefit to the research participants. The researcher must make every effort to do no harm and to reduce risks involved in research according to the fundamental principles of research ethics, **beneficence.** The researcher who designs a study using online interviews must consider four interrelated matters: consent, identity, privacy, and protection of data. Although these four matters are not unique to the online environment, particular ethical issues are associated with each one when the study entails online interviews.

Informed Consent

Perhaps the most important ethical principle in research involves actions by researchers to ensure that participants comprehend their roles in the study and grasp that involvement is voluntary. The key question researchers need to address can be succinctly stated: "how to treat individuals as autonomous agents who should decide for themselves if they wish their personal information and interactions to be studied" (Stern, 2009, p. 95).

The U.S. Code of Federal Regulations (U.S. Department of Health and Human Services, 2013) mandates that researchers obtain informed consent to do the following:

- Protect human subjects/volunteers
- Ensure that potential study subjects clearly understand the benefits and risks associated with their participation in a study
- Provide the potential study subjects with all information needed to reach a decision on whether or not to participate in a research study

Ethical researchers disclose any potential risks and clearly explain the nature of the study, intended use of the data, and expectations for the research participant. To protect human subjects' rights to privacy, confidentiality, and autonomy, the researcher needs to approach subjects at the very beginning of the research to ask for consent. The researcher must discuss any data collected from or about participants prior to consent as part of the agreement.

Participants in any study must understand the researcher's purpose and anticipated commitments, and freely agree to participate—without repercussions if they do not. The onus is on the researcher to ensure that prospective participants understand the information given and that they have capacity to give consent (Loue, 2000). Capacity to consent includes legal age. If the participant is under the age of 18 or cannot legally sign for other reasons, an appropriate individual, such as a parent or guardian, must sign on the participant's behalf. Depending on the nature of the study, information provided to participants may include the following:

- The purpose of the study
- The nature of the study and a general description of other participants
- The expected duration of the individual's participation
- A description of the procedures, including expectations beyond the interview for follow-up comments, review of transcripts, and so on.
- A description of the extent to which confidentiality will be maintained
- A description of who will have access to the data
- A statement that participation in the study is voluntary and response to a given question is voluntary
- A statement indicating that the participant may withdraw at any time without penalty

The informed consent form or letter documents researchers' and participants' agreements, and formalizes study participation. Informed consent, at its simplest, is based on the premise that participants are fully "informed" about what the research involves and have the opportunity to decide whether or not to participate (Wiles, 2013). To ensure that all materials describing the study, including all the implications of the consent agreement, are understood, if the researcher gives any information orally, it should be presented in written form as well. Written materials should be provided in the language best understood by the participant and at an accessible reading level. Use alternative mechanisms to convey the necessary information, as appropriate, if the participant has hearing or vision impairments (Loue, 2000).

> **Ethics Tip:** When discussing conditions for consent, let the participant know that you may need to add to or revise the agreement.

The goals of a research project may shift over the course of the study as emerging patterns suggest new questions. In other cases, the researcher may decide to ask different questions or pursue different directions from what was agreed on in the original consent form. To prepare for this possibility, the researcher should try to create a comprehensive agreement. While many researchers view consent as an ongoing process throughout the study and renegotiate the agreement as appropriate, such renegotiation has its own perils. It can interrupt the process of developing rapport, or researchers could find themselves in an uncomfortable situation mid-study in which the participant refuses to agree to further disclosures (Duncombe & Jessop, 2012). The researcher can include a statement describing the scope of the agreement and indicators for renegotiation if new research interests or directions emerge.

Assumptions embedded in the premise of informed consent are anything but simple. In exploratory studies, even the researcher may not quite know what direction the study will take and thus may be unable to fully inform the participant about what to expect (Bell & Nutt, 2012). Even when researchers have explicitly described the study expectations, they cannot be certain that participants have read or understand them. Still, it is the researcher's responsibility to make a sincere effort to provide clear and reasonable information about the study.

Informed Consent and Online Research

When the informed consent negotiation occurs online, researchers need attention to detail. The first stage is to provide comprehensive information about the study and parameters and expectations for participation. As described in Chapter 3, one way to communicate this information is through a researcher blog, page, or site. Such a page can introduce the researcher and the research purpose, and link to the researcher's institution and its research ethics practices, for the participant's added reassurance. If the researcher is concerned that participants do not fully grasp the information, an audio or video recording or translations in other languages can be posted. A link to this descriptive page can be provided in short posts, texts, or e-mails with participants. Participants can refer to this page at any stage of the study.

Research participants should have a chance to voice any questions or concerns about the study or their participation. This preconsent discussion can occur by text chat, e-mail, or telephone.

In addition to data collected from interviews, the researcher may want to make note in the agreement of any data to be collected from observations of the participant's avatar, personal profile, social networking pages, website, or other user-generated content posted online.

Some institutions accept verbal consent, usually recorded at the beginning of the interview, but typically a written form is required. Depending on institutional or other requirements, the signed form is returned via surface mail, faxed to the researcher, or signed digitally and returned electronically. If acceptable, the researcher can provide the consent form as an e-mail attachment or a download. Participants can be asked to indicate agreement using a check box ("By checking this box, I accept...") on an online form or in an e-mail (Madge, 2006; Walther, 1999). A signed copy of the consent should be returned electronically or via conventional mail.

> **Ethics Tip:** You can download sample consent agreements from the book's website, located at www.sagepub.com/salmons2e.

There are exceptions to every rule, and sometimes a case can be made that consent itself can potentially harm participants. If faced with this situation, consult the relevant IRB or research ethics board policy.

> **Ethics Tip:** Online researchers can use free survey software to create consent forms. These tools allow participants to answer quick yes/no questions or write in comments about their preferences. See this website for an example: www.surveymonkey.com/s/RP7W5VY.

INFORMED CONSENT IN ONLINE INTERVIEW RESEARCH

Interview participants must consent to being a part of the study before an intentional exchange—no matter how seemingly casual—occurs between researcher and participant and is recorded. Many studies might be enhanced by observational data collected during interviews, along with the direct responses of the participants. In a video conference exchange, for example, observing the participant's facial expressions is as much a part of the interview as it would be in a face-to-face interview. Still, a researcher who wishes to use such data should make this level of data collection clear to the participants when obtaining consent.

Description of interview procedures should include specific technology requirements. Consider whether you need to spell out answers to any of the following questions:

- Will participants need a headset to communicate vocally?

- Do they need broadband or a high-speed connection to participate?

- Do they need a web camera?

- Is a computer needed, or can the interview be conducted on a tablet or a smartphone?

> **Research Tip:** When designing your research, think about the setting for the online interview and the kinds of information you may want to gather from observation. Discuss your goals and preferences with the participant and include your agreement in the consent letter.

Another topic online interview researchers need to consider is protection not only of the human subjects but also of their multiple identities in cyberspace. Consider whether you need to discuss the following issues with participants in the consent agreement:

- Use of pseudonyms in data collected or in reports on the study
- Description of appearance of avatars or other digital representations

While the need for agreements from interview participants is generally accepted, the requirements for consent agreements for other kinds of online data collection are not as straightforward. When researchers want to use a multimethod approach for a study that may involve observations and/or collection of user-generated posts, documents, images, or media, a different set of ethical issues arises.

INFORMED CONSENT IN ONLINE OBSERVATION RESEARCH

Distinctions are provided here for two types of observation of behaviors and activities online. While language may vary in different research traditions, the following definitions will be used for the purpose of this book:

- *Observation* to collect posted but not personally identifiable information or look for patterns in such posts on websites, blogs, or microblogs, or in discussion group interactions. In this form of observation, the researchers do not actually create posts or otherwise involve themselves in interactions with the online community, group, or social media site.
- *Participant observation* to collect data in a process that includes the researchers' involvement in communications—for example, posting to forums, blogs, or walls in online communities or on social media sites.

It might seem that a study using data from observation of posted information would *not* require consent from participants and/or agreement from the community, and that studies using participant observation would. However, the answer is not so straightforward. One factor is that either type could be conducted as open or covert observation. Another factor to be considered is this: Is the setting considered *public* or *private*?

Observing people on the street or noting responses to a civic event—where individuals are not identified—could be described as covert data collection in public. Data collection based on observations in "public" settings is typically exempt from informed consent when individuals are not identified and sensitive information is not being collected. However, the determination of public versus private space online is not clear-cut or universally defined. This creates a dilemma for online researchers: When should a researcher explicitly announce his or her presence and obtain consent? Does it matter whether the researcher intends to remain passive or to participate in the group's discussions?

Researchers disagree on these points. Some suggest that user-generated posts in openly accessible forums or on social networking sites are public so there is no need to disclose research activity, particularly when the participants' identities are not recorded. From this view, reading and drawing from postings on a public site may be comparable to reading a newsletter or other informal writing, where proper attribution is accomplished by citing the source. They argue that observing people's activities on a public website is equivalent to observing activities on the street where, as one pointed out, "they would never think of wearing large signs identifying themselves as 'Researcher'"(Sixsmith & Murray, 2001, p. 425). Hughes (2012a) points out that much of the published virtual ethnographic work has been "conducted covertly, with researchers effectively rendered invisible to those who are researched" (p. 17).

Others, such as early online researchers Frankel and Siang (1999), argue that unethical deception can occur when researchers do not identify themselves.

> On the Internet, group discussion formats make it relatively easy for researchers to engage in covert or unobtrusive observation. An investigator can record the online conversations of a community without making her presence as a researcher known. Alternatively, she can pose as a member of the community, giving false information in order to study the reactions and behavior of community members. (p. 9)

Madge (2006) similarly noted that whether an online community is open to all or requires a fee, lurking without participation and collecting data without notice or permission are generally frowned on. Hine (2013) pointed out:

> The Internet makes observable a broad array of social phenomena that have not been readily available to qualitative researchers before. . . . Now, the extent to which otherwise "private" discussions go on in public spaces of the Internet . . . makes these previously impractical studies more achievable. In ethical terms, then, are some studies now possible that we should still refrain from doing because they threaten privacy, well-being or dignity? (p. 13)

The British Educational Research Association's (BERA, 2011) ethics guidelines also highlight concerns about covert observations for the purpose of data collection:

Social networking and other on-line activities, including their video-based environments, present challenges for consideration of consent issues and the participants must be clearly informed that their participation and inter-actions are being monitored and analysed for research. (p. 5)

Waldron (2013) and Bruckman (2002) take the position that covert "lurk-ing" is ethically permissible if the online setting is perceived as public. They posit that researchers can freely quote and analyze online information if the following four criteria are met (cited in James & Busher, 2009, p. 123):

1. It is officially and publically archived.

2. No password is required for archive access.

3. No site policy prohibits it.

4. The topic is not highly sensitive.

This definition raises another question: perceived as "public" by whom? Although free and open websites or e-mail lists may seem comparable to pub-lic places in the real world, the distinction is even more uncertain when access requires some type of membership or registration. Although free and available to anyone willing to sign up, are such sites "public" in research terms? The expectations of the users of an online resource should be taken into consider-ation. The concept of "perceived privacy" has been defined as the "expecta-tions that Internet users may hold concerning the privacy of their online activities, their control over personal information, and their protection from harm" (Lomborg, 2013, p. 23). The size of the user group is also a factor. Users posting content to a group of 10 may have a greater expectation of privacy than would users posting to a group of 1,000 (Eysenbach & Till, 2001). The researcher must discern whether users expect that communication will be confined to the community or whether they expect the general public to observe, read, and/or document their actions, interactions, and postings.

One place to start is in the community itself. Do posted policies or guide-lines preclude research activities (Buchanan, 2011)? Do terms of service articulate privacy of content and/or how it is shared with third parties? Perceptions of privacy, norms, and codes are often spelled out in "frequently asked questions" or "about us" areas of online communities or social net-working sites. Subscription-based sites may have community use guidelines or membership policies. When such sites require registration for log-in but no fee, users typically assume anything posted will be read by a broad range of people. When a subscription or membership fee is required, researchers may assume that users expect privacy and confidentiality (Markham & Buchanan, 2012). Community managers, moderators, or facilitators are another source of information for membership-oriented sites. If present, contacting them to get a sense of formal and tacit expectations or to ask for permission to be more actively engaged is a best practice.

ESOMAR and the International Chamber of Commerce's (ICC) guidelines for market and social research are designed to address different regulatory and consumer expectations (ESOMAR, 2011; ESOMAR & ICC, 2008). Their distinction between public and private social media is clearly defined and thus may be useful to scholars. It is as follows:

- *Public social media:* This category covers the majority of social media, where access to entry is without any form of barrier. It can also include those where a username or password is required, but for identification or site revenue reasons rather than to protect the privacy of the data posted. Examples include public profile pages on social media networks, public micro-blogging posts, and many forums (including those where a username may be required but is automatically granted; that is, they are not moderated).

- *Private social media:* This label covers areas where the user or the website does not want the data to be publically accessible. All such media require username identification for access. Examples include "private wall-to-wall" or individual communications on social media networks, protected posts on micro-blogging sites, or forum/group areas where admittance is controlled by an administrator or moderator. As a general rule, researchers should not copy or scrape content from private areas, even if they have permission from the site owner. If researchers do so, they should make clear to all users that this is happening and should provide individuals with a process to be excluded from the data collection if desired.

Social networking and online community sites may have stated norms or rules, but e-mail is more ambiguous from an ethical standpoint. Although e-mail can be compared to paper mail, unlike paper mail, e-mail can be archived and/or easily replicated. Messages the writer assumed were private may be passed on to unintended recipients or saved in ways others could access. These characteristics can blur a number of boundaries taken for granted with paper mail. E-mail thus poses a dilemma for the researcher, who must assess whether the writer is the original source of the comments sent by personal e-mail, and must determine the appropriateness of citing comments received through an e-mail list.

The Association of Internet Researchers Guidelines offers another approach for considering ethical practices vis-à-vis consent, researcher openness, and participant privacy: the distance principle (Markham & Buchanan, 2012). As Lomborg (2013) described:

The distance principle concerns the conceptual or experiential distance between the object of research and the person who produced it. It is thus not merely a description of the closeness between researcher and subject, but of the relationship between the online data that the researcher wishes to collect and analyse (posted texts and images, a set of relationships among entities, demographic information posted on social network profiles, online survey responses etc.) and the person(s) whose activities created the data. The distance principle also applies to reflections regarding what types of analysis the data are used for: for example, a close content or discourse analysis of a (large) data set, using text examples, may more likely invoke the idea of dealing with human subjects than might an analysis of a similarly large data set, say, link patterns, temporal structures, languages, use of third party applications, or the prevalence of conversations on Twitter, which presents data only in aggregate form. (p. 22)

Elm (2008) suggests that when differentiating between public and private on the Internet, a continuum is more appropriate than a dichotomy. Figure 8.2 expands on and illustrates this suggestion.

The debate about what is ethical or not in Internet research will continue to evolve. As Hughes (2012a) sees it, issues in social research surrounding obtaining participant permissions and informed consent persist, and "researching on and in the Internet presents a range of ethical, epistemological, ontological and practical issues, debates and controversies" (p. 17). Universities and professional associations may have their own sets

Figure 8.2   Public–Private Internet Continuum

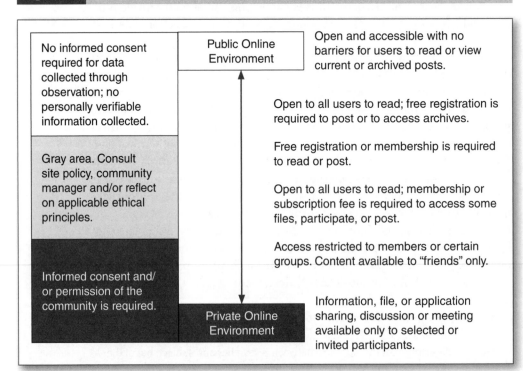

Source: Vision2Lead, Inc (2013).

of guidelines or parameters that researchers must respect. However, on review of many of them, specifics are often missing. In the midst of this unsettled state of affairs, researchers have to answer these questions for themselves as they design (and defend) their research. The Public–Private Internet Continuum with examples (Figure 8.3) is offered here as a model online researchers can use to distinguish between public and private research settings, and to make decisions about the appropriateness of consent and open or covert data collection.

On one end of the continuum is the free and open Internet, where no registration, membership, or log-in is required. These websites or social media sites can be defined as "public" when they are online spaces where companies, organizations, or individuals post information about themselves and allow anyone to view or read it. On the public web, observations and passive analysis of individuals' behaviors, posts, or writings can be collected with proper citation of the source. No personally identifiable information should be included in the data or reports.

On sites where access is restricted to members who register and use a secure log-in, informed consent and/or permission from the community manager, and in some cases site members, should be obtained. In such studies, the agreement should include defined parameters for use of information posted in profiles and use of images or media.

Types of environments in the "gray area" are those that allow anyone to read or view material but require some type of registration to contribute, post, or comment. These settings might include most blogs, media, or e-commerce sites that offer free content and encourage participation or feedback from consumers. Because the public can read any posts, one might assume that people who leave comments expect wide readership. Also in the gray area are sites that are free but require membership and approval from the content owner before visitors can access the material. Such online communication includes most subscription e-mail lists and social networking sites such as Facebook and Twitter. More clear-cut examples include sites, events, or communications that require a fee, membership, employment in the company, or enrollment in the class to access content and participate (see Figure 8.3).

Researchers must weigh the benefits and risks and make appropriate and ethical decisions for studies in the "gray area"—the online spaces or e-mail lists where membership is required but free to anyone who cares to join. Researchers must decide whether to collect data and remain anonymous or to possibly disrupt or change

> **Ethics Tip:** When you plan observational activities, before you collect data, review any posted terms of membership or behavior and try to gauge the culture and norms in terms of personal disclosure and privacy. If possible, discuss research goals with the moderator and/or members, and act accordingly in terms of consent or disclosure of your identity as a researcher.

Figure 8.3	Public–Private Internet Continuum With Examples

Public websites or blogs	**Public Online Environment**	Open and accessible with no barriers for users to read or view current or archived posts
News, magazine and media sites, blogs, consumer reviews, YouTube		Open to all users to read; free registration is required to post or to access archives
Social networking, Second Life, Facebook, Pinterest, Twitter, e-mail lists		Free registration or membership is required to read or post
Clubs, professional associations, journals		Open to all users to read; membership or subscription fee is required to access some files, participate, or post
Intranet, membership organizations, e-learning classes, profile pages on social networking sites		Access restricted to members or certain groups. Content available to "friends" only
Online meeting, video conference, some virtual worlds or games	**Private Online Environment**	Information, file or application sharing, discussion or meeting available only to selected or invited participants

Source: Vision2Lead, Inc (2013).

the course of events by announcing research intentions. Researchers should reflect on points made throughout this chapter about the distance principle and perceived privacy (Lomborg, 2013), as well as on two additional questions: What risks to the observed subjects may be associated with the study? Would the credibility of the study be jeopardized without consenting participants?

Online interviews are typically conducted in a "private online environment" where the interviewer and interviewee are the only participants. In consensual, participatory interview research, interviewer and interviewee arrange to meet. They are both aware that they are engaging in online interactions for purposeful data collection. In this type of research, informed consent is unquestionably required.

Identity and Privacy

Many research ethics issues are comparable online or off, but identity may generate unique issues online. As the saying goes, no one knows if you are a dog on the Internet. How does the researcher know whether a potential research participant is the proverbial dog? In some cases, research participants have verifiable identities. Researchers may be able to corroborate identity through academic or other affiliations. In other cases, identity may be ambiguous since online, people commonly go by first names only, nick-names, and/or avatar names. Association of data to the interviewee raises questions such as, Will the material be attributed to a specified person? Will this person be referred to by real name, a pseudonym, or an avatar name? Should the name and identity used on the Internet be protected in the same way as the name and identity used off the Internet?

These issues are under debate, and online research protocols are not yet clearly defined. In the meantime, there are some clear guidelines all researchers should observe when it comes to identity. First, ethical researchers must begin by being honest about their own identities throughout all stages of the research. Just as research subjects can be cloaked in anonymity and pseudonymity, so can researchers, raising the potential for deception. "Deception can occur when a researcher inten-tionally misinforms or does not fully disclose relevant information to subjects in cases when informed consent is required" (Frankel & Siang, 1999, p. 9). Ethical researchers are careful to introduce themselves. Where possible, academic e-mail addresses or other evidence of institutional affiliation should be used to affirm trustworthiness and inspire confidence.

Second, researchers must verify that the potential interviewee is over the age of 18 or the age of consent in the country where the research is conducted. If there are any doubts about age, corroborating records or copies of photo identification should be requested as part of the informed consent process. Third, researchers must respect participants' privacy.

Privacy in the research context refers to steps taken to safeguard interviewees' right to integrity and self-determination. This means research participants have the right to decide what kinds of information to share with the researcher and under what conditions (Elm, 2008). Carusi (2008) feels it is important to distinguish between infor-mation related to "thin identity" and to "thick identity":

> Thin identity is the identity of a particular indi-vidual as a re-identifiable identity. Proper names pick out particular individuals and have

 Ethics Tip: Avoid any confusion about your identity as a researcher. Use an institutional, corporate, or foundation e-mail address. Create a research site or blog where participants and others can verify the researcher's identity and learn more about the study.

Research Tip: Is there publicly accessible information about you online that could undermine your credibility as a researcher? If so, to the degree possible, remove it before you begin recruiting participants.

⚖️ **Ethics Tip: Respect both thick and thin identity of participants when data are collected from public sites.**

to do with thin identity. Thick identity is a matter of that individual's experience of their own personhood, their own subjective or psychological sense of who they are. [T]hick identity can be a matter of ethical concern even when it has been detached from thin identity. (p. 41)

Carusi (2008) illustrates the distinction with this example: If *thin* identity has to do with a particular individual and the fact that she has a certain medical condition, then *thick* identity concerns her representation as a victim, a fighter, or a survivor of that condition. An online researcher may breach the participant's confidentiality by appropriating images, quotations, stories, or other representations even if the researcher removes any personal information and thick identity has been detached from thin identity. Search engines allow people to enter phrases and locate the original post, with the writer's name and geographic location. This means researchers can easily and unintentionally violate individuals' privacy by quoting the exact words of an e-mail list or online community posting—even though they have not attributed it directly.

Ethical dilemmas described in this chapter can be further complicated by the fact that online research—with easy access to participants across the globe—may cross cultural as well as geographic boundaries. Sensitivities about privacy, identity, the types of information to be shared, and the conditions for the exchange may vary widely. In addition, crossing geographic boundaries may mean different legal jurisdictions must be considered, with their own rules about privacy and protection of human subjects in research. For example, when data are transferred from a European Union (EU) country to a non-EU country, the data must be adequately protected under EU regulations. Researching groups, such as indigenous peoples, may mean notions of harm, risk, privacy, and confidentiality have to be considered at the level of the community, not just the individual (O'Hara, 2005). A uniform standard is not possible, and researchers clearly must honor the codes and expectations in place in the culture or the community where the study participants reside or interact.

Withdrawal From the Online Study

The ability to withdraw from the research at any time is a central tenet of informed consent and should be clearly spelled out in the consent agreement. In reality, a participant can withdraw from a virtual interview by simply closing the chat window or logging out of the meeting space. During virtual interviews, sudden withdrawal of a participant can be disconcerting to the researcher. It may be unclear whether the interviewee no longer wishes to participate or there is simply a technical or connection problem. Researchers may feel some ambiguity about whether and how to follow up with a participant after contact is lost. To help avoid these potential problems, it is advisable to discuss a withdrawal protocol when negotiating the consent agreement. However, in any study, impromptu abandonment is a risk researchers must accept.

> ⚖️ **Ethics Tip:** You may want to discuss a withdrawal protocol. Let participants know that, while they can withdraw from the study without penalty, you would appreciate a message confirming a decision to discontinue participation. This can save the researcher the time of sending inquiring e-mails, and avoid the participant's embarrassment or annoyance at receiving such inquiries.

When do researchers need to obtain informed consent? Interview research requires informed consent. Also, in interview-based studies, the researcher's identity is known. It is difficult to imagine a circumstance where an interviewer would not disclose his or her identity to the participant. As noted in Chapter 3, the online researcher may want to take additional steps to establish credibility and a scholarly identity. These decisions are more ambiguous in other types of online data collection. It may not always be clear when consent is needed or whether the researcher must be identified and data collection activities disclosed. Since interviews may be one stream of data in a multi-method or mixed-methods study, online researchers should consider a broad range of ethical issues.

Protection of Data

For many Internet studies, potential breach of confidentiality may be the gravest risk the participant could face. Researchers must be aware of the vulnerability of the data at every stage of the research process. Data are vulnerable during collection, transmission, and storage. Given the ease with which researchers can digitally manipulate data, the agreed use of data must be honored.

Mann and Stewart (2000) described a set of Principles of Fair Information Processing Online (see Table 8.1). While these principles were articulated before many current interactive and archival technologies were invented, they are still relevant for ethical online interview practice.

Storage of data used to be an uncomplicated task: One downloaded the files onto a disc or drive and locked the file in a safe place. With today's technologies—online video conferencing, web conferencing, and

> ⚖️ **Ethics Tip:** Consider implications of the Principles of Fair Information Processing Online when articulating the consent agreement.

Table 8.1	Fair Information Processing and Online Interviews
Principles of Fair Information Processing	**Implications for Online Interviewers**
• Personal data should be collected for one specific purpose. • People should have access to the data collected about themselves. • Personal data should be guarded against risks such as unauthorized access, modification, or disclosure. • People have the right to have inaccurate data corrected. • Data should be collected in a context of free speech. • Personal data are not to be communicated externally without the consent of the subject who supplied the data.	• Be clear about the possible future uses of the research findings, such as in publications. • Be clear about the data you want to collect from the interview and associated observations, as well as from the participant's website, blog, or social networking profiles or posts. • Allow participants to see transcripts or notes, and to make corrections or additions. • Protect the data. If the interview is occurring on a proprietary site, make sure you can download the recording and then delete it from the server.

Source: Adapted from Mann and Stewart (2000).

social media in particular—the whole archive is stored on the platform's servers, known as the cloud. This presents an ethical dilemma for researchers. Can you be confident that the company adequately protects data from unauthorized access? Do you have the ability to download and delete the files from the company's servers once the interview is completed? Does the site's user policy state that anything posted becomes the intellectual property of the company that runs the site or platform? These factors may influence the choice of information and communications technology (ICT) and milieu for the interviews.

Bakardjieva and Feenberg (2001) use the term **alienation** to describe "the appropriation of the products of somebody's action for purposes never intended or foreseen by the actor herself, drawing these products into a system of relations over which the producer has no knowledge or control" (p. 206). As noted earlier in the chapter, if the purpose of the study or the kinds of data the researcher wants change in the course of the study, then the consent agreement must be updated. The research design should include a feedback loop; that is, the person interviewed should be able to see, review, and clarify information in the data. With these safeguards in place, the researcher can honor fairness and respect for research participants' preferences.

Another ethical minefield for electronic data involves the researcher. When words, paragraphs, or entire documents can be easily (and selectively) copied, rearranged to alter the meaning, or deleted altogether, the researcher's own integrity is essential to maintain the verbatim raw data and use them properly. Davis (1999) elucidates situations in which lapses in integrity can occur:

- "Smoothing out" reported data by dropping certain results because they show weaknesses in research design or implementation

- Suppressing data clearly inconsistent with one's conclusions ("cooking")

- Fabricating data ("forging")

- Keeping incomplete records of research, discarding records after research is complete, or denying others access to data on which published research relied

> Ethics Tip: Create a checklist that articulates your own standards of values and ethics before you start collecting and analyzing data. Keep it handy and consult it when you confront sticky situations.

Ethical researchers spell out the standards they will uphold—and they stick with them. Although the data themselves must be kept private, the process and procedures of research should be transparent to reveal honesty at all stages of the study.

Ethical Frameworks

Traditional ethical concepts offer today's researchers varied ways to think about their studies. Ethical frameworks afford a means of thinking about ethical dilemmas by providing criteria researchers can use to determine whether an action is right or wrong (Wiles, 2013). Those frameworks relevant to researchers include deontological, consequentialist, and virtue ethics. Brief descriptions of each are provided here.

THE DEONTOLOGICAL APPROACH

Deontological ethics, building on the philosophies of Immanuel Kant (1785/2008), has at its simplest views morality in terms of duties and principles. Deontologists have less regard for the outcomes resulting from following their principles, believing that some choices are morally wrong, no matter how good the consequences (Baggini & Fosl, 2007; Zalta, 2008).

A primary tenet of deontology is respect for the individual; individuals are not seen merely as a means to an end. "Informed consent becomes a way of operationalizing that tenet, through an acknowledgement of an individual's values and choices that are freely made" (Loue, 2000, p. 97). Deontological researchers are concerned with following ethical rules, codes, or formally specified guidelines (Berry, 2004). *The Belmont Report*, which is the basis for protection of human subjects regulations in the United States, and the Association of Internet Researchers' professional codes of ethics have their origins in Kantian deontological theory (Ess, 2002; Pedroni & Pimple, 2001). As noted at the beginning of this chapter, researchers proposing new approaches may need to show review bodies that they can follow established guidelines for research even when the study is conducted using new techniques.

THE CONSEQUENTIALIST OR UTILITARIAN APPROACH

Consequentialism, or **utilitarianism**, building on the philosophies of John Stuart Mill (1863/1985), is concerned with moral rightness of acts. It emphasizes that ethical action provides the most good or does the least harm (Baggini & Fosl, 2007; Zalta, 2008). Ethical decisions, then, are based on the consequences of specific actions judged to be moral when the outcome is good for the individual or society (Wiles, 2013, p. 4).

Because utilitarianism seeks to maximize good, involvement of individuals in research without their understanding or permission, or against their will would be considered clearly unethical (Loue, 2000). Consequentialist researchers might prioritize the potential of research findings to add to the greater common good over strict adherence to established rules or guidelines. For Internet researchers, this could mean taking a flexible approach to applying principles, believing that the value of the study outweighs adherence to rules the researchers perceive as outdated. They may believe that by doing so they can advance more appropriate ground rules for future Internet researchers: a positive consequence. Alternatively, consequentialism could be used to justify deception, in that informative research findings would outweigh covert online observation (Berry, 2004).

THE VIRTUE ETHICS APPROACH

Virtue ethics is grounded in ideas from Plato and Aristotle. This approach suggests that ethical actions ought to be consistent with certain ideal virtues that provide for the full development of our humanity (Velasquez et al., 2008). These virtues enable us to act in ways that demonstrate values such as honesty, courage, compassion, generosity, tolerance, and fairness. People are best able to practice virtue ethics when they possess *phronesis*, moral or practical wisdom (Zalta, 2008).

Virtue ethics emphasizes the qualities of respectfulness and benevolence, which again argue for the recognition of and respect for an individual's freely made choice and informed consent (Loue, 2000). Virtue ethics in research are based on the "moral character of the researcher rather than principles, rules or consequences of an act or decision" (Wiles, 2013, p. 5). Using virtue ethics, a researcher relies on his or her personal value system and moral code and character to make the right decisions and to treat the research subject with fairness and integrity.

TOWARD AN UNDERSTANDING OF INTERNET RESEARCH ETHICS

Ethical Internet researchers must somehow reconcile elements of these frameworks. Berry (2004) argues that "they are all necessary components of a dialogical and relational process of ethical responsibility" (p. 330). Whether or not researchers see themselves as adhering to deontological positions, they need to be accountable to some degree to rules established by the relevant academy or agency. Whether or not they see themselves as consequentialist, they must subscribe to the principles of beneficence and aim to maximize possible benefits and minimize possible harm. Whether or not they see themselves as virtuous, they will need to use fairness and honesty to achieve credible research findings. If the researcher believes that all persons have an inherent capacity for self-determination, this belief provides the grounds for an obligation to avoid interfering with participants' actions and decisions by withholding relevant information (Pedroni & Pimple, 2001). During research, all these positions argue that questions should be raised: "Is the researcher responding to the needs of others? Do they care about the activities of members of online groups as people with feelings like themselves?"(Berry, 2004).

Research Design, Ethics, and Review Boards

Faculty members and graduate students typically submit proposals for research with human subjects to an IRB, research ethics board, or similar entity. While each researcher should consult his or her own institution's guidelines, this section discusses IRB reviews and offers suggestions for proposals that include online interview data collection.

RISK/BENEFIT ANALYSIS

The review or ethics board will try to determine whether research subjects could be exposed to physical, economic, or social harm. Even small risks will be of concern to the IRB if the population is vulnerable, especially if it includes children or people who are incarcerated.

Most online research entails little or no physical risk. Psychological harm is typically minimal or transitory. It is the job of the IRB to discern whether risks are such that long-term harm could occur. IRB reviewers realize the following:

> Stress and feelings of guilt or embarrassment may arise simply from thinking or talking about one's own behavior or attitudes on sensitive topics such as drug use, sexual preferences, selfishness, and violence. These feelings may be aroused when the subject is being interviewed. (Penslar & Porter, 2009)

Questions reviewers will ask include the following:

- Are both risks and anticipated benefits accurately identified, evaluated, and described?

- Are the risks greater than **minimal risk**? Has the proposal taken into account vulnerabilities among prospective subjects that might be relevant to evaluating the risk of participation?

- Has due care been used to minimize risks and maximize the likelihood of benefits?

- Are there adequate provisions for a continuing reassessment of the balance between risks and benefits? Should there be a data and safety monitoring committee (Porter, 1993)?

Because the IRB committee may not have evaluated many proposals for online interviews, the researcher should offer either sample questions or interview themes so reviewers can be assured that research participants will not be deceived and psychological stress will be minimized. See the sections in this chapter about interviewer deception, and articulate your approach for disclosing your presence and stating the purpose of the study.

REVIEW ISSUES FOR INFORMED CONSENT

This chapter has explored issues for consent for interview and observational research. Adequacy of information provided to the participants and credibility of their voluntary agreement to participate are subjected to scrutiny in the IRB review. In the United States, researchers are required to provide participants certain information, including the following:

- An explanation of the purposes of the research and the expected duration of the subject's participation, a description of the procedures to be followed, and identification of any procedures that are experimental

- Description of any reasonably foreseeable risks or discomforts to the subject

- A statement describing the extent, if any, to which confidentiality of records identifying the subject will be maintained

- An explanation of whom to contact for answers to pertinent questions about the research and research subjects' rights, and whom to contact in the event of a research-related injury to the subject

- A statement that participation is voluntary, refusal to participate will involve no penalty or loss of benefits to which the subject is otherwise entitled, and the subject may discontinue participation at any time without penalty or loss of benefits to which the subject is otherwise entitled

- Anticipated circumstances under which the subject's participation may be terminated by the investigator without regard to the subject's consent (U.S. Department of Health and Human Services, 2010)

Researchers must consult the laws and regulations governing the institution, as well as the laws and regulations governing the country where research participants reside. Institutional Review and International Research Regulations governing research to be conducted outside of the United States by U.S. investigators may require that the protocol be reviewed and approved not only by a review committee based in the United States but also by the appropriate review committee in the country hosting the research.

Generally, the agreement to participate based on these terms should be signed by the participant. This requirement can be waived in some situations where risks are associated with a breach of confidentiality concerning the subject's participation in the research. If the nature of research participation can potentially change midstudy, reviewers may want to know how consent will be renegotiated during the course of the research (Porter, 1993). They may or may not require resubmission to the IRB, depending on the extent of the changes.

The IRB is concerned with the possibility of psychological harm when reviewing behavioral research that involves an element of deception, so reviewers will look at evidence of honesty and disclosure. Reviewers will want to know whether researchers intend to withhold information about the real purpose of the research or to give subjects false information about some aspect of the research, meaning that the subjects' consent may not be fully informed (Porter, 1993). Questions reviewers may ask about the proposal include the following:

- Is the language and presentation of the information to be conveyed appropriate to the subject population? (Consider the level of complexity and the need for translation into a language other than English.)

- Are the timing of and setting for the explanation of the research conducive to good decision making? Can anything more be done to enhance the prospective subjects' comprehension of the information and their ability to make a choice?

- Who will be explaining the research to potential subjects? Should someone in addition to or other than the investigator be present (Porter, 1993)?

To pass this part of the review, online researchers will want to plainly spell out the ways they will provide information participants need before agreeing to be interviewed. In addition, researchers need to discuss ways to verify that participants fully understand the expectations and requirements of the study. If an emergent design anticipates that another phase may be added to the study, then the researcher should outline the frequency and/or events that will trigger the sharing of additional information about the study or another signed consent form.

REVIEW ISSUES FOR PRIVACY AND CONFIDENTIALITY

IRB reviewers want to be sure that adequate safeguards for privacy and confidentiality are in place for the proposed study. Reviewers want to be sure that participants have control over the extent, timing, and circumstances of sharing information. They look for ways confidentiality will be handled. Confidentiality refers to treatment of information that an individual has disclosed and protections to prevent that information from being divulged without permission in ways that are inconsistent with the understanding of the original disclosure (Porter, 1993).

Questions reviewers may ask about the proposal include the following:

- Does the research involve observation or intrusion in situations where the subjects have a reasonable expectation of privacy? Would reasonable people be offended by such an intrusion? Can the research be redesigned to avoid the intrusion?

- Will the investigator(s) be collecting sensitive information about individuals? If so, have they made adequate provisions for protecting the confidentiality of the data through coding, destruction of identifying information, limiting access to the data, or whatever methods may be appropriate to the study?

- Are the investigator's disclosures to subjects about confidentiality adequate? Should documentation of consent be waived to protect confidentiality (Porter, 1993)?

To pass this section of the IRB review, online researchers need to answer these questions and thoroughly explain how they will protect confidentiality and the data.

Closing Thoughts

Research design is a complex and often lengthy process. In addition to the typical elements every researcher must address, the online researcher must also consider implications related to the online milieu. This chapter focused on the ethical dilemmas inherent in the evolving online environment. Real ethical issues, as well as fears of ethical pitfalls in little-known online research settings, must be addressed to meet institutional demands. Attention to ethical practice is needed at every stage of the research process. Ultimately, the quality of the design and attention to ethical conduct allow the researcher to generate credible findings.

Researcher's Notebook

THE E-INTERVIEW RESEARCH FRAMEWORK: ADDRESSING ETHICAL ISSUES

The E-Interview Research Framework reminds us of the holistic nature of research design. Ethical issues are central to every step of the process. Key questions related to decisions about research ethics are included in Table 8.2.

Table 8.2	Applying the E-Interview Research Framework: Addressing Ethical Issues
	Addressing Ethical Issues
Aligning purpose and design	• What known risks or ethical issues exist with this research design? • What benefit to individual or public good will this study generate? • What specific tenets of the selected theoretical or methodological frameworks apply?
Choosing online data collection method	• What is the ethical rationale for the selection of online interviews (and, as relevant, observations)?
Handling sampling and recruiting	• Is the study investigating online behavior? If so, does the site or community allow researchers to recruit participants? • Does the desired population have access to and comfort using the selected ICT?
Taking a position as a researcher	• Is the researcher a known insider or outsider in the selected research setting? • If an insider, will status or prior knowledge add a risk for researcher bias? • How will the researcher avoid deception in interactions with the participants?
Determining e-interview or observation styles	• What questions are appropriate to ask? • How will trust and rapport be developed through honest dialogue with the researcher? • How will privacy be maintained?

(Continued)

Table 8.2   (Continued)

	Addressing Ethical Issues
Selecting ICT and milieu	• What specific ethical issues (e.g., privacy, protected areas, use of avatars, need for community agreement) are present in the selected milieu? • What aspects of the selected ICT (e.g., use of video or images, avatars, profile info) should be discussed and mentioned in an agreement? • Can you be confident that the company adequately protects data from unauthorized access? • Do you have the ability to download and delete the files from the company's servers once the interview is completed? Does the site's user policy state that anything posted becomes the intellectual property of the company that runs the site or platform?
Collecting the data	• How will participants and their digital identities be protected? • Will data be collected using open or covert observation? • How will data be protected?

STORIES OF ONLINE INQUIRY: THREE RESEARCHERS—ETHICAL OR NOT?

Researcher 1 plans to study citizen journalists and their blogs. For the first phase of the study, the researcher intends to observe dialogue between bloggers and their readers. After observing a number of blogs for several months, the researcher plans to identify key themes and questions to guide online interviews with a sample of the bloggers and regular commenters. The researcher chooses a number of blogs to observe on a daily basis for a month. She makes notes about the length, frequency, and content of the postings by the bloggers and contributors. She remains an anonymous reader; like any number of other visitors, she does not post any comments on the blogs or complete the registration form that would enable her to make such posts. She does not solicit consent at this stage or announce her presence as a researcher. After reviewing her notes and reflecting on her observations, she identifies some criteria she will use to select interview participants. She contacts those individuals to introduce herself and discuss the purpose of her study. The bloggers and contributors who are willing to participate in the study sign a consent agreement and arrange to meet in a private online space for the interview. The agreement spells out terms of the interview, as well as the scope of information the researcher can use as data.

A researcher with a similar research intention takes a different approach. Researcher 2 chooses a number of blogs to observe on a daily basis for a month. Like the first researcher, she plans to do so without obtaining consent. This researcher completes the registration using a pseudonym and posts comments to the blogs to elicit responses on topics of interest to her research. Because the other visitors assume a public readership, the researcher believes it is acceptable to take notes on the content of the responses. With registration, she can access a profile of the blogger, including other affiliations. She finds other sites and e-mail lists where these bloggers are members and joins to track participation and view their profiles, posts, and comments. These steps allow her to gain more information about the bloggers' interests and backgrounds. She continues to participate and take notes on any responses to her postings. She believes her actions are consistent with the role of a participant observer in a public environment. She does not solicit consent or announce her presence as a researcher.

After reviewing her notes and reflecting on her observations, she identifies some criteria she will use to select interview participants. She selects posts the bloggers have written to use as the basis for further discussion during the interview. She contacts those individuals to introduce herself and discuss the purpose of her study. The bloggers and contributors who are willing to participate in the study sign a consent agreement and arrange to meet in a private online space for the interview.

Researcher 3 also plans to study citizen journalists and their blogs. Her research design includes use of one-to-one interviews with bloggers as the first stage, followed by observation of each blogger for 3 months. She creates a recruitment message and posts it online; it yields six consenting participants. The consent form indicates that she will use public posts by the blogger as data for the study.

As the study progresses, Researcher 3 notices that one of the bloggers also has a Facebook page. After she "friends" the participant on Facebook, she begins to notice posts that show an entirely different side of the participant than was shared in the interview and business-oriented blog. She decides that since she already has the participant's consent to quote from posted material, using these posts as data will be acceptable.

If you were advising these three researchers about ethics, what would you say and why?

Key Concepts

- Attention to ethical online research begins with the research design and continues throughout the study.

- Simplistic either/or explanations will not be adequate for researchers who want to propose online research. They must navigate dichotomies such as public versus private definitions of online space and deontological versus consequentialist thinking about ethics to find workable approaches.

- Robust justifications may be needed for review boards, which lack experience with online research—especially in the areas of privacy, confidentiality, and informed consent.

Discussions and Assignments

1. Before you start collecting and analyzing data, create a checklist for ethical online research that articulates your own standards of values and ethics. Compare and contrast your checklist with your peers' lists. Discuss similarities and differences. Refine your checklist based on new insights.

    - Justify your choices using principles from one or more ethical theories.
    - Compare and contrast your ethics checklist with the ones your peers developed. Were your priorities the same? Were your theoretical justifications the same?

2. Review at least two studies conducted with data collected online (observation, participant observation, interviews, or focus groups).

    - Do you feel that the researchers acted ethically? Why or why not?
    - Where would you place the research setting on the Public–Private Internet Continuum (see Figure 8.2)?
    - What advice would you give the researcher to improve ethical practices with the research participants?

3. Reflect on the ethical risks for researchers. Discuss the steps you will take to conduct research in a transparent, honest way.

On the Web

www.sagepub.com/salmons2e
You will find media pieces sample consent forms and a list of research ethics codes and resources from various disciplines.

Preparing for an Online Interview

9

A discovery is said to be an accident meeting a prepared mind.

—Albert Szent-Gyorgyi (1893–1986)

> After you study Chapter 9, you will be able to do the following:
> - Understand the steps needed to plan an online interview
> - Outline specific preparations needed based on technologies; synchronous, near-synchronous, and/or asynchronous communications; and the type and research context of the online interview
> - Describe the essential pre-interview groundwork online interviewers must complete

Chapters 9 and 10 together address the E-Interview Research Framework category "Collecting the Data." Collecting data begins with preparation. This chapter explores three interrelated areas of interview preparation: preparing questions or discussion themes, preparing to use the selected interview technology, and individual interviewer preparation.

Planning to Interview

Once the researcher has discerned the research purpose, designed the study, considered ethical issues, obtained approval, planned for sampling, and recruited sample participants, it is time to move to the practical steps of interview planning and preparation. Preceding chapters have shown that online interview researchers can and should draw principles from relevant qualitative research methods and methodologies and adapt them as appropriate for use in online interview research. Interview preparation is no exception. This chapter draws relevant suggestions for interview preparation from research theorists and points to additional considerations for online interviewers.

Eliciting descriptions of experiences and perceptions of interviewees is the goal of any research interview. In-depth interaction with research participants should occur at each stage of the process: preparing to collect data, collecting data (see Chapters 10 and 11), and analyzing data (see the Appendix). Once consent has been obtained, every interaction can be used to collect data. In studies where the researcher conducts more than one interview with each participant, or where the researcher communicates with participants outside of the formal interview, more than one online approach can be used. Synchronous, near-synchronous, and asynchronous communications can be used strategically at different points of the study. Researchers are wise to view all communications, both informal and formal, conducted throughout the planning process as opportunities for building the relationship, fostering comfort with the process, and instilling trust in the interviewer.

Preparing the Questions

Questioning is central to any interview. Whether the interview is structured, semistructured, or unstructured, the interviewer must discern how the interviewee can contribute insights needed to understand the research questions the study was designed to answer.

Researchers planning for structured or semistructured interviews will articulate all or most of the **main interview questions** in advance and plan the sequence for asking them. Open-ended questions solicit participants' stories, thoughts, and feelings. These queries are crafted to align with the research questions and purpose of the study. Methodologists suggest a number of strategies for scripting questions. Weiss (1994) observes that "any question is a good question if it directs the respondent to material needed by the study in a way that makes it easy for the respondent to provide the material" (p. 73). Kvale (2007) describes *thematic* questions that relate to the "what" of the interview and *dynamic* questions that pertain to the "how" of an interview. Dynamic questioning refers to building rapport needed to keep the conversation flowing (Kvale, 2007, p. 57).

Researchers may ponder ways to encourage interviewees to dig deeper and determine how far they want to go with any particular question. Is it worth possibly sacrificing breadth and leaving some questions unasked if the interviewee wants to keep talking on one topic? If not, how will the interviewer encourage the participant to move on? Rubin and Rubin

(2012) spell out a number of kinds of **probes** that encourage the participant to continue the line of comments or redirect the participant to a new topic. The simplest probes, such as "Tell me more" or "How did you feel when that happened?" help keep the conversation flowing. To be more strategic, Rubin and Rubin identified three types of probes (pp. 139–140):

- *Attention probes* ("Okay, I understand," and so forth) let the interviewee know the researcher is listening.

- *Conversation management probes* keep the conversation focused on the research topic and help regulate the desired level of depth. Researchers use such probes to confirm answers or ask for better definition or clarification if they cannot follow the thread of the comments.

- *Credibility probes* aim to find relevant evidence to support participants' claims.

- These verbal probes are complemented with *nonverbal probes*: the eye contact or timing patterns researchers use to show participants that they are interested in hearing them continue.

The sequence of main questions may be predetermined or arranged as the interview proceeds. Although subquestions, **follow-up questions,** or probes can be outlined in advance, the researcher will refine or add to the planned list as needed based on interviewee responses.

In less-structured interviews, researchers may want to be more spontaneous than is possible when questions are formulated in advance. To be more flexible, such researchers may develop an **interview guide,** a kind of "cheat sheet" to remind them of the key points to cover. Guides can be very detailed or simply list or outline the subject areas to be covered and key words the researcher wants to use when posing the questions. Researchers can modify Moustakas's (1994) suggested list of questions to fit their own research designs:

- What dimensions, incidents, and people connected with the experience stand out for you?

- How did the experience affect you? What changes do you associate with the experience?

- How did the experience affect significant others in your life?

- What feelings were generated by the experience?

- What thoughts stood out or are memorable?

- Have you shared all that is significant with reference to the experience? (p. 116)

Researchers at the unstructured end of the continuum approach the interview with the larger purpose for the inquiry in mind; they develop specific topics and articulate questions as the interview unfolds.

Whether the interviewer spells out each question or maps out key topics, if the interview is to be conducted online, the nature of the technology will influence the options for conveying the question and for receiving and responding to the answer. Will the participant be typing responses using text on a mobile device or chat software on a computer? Will the participant be speaking? Will the participant and interviewer be able to see each other's natural visage or an invented persona? Will they be able to observe and respond to visual examples or media? (See Chapter 6 for more about online visual methods.) Each is a distinctively different communication experience. This means selection of interview technology relates specifically to the kind of planning the interviewer needs in advance of the interview (see Figure 9.1).

| Figure 9.1 | Interview Preparation by Type |

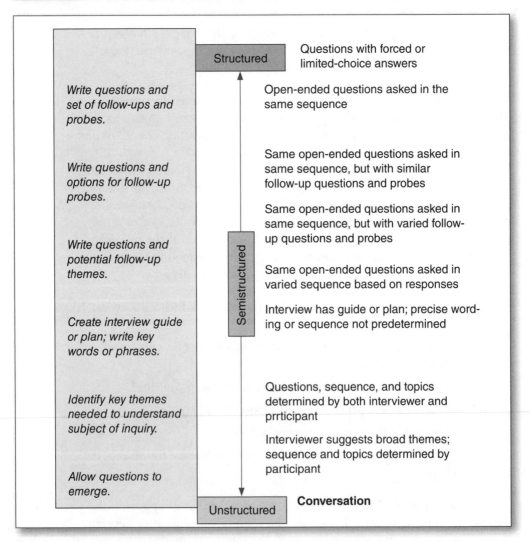

Source: Vision2Lead, Inc (2014).

Communications Technologies and
Online Interview Preparation

CONSIDERATIONS FOR ICT SELECTION

In synchronous interviews, researchers and participants interact in real time. In near-synchronous interviews, researchers and participants post questions and answers with the expectation that a response will be posted as soon as the other logs on next. In asynchronous interviews, there is a gap in time between question, answer, follow-up, and response. Chapter 5 offered an overview of types of information and communications technologies (ICTs) that researchers can use for interviews and related observations. This book classifies ICTs into four main types: text based; video conference, video chat, or video call; web conferencing meeting space; and immersive virtual worlds or games.

The selection of technologies to use in the interview, and in other communications between researcher and participant, may depend on a variety of considerations. As discussed in previous chapters, besides the obvious practical matters of cost and access, technology selection may also be influenced by the research design and sampling and recruiting plans.

When online interviews are conducted to investigate face-to-face phenomena, as noted in Chapter 3, the online environment is the meeting venue, not the subject of investigation. Such a researcher may have limited opportunities to introduce unfamiliar technologies, and the participant may have limited interest in learning new ICTs. In this type of interview, access to and comfort with the ICT might be the critical factors for success.

A different set of factors may influence technology choices for online interviews to investigate online behaviors, events, transactions, or experiences. Researchers may want to use the same ICTs the participants are using in the circumstances being studied. Would a researcher who wants to understand the ways facilitators stimulate discussion in online meetings want to carry out the interview in the same meeting space? Using the same example, does the researcher also want to conduct some observations of the facilitator in action? Might the researcher find conducting interviews in a variety of spaces beneficial, or might it be impractical? Considering that each type of communication medium needs a slightly different preparation, researchers may want to offer a limited selection from which to choose so every interview does not require additional preparation.

LEARNING THE ICT

Some ICTs require researchers to actively manage various communication and recording features during the interview. Others, such as text chat, are simple to operate or, as with video conferencing in a facility, involve technicians who manage the equipment. Researchers must be fully cognizant of the operation—and perils—of selected interview technologies. Communicating in the medium should come naturally by the time the first interaction with a participant occurs.

It is important to anticipate types of technical problems and either learn to fix them, work around them, or find alternatives that could be quickly made available. Implications of last-minute changes must be considered. For example, if it is necessary to switch from Voice over Internet Protocol (VoIP) to telephone, do you have the participant's phone number and alternate contact information? Given the importance of the interview recording, do you have a backup option if there is a problem? To avoid last-minute stress, pre-interview communications must include an assessment of the research participants' experience and comfort level with the selected technology or technologies. Make available clear log-in or call-in procedures, and provide any technical support service phone numbers or links to live-chat help.

Practice interviews are essential, whether or not the researcher is familiar with the ICT. The ideal practice partner is candid and generous with constructive feedback. Consider rehearsing with fellow researchers (or fellow students), friends, or colleagues who will provide candid advice. Such practice is even more essential for the online researcher, who must be confident and fluent in the selected technology tools before conducting interviews with research participants. The online interviewer also may ask for impressions conveyed by written and visual communications. Another suggestion is to ask a colleague or more experienced interviewer to observe a practice interview or interview recording and offer suggestions.

Record the practice interview and listen to it. Were your explanations of the study expectations and/or any background information concise and clear? Were questions asked in a supportive but neutral tone? Did you avoid emotional reactions to responses that participants might interpret as judgmental or disrespectful? Researchers may benefit from practicing both roles: interviewer as well as interviewee. By taking the research participant's side, the researcher may gain new insights about how to proceed.

If possible, arrange a time when you can meet, using the interview technology as part of the preparation. A brief online planning session and orientation to the software will reduce the pressure on both researcher and participant in the interview. This planning session can be used to reiterate expectations spelled out in the recruitment statement (Chapter 7), to discuss the informed consent form (Chapter 7 and 8), and/or to answer any remaining questions, in addition to practicing communication with the selected technology. Such informal dialogue is valuable for building the trust and relationship needed for productive and open dialogue in the interview.

Interview Preparation by ICT Type

Some preparation steps common to all online interviews and some specific to ICT types are outlined here.

PREPARING FOR ANY ONLINE INTERVIEW

- Confirm time frame, anticipated length for interview.
- Confirm online setting for the interview.
- Schedule time as needed to try the ICT prior to formal data collection.
- Schedule interview(s).
- Establish protocols for the interview, including basic logistics. These may include agreement on signals to indicate need for more time to answer or time for a break. Protocols may also include discussion expectations for level of focus expected during the interview.

PREPARING FOR A TEXT-BASED INTERVIEW

Synchronicity and Synchronous/Near-Synchronous Text-Based Interviews

Synchronous or near-synchronous text-based interviews are conducted in a chat or instant message application. These may be free-standing applications or features of a social networking site. In this type of interview, the interviewer posts main questions first, then posts follow-ups and probes based on the participant's written responses. Synchronous or near-synchronous text-based interviews can also occur as part of multichannel communications in a virtual environment or on a web conferencing platform. In such interviews, other audio and/or visual elements may complement the written exchange.

When both parties are engaged in a live exchange, fully focused on the question–response interaction, synchronicity is achieved (Dennis, Fuller, & Valacich, 2008). In other cases, the interview may be ostensibly synchronous but the participant is not devoting full attention to it. While a pause in response might indicate participant reflection on the question, a time lag can also mean the participant is engaged in some other activity. A key risk is participant distraction, which can cause lost momentum or a premature termination of

> **Ethics Tip:** Make sure all plans are consistent with the protocols laid out in pre-interview discussions and verified in the consent agreement signed by research participants.

the interview. Multitasking participants may engage in several synchronous events, without truly focusing attention on any one conversation. While the interviewer is thinking about, then typing, the next question, the participant may find other, more fast-paced activities to engage his or her attention. An interview that the researcher intends as "synchronous" can become "near synchronous." Or participants could simply close the window and be gone! When discussing the interview protocol, consider asking the participant to signal you when he or she needs a break or needs to respond to another conversation.

Preparation is essential to keep the dialogue moving. Preparation entails decision making on the interviewer's part about the level of structure versus spontaneity desired. For more structured interviews, the researcher may type out main questions and frequently used probes to be quickly cut and pasted into the messaging window. Even for less-structured interviews, definitions of terms or clarifications of concepts related to the research phenomenon may be written out beforehand. At another level, preparation starts at the research agreement and consent stage, which can include discussion of the researcher's expectations for focused synchronicity during the interview, or for a less-restrictive time frame between question and response.

To avoid lengthy chat sessions that carry the risk of distractions, text-based interviews can be conducted in near-synchronous episodes. Instead of one significant interview, consider arranging for multiple short sessions. Plan to post initial main questions before the participant logs in for the interview to allow time for reflection on the research problem. Or questions could, for example, be posted every morning for a time-limited series of interactions, with the expectation that at some point during the day the participant will answer. Mobile, on-location access makes it possible for participants to check in and report on observations or experiences as they happen. For example, the interviewer and participant could log in for a couple of short questions on a daily or weekly basis, allowing data collection at strategic times relevant to the purpose of the study.

Whether the researcher and participant are using full-sized or tiny virtual keyboards, the process of posing and responding to questions is slowed by the act of writing those questions and responses. To hurry along the typing of a conversation, texters use various shortcuts. Electronic paralinguistic expressions such as *lol*, meaning "laugh(ing) out loud," or *ttyl*, meaning "talk to you later," have evolved as part of a large system of shorthand (Varnhagen et al., 2010). Emoticons (Laflen & Fiorenza, 2012) and emoji (Baron & Ling, 2011; Ueda & Nojima, 2011; Wortham, 2013) have emerged as a kind of visual, digital shorthand. Text users allow emoticons to substitute for social cues ☺, to add meaning, or to soften difficult messages (Amaghlobeli, 2012). However, like facial expressions or gestures, they do not all have universally shared meanings ☺. In speech, nonverbal signals such as intonation can provide nuance or clarify the intended meaning better than the verbal context can, and, similarly, emoticons can radically alter the meaning of the message.

When an interviewer conducts a text-message interview with an interviewee from another cultural background or communication style, the interviewer must pay careful attention to the use of emoticons. Emoticon use varies by age and gender (Amaghlobeli, 2012). It cannot be assumed that emoticons will be interpreted in the manner the interviewer intended ☺ (Opdenakker, 2006). Miscommunication can occur during a text interview when a participant is more competent or comfortable with the use of emoticons or text abbreviations than the interviewer is (O'Connor, 2006). In preparing for an interview, think about whether and how you will use emoticons. If you decide to use them, will you determine some kind of consistent meaning you associate with each one? Preparation also entails decisions about whether or to what extent to use nontext elements, including shared files or links to images or media. (See Chapter 6 for more about visual research options.)

Even with the use of shortcuts, keep in mind that online interviews in the synchronous mode are slow. In one study, researchers reported that text-based synchronous interviews took about twice the length of in-person interviews and produced far fewer words.

> A 120-minute online interview produced about seven pages of text. A 90-minute face-to-face interview produced 30 to 40 pages of text. The exchange of questions and responses was clearly influenced by the reading, reflection and typing skills of the respondents. (Davis, Bolding, Hart, Sherr, & Elford, 2004, p. 947)

To adapt, they resorted to short, closed-ended questions that fostered simple question-and-answer sequences (Davis et al., 2004).

To prepare for a text-based interview, the researcher should do the following:

- In absence of face-to-face introductions, decide whether you want to share images, a recorded introduction, or other information about yourself and the study. You might decide to create a research website that participants can visit to learn more.

- Select a text interview technology with which participants are familiar; discuss platform choice as part of the consent agreement. Provide any instructions or tech support information the participant may need.

- Familiarize yourself with communications options in that setting; review archiving function for saving the transcript.

- Make sure you and the participant agree on the expectations for the exchange, using the Time–Response Continuum.

- Familiarize yourself with electronic paralinguistic expressions, emoticons, or other communication shortcuts or slang used by the target population. Decide how you will use these shortcuts to save time and keep the conversation moving.

- Articulate a greater number of questions that elicit shorter responses; break big questions into a series of subquestions.

- Write out questions or key phrases in advance so you can cut and paste them into the text window to save time and keep the interview flowing.

- Provide any background information in advance so you can move quickly into a dynamic exchange.

- Determine what protocols are needed for the interview and how you will communicate them to the participants.

- Choose at least one person who is not a research participant with whom to practice the interview. After the practice session, make any needed adjustments to wording of questions, use of emoticons, and timing.

Preparing for an Asynchronous Text-Based Interview

Asynchronous interviews are conducted by e-mail, or by posting in a private forum, blog, or wiki. Like the interviews described earlier, they are conducted primarily in writing, with the potential for shared images or links to other media. Many of the issues discussed above are relevant to this type of interview, with one big exception: While text-chat interviews require close attention to fast timing, the timing in asynchronous interviews is more relaxed. The researcher can be much more flexible and allow for an iterative process in this type of interview. The interviewer can read and reread the participant's response and think carefully about the next question. Indeed, the main attribute cited in favor of asynchronous interviews is the opportunity for reflection by researcher and participant between question, response, and the next question. In either synchronous or asynchronous text-based interviews, the researcher needs to design the study carefully and prepare for the interviews.

Either structured or unstructured interviews are possible, each with distinct advantages. In a structured interview style, researchers can interview more than one participant at a time because questions can be sent individually to several participants at once (Meho, 2006). In less-structured interviews, participants can more freely discuss general themes, perhaps contributing unexpected perspectives.

The researcher needs to be clear about expectations and gain agreement from participants. The overall time frame for the study should be spelled out, as well as the turnaround time for responses. Do you want participants to respond within 24 hours, or within a week? What should participants expect from you in terms of feedback, probes, or follow-up questions, and within what time frame? The longer the interview, the larger the number of expected iterations and the greater the risk that participants will lose interest or become distracted and not provide complete data.

To prepare for an e-mail interview, the researcher should do the following:

- In absence of face-to-face introductions, decide whether you want to share images, a recorded introduction, or other information about yourself and the study. You might decide to create a research website that participants can visit to learn more.

- Set up a separate e-mail account to ensure privacy. If you are associated with an institution, use your academic e-mail address.

- Develop an interview schedule and guide. More-structured interviews may be laid out with main questions to be asked at specific intervals, such as each week. A less-structured interview should offer an outline of the themes or topics to be explored within a defined time frame.

- In addition to the informed consent agreement, create a procedural agreement with expectations for length of the interview and turnaround time for responses.

- Enlist at least one person who is not a research participant with whom to practice the interview (or a partial interview). Refine questions and approach as needed.

PREPARING FOR A VIDEO INTERVIEW

Not long ago, studios with costly setups were the only way to meet via video conference. However, desktop and mobile options are emerging with the advent of low-cost web cameras and free online services. These informal video calls or video chats can be carried out almost anywhere.

Facilities, including video conference/integrated classrooms, offices, and meeting rooms, offer high-quality options for research purposes. Multiple cameras and assistance from trained technicians mean video conferencing facilities enable either close-up or room visibility, can accommodate groups, and allow for complex interactions or the presence of observers. Many multisite businesses, governmental agencies, and educational institutions have invested in such video conferencing systems. Per-session rentals are available at commercial sites such as those that provide office and business services.

Movement toward greater access and flexibility for desktop video conferencing is advantageous for interview researchers with small budgets or those without access to such facilities. Many text-messaging and chat services now allow users to plug in a web camera; other services, such as **Skype**, offer two-way audio, video, and chat in free Internet calls. Depending on whether the technology is a video conference facility or video call, the researcher will need to decide whether a close-up, waist-up, or wider picture of the person in the room will work best. Testing the setup and communications options is a crucial part of preparation. Additional preparations include the following:

- Experiment with setup and camera positioning options.
- Review other features, such as text chat or areas for presenting visuals, and determine whether or how to use them in the interview.
- Decide how you want to present yourself. Just as in a face-to-face live interview, the background, your attire, and style all convey messages.
- Carefully review questions or interview guide so you can minimize the need to look down at notes. Take the time, before looking down to read notes, to make the best "virtual eye contact" possible.
- Discuss options and parameters for the participant's web camera. Is it acceptable for the participant to turn the camera off and use audio only?
- If using a facility where others (e.g., technicians, camera operators) will be present, determine policies for confidentiality. Depending on the setting, technical personnel, and policies, you may decide to ask more sensitive questions in another way.
- Enlist at least one person who is not a research participant with whom to practice the interview (or a partial interview). Refine questions and approach as needed.

PREPARING TO INTERVIEW IN A WEB CONFERENCING MEETING SPACE

Online meeting or web conferencing platforms integrate text chat, audio, and video conferencing functions with various combinations of tools that may include shared applications and shared whiteboard. The entire interaction is captured and archived, thus providing a data record for the researcher to review and analyze.

Such software suites are typically used for online meetings in business or for instructional purposes. Some are fee-based or subscription services. These services often offer free or low-cost versions for personal use. Other ad-supported or nonprofit services also are available.

When people log in to an online meeting space, they typically see a screen divided into different areas, with space for text chat, various toolbars for drawing and writing, and icons linking to other services. The central workspace can be used to share written or visual details about the study using PowerPoint slides, diagrams, photographs, or other visual elements. Depending on the level of access the researcher sets, the participant has access to some or all of the tools that allow for content sharing or generation.

To plan for an interview in an online meeting space, the researcher reviews the various communication features to determine which to use to convey questions, and what options to make available to interviewees. How will visual, verbal, and/or text options be used?

See the points provided earlier in this chapter to prepare for using the text and video conference applications in the interview. See Chapter 6 for more about the visual research potential for interviews in a web conferencing space. Three other components found in most online meeting platforms are considered here: the shared whiteboard, shared applications, and the web tour.

Preparation for a structured or semistructured interview in a web conferencing space entails outlining questions in advance. These questions, discussion themes, and/or diagrams, images, or media clips for elicitation can be presented on PowerPoint slides or other documents loaded into the meeting space. (See Chapter 6 for more about the visual studies that can be conducted with these tools.) By preparing question prompts, the interviewer is able to focus on the conversation, without the need to cut and paste from another document or type during the interview. Interview questions or themes can be presented one by one by advancing through the slides or pages. It is also possible to move back and forth through the preset questions if changing the sequence is desirable. The interviewer can speak and explain the questions, and the interviewee can also read or view the prompts. Because the medium is flexible, additional questions, follow-ups, and/or probes can be either spoken or written during the interview.

For less-structured interviews, themes for discussion can be written, drawn, uploaded, or linked to on the shared whiteboard during the interview. The interviewer can speak and write the question or pose a question related to a visual element presented on the shared whiteboard.

Three other components found in most online meeting platforms can also be beneficial for visual elicitation, communication, and/or collaboration in the interview: the central whiteboard, shared applications, and the web tour. The whiteboard allows the researcher and/or participant to draw on the screen. The whiteboard can be used to generate or build on existing models, visual maps, or diagrams. In studies that relate to software or other technologies, shared applications allow the participant, for example, to demonstrate how he or she would solve a particular problem. The web tour option can be used to view websites or media that may illustrate some aspect of the research phenomenon.

All elements the researcher intends to share must be selected and tested in advance of the interview. Any intellectual property issues, such as permissions for use of images or media, should be obtained before finalizing the interview plans.

The main issue that is both an advantage and a disadvantage of the meeting space is the diversity of tools, which some researchers may find overwhelming. With a little practice, researchers can overcome this potential challenge. Highly engaged participants may be less likely to exit out of the interview prematurely. Diverse options for communication make the online meeting environment an ideal choice for the interviewer who wants to cultivate answers from and with participants as the metaphorical gardener or explore answers by traveling through the interview with the participant.

Once the tools, process, and approach have been selected, steps to prepare for the interview include the following:

- Check audio features. If the space allows for only one speaker at a time, determine protocols for turn-taking in conversation and conduct a pre-interview run-through.

- Check recording/archiving features. You may want to set up an external voice recorder as a backup to ensure audio capture.

- Select or develop relevant diagrams, illustrations, examples, photographs, visual maps, and so on that can be used to show, rather than ask or tell, the participant what you want to discuss. (See Chapter 6 for further discussion of visual methods in online interviews.)

- Some platforms allow for PowerPoint slides, while others allow for shared documents. In addition to posing questions using audio, questions or key topics can be written out on the shared whiteboard. If this approach will be used, develop the slides and documents.

- Some platforms allow for the use of media, such as video clips. If you are incorporating media, make sure you can easily access, run, and close out of the media element, and return to the main discussion area.

- Review the interactive features of the platform. Can any of them be used in the course of the interview? For example, could you ask participants to draw or diagram answers to some questions?

- Enlist at least one person who is not a research participant with whom to practice the interview (or a partial interview). Refine questions and approach as needed.

If the meeting space allows for a webcam option, add the following preparations:

- Follow preparatory steps for video conferencing.

- Practice using the webcam.

- Adjust the webcam to allow for close-up view.

- Determine whether you want to use the webcam during all or part of the interview. For example, you could use it to make contact in the introduction and then turn it off.

- Decide who gets to choose when and how to use the webcam. This decision may be one to discuss in advance of the interview.

PREPARING TO INTERVIEW IN AN IMMERSIVE VIRTUAL ENVIRONMENT

Preparing for an interview in a virtual world or game includes creating (or updating) an avatar that represents the researcher. Williams (2007) calls the avatar a "graphical pseudo-presence." The avatar "explicitly communicates a wealth of information upon the observer's online identity. The choice of pseudonym for the day and the dress and stature of the avatar chosen impact on how the observed react to the observer" (p. 11).

Avatars are not neutral; they are "created by people who sit in front of a computer with a set of lived experiences, identities, characteristics, and beliefs" (Anarbaeva, 2012, p. 2). The influence of "real" identity on avatar development is seen in multiplayer games as well: "Even those who role-play necessarily bring their attitudes, education and 21st century interpretation of knightly values into the MMO [massively multiplayer online game], so the two identities are never disconnected" (Lehdonvirta, 2010). To examine the relationship between person and avatar, Messinger's research team (Messinger, Ge, Stroulia, Lyons, & Smirnov, 2008) draws on earlier theories by Hull (1943), Kaplan (1975), Swann (1987), and Swann, Pelham, and Krull (1989) to analyze whether people act more in accordance with motives for *self-enhancement* or *self-verification* when creating avatars. Self-enhancement theory is based on the notion that individuals are motivated to promote a positive self-concept and solicit positive feedback from others. People with negative self-views tend to distort personal information in a positive direction, referred to as *compensatory self-enhancement*. In contrast, self-verification theory contends that people are motivated to maintain a consistent self-concept, preserve the truth about themselves, and seek objective feedback from others. People are motivated to self-verify because portraying one's self-concept in a stable, self-congruent manner bolsters a person's confidence in predicting and controlling the world, and facilitates social interactions (Messinger et al., 2008). Messinger and colleagues found that people generally balance motives for self-verification and self-enhancement, customizing their avatars to bear similarity to their real selves, with moderate enhancements.

Researchers need to decide how to present themselves as avatars, based on the focus and the setting of the study. What self-view applies for the researcher in the development of his or her avatar? How does the self-view of the participant play into the data to be collected from the participant? Researchers can embody their online identity any way they see fit (Dunn & Guadagno, 2012), to appear in a way that others in the game or virtual world will accept (Martey & Shiflett, 2012). Anarbaeva (2012) observes:

> Some social norms of Second Life culture vary from region to region, though, in particular dress codes. This can be compared to the offline life of an avatar where rules and norms differ when one enters a different location (e.g. country, state, etc.). Once new residents have spent some time in Second Life and learned how to get around and how to customize their avatar, their "newbie" status becomes less visible and they are seen as "true" residents of this virtual community.
>
> . . . Second Life encourages us to look beyond our offline identities. Although avatars may start out with an identity similar to their user's offline identity, we are able to experiment with characteristics of a different ethnicity, race, and gender in a cyber-location. (pp. 7, 12)

Preparation, then, includes learning the social norms of participants' culture(s) and deciding whether to appear as a new or experienced member of that culture—or as an outsider.

Additional preparation points include the following:

- Test your "image" with colleagues or friends to assess whether you convey the persona you intend to present to research participants. Enlist at least one person who is not a research participant with whom to practice the interview (or a partial interview). Refine questions and approach as needed.

- Familiarize yourself with the selected virtual world or game's functions and norms, including teleporting and sharing items with other avatars.

- Decide where and how to conduct the interview. If you create a space, consider making it private and requiring permission to enter (make sure space is large enough so that audio exchanges are out of range of others who could eavesdrop).

- If it is not your own property, make arrangements to use it for interview purposes. Schedule and plan to minimize the presence of others and the likelihood of eavesdropping.

- If you select a place such as a library or academic meeting area, determine what ethical expectations are established by the setting.

- Make sure the participant has all information needed, including meeting place.

- Offer to meet ahead of the interview so both researcher and participant are familiar with the location and features. If you decide to meet on the participant's property, ask to visit in advance of the interview.

- Decide whether to use text chat or audio features for dialogue in the interview.

- If you are using text chat, see the suggestions for text-based interviews.

- If using VoIP or telephone, check audio operations. Arrange for audio recording.

> ⚖️ **Ethics Tip:** If you want to collect data through observation, the style of avatar the participant chose, or the space the participant built, make sure you have asked for permission in the consent agreement.

Getting Ready to Interview

As noted, the online interviewer has three kinds of preparations to make: One is related to preparing questions or discussion themes apropos to the empirical and theoretical basis of the study; a second is related to preparation for the use of selected technology; the third is the personal preparation needed to serve as guide and facilitator of the interview—as the person behind the monitor in a human-to-human conversation with a purpose.

DEFINING ROLES

Earlier sections have explored researchers' roles in terms of the miner who excavates information, the gardener who cultivates exchange, or the traveler who journeys with the participant (see Chapter 3). Researchers need to have clear intentions in mind. They also need to consider how participants perceive these intentions. Rubin and Rubin (2012) point out that people relate to one another through culturally understood roles in which obligations and responsibilities are known to both parties. In establishing an acceptable role as researcher, it is important to decide how you want to present yourself and how much of your own experience you want to share. In the online interview, unless a full video conferencing system is used, your visual image may be limited and, as a result, may seem even more significant. What image do you want to convey as it relates to your role in this study?

> ⚖️ **Ethics Tip:** If you want to collect data on the participants' activities, group memberships, and so on by reviewing their profiles or other information, make sure you have asked for permission in the consent agreement.

EPOCHE, SELF-REFLECTION, AND PREPARING TO LISTEN

As the researcher, it is important to approach each interview with a clear and fresh perspective; this is what phenomenological researchers call

Epoche (Moustakas, 1994). Whatever methodological tradition guides the study, starting with an open mind is important for data collection through interview research.

Moustakas (1994) points out that Epoche is "preparation for deriving new knowledge" by listening without expectations for any particular outcome (p. 85). "In the Epoch, we set aside our prejudgments, biases, and preconceived ideas about things" (p. 85). It is, of course, impossible to pretend that researchers have no biases and can listen to answers without sifting through their own experiences and cultural lenses. Rubin and Rubin (2005) suggest that self-reflection is essential: "Researchers need to continually examine their own understandings and reactions" (p. 31). Moustakas calls this being "transparent to ourselves" (p. 86).

The attitude of Epoche emerges when the researcher is self-aware and sets aside time to mentally refresh before beginning an interview. The attitude of Epoche emerges when the researcher has a sense of deep respect and appreciation for each participant's unique contribution. When online researchers are confident about the intended direction for questioning and the smooth application of the ICTs, they enter the interview ready to listen deeply and respectfully to the participant.

With ongoing self-reflection and Epoche, each new interview is a fresh experience. This kind of preparation is needed before every interview. Once the interviewer has conducted several interviews, certain responses to particular questions may be anticipated; the interviewer who has made a conscious effort to set preconceived notions aside may hear subtle or profound nuances that might otherwise be overlooked.

Closing Thoughts

Preparing for an online interview involves personal, theoretical, and technical steps for the researcher and participant. The exchanges throughout the process—whether routine or substantive—should be seen as meaningful aspects of the overall research relationship. The interaction begins when the researcher describes the study, clarifies expectations, and obtains informed consent agreements (see Chapter 8). The process of planning for the interview offers additional opportunities to communicate and build trust, which are foundational to the successful research interview.

In the Chapter 4 discussion of interview structure, a range of very structured to very unstructured interviews was defined. Some interviewers prefer an unstructured conversational style of interviewing. Online, even these interviewers will do best by writing out key phrases or themes in advance if text will be used in the interview.

Although new tools for communication will undoubtedly appear, the basic distinctions of synchronous and asynchronous, visual, and text-based interview styles will likely persist. Decisions about the ICT and means of communication are closely interwoven with the research purpose, methodology, and theoretical framework. There is no simple recipe for how to mix them; finding the right synergy will be part of the learning and new knowledge that result from the study.

Researcher's Notebook

STORIES OF ONLINE INQUIRY

Interviews described in previous Researcher's Notebooks generated data for studies on collaborative e-learning and on women e-entrepreneurs. Two studies are referenced as exemplars:

- A study about collaborative e-learning that aimed to explore instructional practices and organize results into a Taxonomy of Online Collaboration. Findings of the study were published in several articles and chapters (Diaz, Salmons, & Brown, 2010; Salmons, 2007, 2009).

- A study about women e-entrepreneurs that aimed to explore their uses of technology (Salmons, 2014).

In both studies, the interviews took place online in a web conferencing meeting space. The selected platforms allow for dialogue through VoIP, telephone, and/or text chat. A webcam can be used for video. Additionally, there is an area where researcher and participant can view slides and use a shared whiteboard. In other words, these are complicated technologies and the researcher needs to know the features well enough to decide, at the design stage, what kinds of interactions to carry out in the interview. Then, when preparing to conduct an interview, the researcher needs to be conversant with use of selected features to avoid disruption or distraction during the interview.

To prepare for these interviews, I took several important steps. I used the selected web meeting spaces for other purposes, including webinars and meetings. Those experiences allowed me to build comfort working in the space and also helped me understand where visitors might encounter obstacles.

In advance of data collection, I developed the main interview questions and related graphics and placed them on slides. These slides could be advanced during the interview to provide structure and consistent sequence that helped keep the interview focused.

(Continued)

(Continued)

Pre-Interview Discussions

Prior to the interviews, selection criteria and agreements were discussed with research participants via e-mail, and any questions about the process were answered. Once participants signed the informed consent form, any interaction was treated as data collection.

Research participants were provided with working definitions of key concepts and relevant background information. Research participants in the first study were encouraged to select a course or program of study that best demonstrated collaborative methods of teaching and learning to discuss in the interview. Participants for the study on women entrepreneurs were encouraged to share links to their websites, blogs, or social media pages so that I could learn about their businesses ahead of the interview. These pre-interview exchanges allowed me to understand more about each participant so I could begin to formulate the follow-up or probing questions I might ask to dig into particular areas of interest.

These preparatory steps resulted in greater confidence on my part, and readiness on research participants' parts, for lively and generative online interviews.

Key Concepts

- Quality of interview research outcomes depends on data contributed by research participants. Establishing productive communications using online technology requires careful planning.

- A determination of whether the inquiry is designed to study online behaviors or face-to-face behaviors may shape the choice of technology tool for conducting online interviews.

- Regardless of technology, the interview researcher must be self-aware and take time to reflect on his or her role, as well as biases or presumptions that could influence the way participants' remarks are understood.

Discussions and Assignments

1. Identify an ICT you are interested in using for an online interview. Discuss the specific options available for communicating, how you would use them, and steps you would take to prepare.

2. Create a planning timeline and checklist for an online interview that uses the ICT you chose in the above assignment.

3. Discuss the concept of Epoche. What could you do to clear your mind in readiness for an online interview?

4. Discuss the point made by Rubin and Rubin (2005): People relate to one another through culturally understood roles in which obligations and responsibilities are known to both parties. When the interview occurs online, how do people know "culturally understood roles" and agree to obligations and responsibilities? Identify any steps researchers (or participants) should make in the planning phase.

On the Web

www.sagepub.com/salmons2e
You will find media pieces and other resources related to online interview preparation.

10 Conducting the Online Interview

> *The important thing is not to stop questioning. Curiosity has its own reason for existing. One cannot help but be in awe when he contemplates the mysteries of eternity, of life, of the marvelous structure of reality. It is enough if one tries merely to comprehend a little of this mystery every day. Never lose a holy curiosity.*
>
> —Albert Einstein (1879–1955)

> *Always be suspicious of data collection that goes according to plan.*
>
> —Michael Q. Patton (2002)

After studying Chapter 10, you will be able to do the following:

- Summarize roles and responsibilities of the interviewer during the interview
- Describe essential practices for conducting a productive research interview
- Conduct a research interview using synchronous or asynchronous technologies

After contemplating the researcher's intentions and position in Chapter 3, interview approach in Chapter 4, options for technology in Chapters 5 and 6, sampling and recruiting in Chapter 7, ethical issues in Chapter 8, and preparation in Chapter 9, you are ready to explore practical

Figure 10.1   E-Interview Research Framework: Collecting the Data

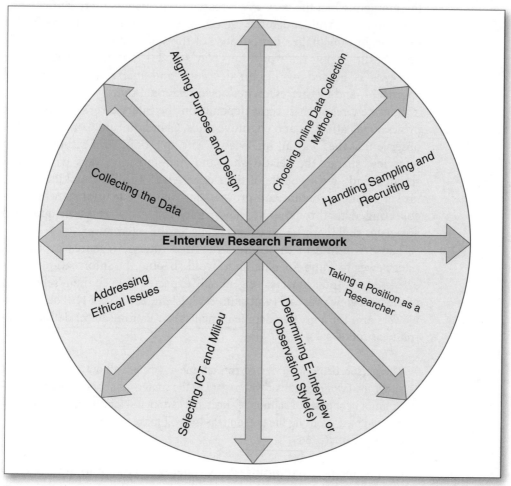

Source: Vision2Lead, Inc (2009–2014).

steps for conducting an online research interview. Such interviews use tools that allow interviewer and participant to communicate with text, audio, visual, or immersive technologies. This chapter continues the discussion of data collection with a focus on practical steps for conducting online interviews.

The Interviewer and the Interview

The moment comes when dreaming, training, practicing, and rehearsing are through. The athlete stands poised at the end of a diving board with an Olympic audience's attention, the actor takes the stage, the nervous lover pulls a ring from his pocket—and it is time for action. Similarly, the researcher moves from intellectual exploration of literature and theory to the moment when the very real research participant is there, anticipating a question that will launch the interview. At that moment, the researcher must begin to actualize the purpose of the study and, as Denzin (2001) describes it, "bring the world into play" (p. 25). The way the researcher proceeds is guided by design decisions and interview structure and approach—and by the researcher's own relational style.

Interview research success depends on the interviewer's personal and professional, affective and cognitive skills. Clandinin and Connelly (2000) observe that the "way an interviewer acts, questions, and responds in an interview shapes the relationship and therefore the ways participants respond and give accounts of their experience" (p. 110). A skilled interviewer balances content and process, and active or neutral stances when collecting data through interviews. Each interview research approach associates slightly different expectations for the interviewer.

Those working in the more structured interview genres expect the interviewer to mine for data and "avoid shaping the information that is extracted. . . . Interviewers are generally expected to keep their 'selves' out of the interview process" (Gubrium & Holstein, 2003a, p. 31). These interviewers aim for a greater degree of neutrality. Patton (2002) defines neutrality as follows:

> The person being interviewed can tell me anything without engendering either my favor or disfavor with regard to the content of her or his response. I cannot be shocked; I cannot be angered; I cannot be embarrassed; I cannot be saddened. Nothing the person tells me will make me think more or less of the person. (p. 365)

This is not an insignificant matter. Interviewers want to draw out stories that interviewees are reluctant to share with others. As a result, they may find themselves called on to move into "realities that are not only different from one's own but also surprising, alien, uncomfortable, a direct challenge to one's thinking, disgusting, horrifying, anxiety-provoking, boring or otherwise difficult" (Rosenblatt, 2003, p. 229). Researchers must engage in continuous honest reflection not only to identify biases and assumptions but also to think about how this background shapes the research focus and show how those reflections lead to insights (Baym, 2009). Maintaining nonjudgmental openness and composure can be a challenge for interviewers who are studying cultures or circumstances greatly different from their own.

Interviewers who want to cultivate exchange in semistructured interviews, using the gardener metaphor, should actively listen for the seeds they want to nurture into new conversational directions. Sometimes it may be necessary to set aside planned interview questions to explore more deeply the participant's thoughts, stories, or reflections. As Fontana and Frey (2003) observe, "Asking questions and getting answers is a much harder task than it may seem at first. The spoken or written word always has a residue of ambiguity, no matter how carefully we word the questions" (p. 61). The researcher working from a gardener position sees this "ambiguity" as an opportunity to use probes and follow-up questions that allow the participant to share additional insights. This approach requires the researcher to be flexible and in the moment.

Postmodern interviewers who aim to cocreate narratives by traveling with research participants believe neutrality is neither desirable nor achievable. Postmodern interviewers look for ways to work with participants to generate knowledge from positions within the interview (Gubrium & Holstein, 2003a). Interviewers need to consider the nature of the research and characteristics of the sample population, and adopt an approach that suits the design and nature of the study.

Regardless of methodological approach, the core activity is the same for any interviewer: to engage in dialogue with the research participant with the purpose of data collection. And regardless of epistemological or methodological stance, the interviewer is responsible for the interview and must take this role seriously. Kvale (2006) argues the following:

> It may be concluded that a research interview is not an open and dominance-free dialogue between egalitarian partners, but a specific hierarchical and instrumental form of conversation, where the interviewer sets the stage and scripts in accord with his or her research interests. The use of power in interviews to produce knowledge is a valuable and legitimate way of conducting research. (p. 485)

Some researchers may chafe at this description of the power dynamic of the interview. But undoubtedly, identifying clear research questions and an appropriate design are the job of the researcher, as are the steps involved in preparing for and carrying out interviews, and ultimately analyzing the data to answer the research questions. With the power inherent in the role comes responsibility for self-awareness, fairness, and respect for the research participant.

Research participants are not without power in the interview. Kvale and Knapik offer these observations:

> The interview subjects have their own countering options of not answering or deflecting a question, talking about something other than what the interviewer asks for, or merely telling what they believe the interviewer wants to hear. (Kvale, 2006, p. 485)

Although participants do have fewer opportunities to explain what is salient for them when interactions are more structured, it does not make sense to assume that responsiveness is eliminated. Answers might still be chosen in response to what is salient for them in the moment or for their anticipated futures (e.g., cherished self-descriptions, perceived goals of the research, what the question is really asking). (Knapik, 2006, p. 6)

Knapik (2006) studied the perspectives of participants' comments, which are useful for those considering interviewer styles and approaches. Participants in Knapik's study observed that the way they reported their experience of the phenomenon of interest in their research interviews was influenced by "continually updated understandings that resulted from their active monitoring of researchers' reactions" (p. 6). In one example, the researcher's expression of surprise indicated to one participant that he was providing an account that ran contrary to her expectations. The participant described how "subsequent back-and-forth exchanges supported his growing sense that his unexpected account was more problematic than interesting for the researcher" (p. 5). Two of Knapik's participants expressed worry over the possibility that their account would contribute to existing stereotypes—a concern that their comments might be misrepresented and too easily categorized. In both cases, this perception had a dampening effect on the participants and limited their willingness for greater self-disclosure (p. 7).

Knapik (2006) observed that we can compromise both quality and ethics when we make interviewees' spontaneous reactions a problem to be managed. She warns that the interviewer needs to be flexible and open to the possibility that what might be seen as the participant derailing the interview may actually be an opportunity to collect data on new aspects of the phenomena. She said, "I do not wish to negate the importance of developing guidelines for researchers; focusing on imperatives can leave unacknowledged the level of improvisation that is inevitably needed and ultimately desirable" (p. 6). Gubrium and Koro-Ljungberg (2005) make a similar point:

> Qualitative researchers are dependent on participant engagement—silences, pauses, refusals to answer, and misunderstandings. On one hand, some engagements can limit the involvement of the participant, thus violating the interactiveness of the interview, but on the other hand, these engagements are the participants' means to share or take over control and power during interviews. . . . [F]rom the social constructionist perspective, if researchers do not relinquish some control during the interview, they limit their data and research process. (p. 696)

To collect data through a purposeful interview, Ritchie and Lewis (2003) and Mason (2002) point out that a researcher must do the following:

- *Establish credibility* so the interviewee is assured of the professionalism of the study and legitimate uses intended for the data.

- *Demonstrate respect for the interviewee* to engender trust and comfort the interviewee needs to reveal personal views or experiences.

- *Listen* actively and reflectively, and decide whether to dig deeper or move on to another topic. Find a balance between talking and listening.

- *Think clearly, logically, and in the moment.* The less structured the approach, the more decisions about the content and sequence need to be made spontaneously within the interview. Flexibility and willingness to diverge from prepared questions and go with the interview flow are essential.

- *Remember* what has been said and make a mental note so you can return to points made earlier in the interview.

- *Be curious* and show interest in the topic of inquiry.

Awareness of the interviewer's role and position is essential for the online interviewer because research participants can withdraw with one click. Online interviewers have a narrower margin of error when it comes to engaging—or alienating—research participants. The need to function as a curious, respectful active listener further means it is essential to develop social presence with the research participant—within whatever information and communications technology (ICT) has been selected for the interview.

Shin (2002), drawing on the work of Lombard and Ditton (1997), points out: "Presence, as social richness, involves the degree to which media are capable of making users perceive other users' sociability, warmth, sensitivity, personality, or closeness in a mediated communication situation" (p. 124).

Online interviewers will most likely use a mix of written, audio, and visual communications, so will need to consider how to develop social presence in each respective medium. Participants' willingness to follow the researcher's agenda or their interest in exerting control over the interview in different directions may be influenced to some extent by their expectations for online participation generally. Bakardjieva (2005) characterizes two distinct orientations toward the social character of the Internet: the consumption model and the community model. The consumption model emerged when online libraries and publications began to offer Internet consumers an unlimited supply of data and media. Such users see the social web as a place to access and share information. The community model emerged when users found ways to build online networks and use interactive capabilities for communicating and collaborating with family, friends, and colleagues (Bakardjieva, 2005, p. 165). They see the social web as a place where they can contribute user-generated information. They seek affiliation with others who share common interests, rather than efficiency in finding answers (O'Sullivan, Hunt, & Lippert, 2004). Understanding whether the study's sample population are more likely to see their relation to the Internet as either consumers or generators of web-based resources may help the interviewer plan accordingly and be more successful at engaging participants. Researchers may need to allow more time to develop relationships and trust with participants who are accustomed to receiving content online without contributing their own perspectives.

Self-presentation and impression formation can influence research relationships and thus take on new significance in the online environment. The face-to-face interviewer might think about issues of identity and credibility when deciding how to present him- or herself. What to wear—will professional or casual dress create the appropriate impression? Should the researcher aim to appear as similar as possible to the research participants and emphasize their common characteristics? The online interviewer must decide whether, when, and how to share his or her pictures. O'Sullivan and colleagues' 2004 research on dimensions of **mediated immediacy** in online communications points to similarity, informality, and self-disclosure as important "approachability cues" that signal to others that "you can approach me" (p. 472). Their findings showed that people were perceived online as friendly and open when they self-disclosed some personal information and shared photos portraying experiences outside of their official role, in informal postures or settings (p. 473).

When considering what kinds of pictures to share—still, moving, graphical—it is important for interviewers to clarify the intended purpose and desired impression. Researchers may want to share their pictures to establish credibility and reinforce the fact that a responsible, caring human exists on the other side of the monitor. Pictures can help build a more personal relationship, establish rapport, and create social presence. On the practical side, there are numerous ways to share pictures online. A research website, blog, or wiki could offer photographs of the interviewer. The researcher should be aware that informal photographs (and personal information from the nonprofessional side of life) posted elsewhere online may be accessed by curious research participants.

Photographs could be shared as part of pre-interview preparation or when introducing the study during the interview. Any medium chosen for dialogue, even text-based channels, offers file sharing for digital picture exchange. Multichannel meeting groupware or video conferencing allow interviewers to share live, real-time images. Interviewers working in immersive virtual environments have an additional challenge when determining what avatar characteristics are appropriate given the context and culture of the setting for the interview. No firm guidelines exist for such interviewers. Observations of avatars in similar environments or of representations used by the target population may offer some clues about whether more realistic or fanciful images would best serve the research purpose.

Although some interviewers believe using visual images (whether real or graphic) adds to the richness of the exchange, other researchers report that lack of visual identification can have advantages. "[Visual] anonymity in text-based CMC [computer-mediated communication] can encourage response in research on sensitive topics" (Fielding, 2007, p. 20). Joinson (2001) made a similar observation: "CMC discussions proved to have higher levels of spontaneous self-disclosure than face-to-face discussions. And visually anonymous participants disclosed significantly more information about themselves than non-visually anonymous participants did" (p. 188). Some welcome the opportunity for online social spaces that are "free of the constraints of the body, (so) you are accepted on the basis of your written words, not what you look like or sound like or where you live" (Kitchin, 1998, p. 387). However, researchers may need to consider the time factor, since communication using leaner media—that is, communication with less immediacy and fewer nonverbal cues—can take longer. Multiple cues available when communicating visually can facilitate "more accurate understanding of others' messages by making their perspectives and expectations transparent. . . . [C]ommunication takes less time when multiple cues are possible because more information can be packed into a message" (Huang, Kahai, & Jestice, 2010, p. 1100).

Whether through words or images, the extent and type of self-disclosure is a consideration for all interviewers. Online, understanding of the sample population may help interviewers decide what will contribute to, or detract from, the social presence and trusting communication necessary for productive interviews. Researchers may want to consider the extent to which rich or lean media will be effective, how much flexibility to offer, and whether participants can choose to disclose themselves visually or not.

Mason (2002) recommends that interviewers practice skills, taking steps such as recording and listening to pilot or rehearsal interviews. As noted in Chapter 6, a part of preparation may involve rehearsing with fellow researchers (or fellow students), friends, or colleagues who will provide candid feedback. Such practice is even more essential for the online researcher, who must be confident and fluent in the selected technology tools before conducting interviews with research participants. The online interviewer also may ask for feedback on impressions conveyed by written and visual communications. Another suggestion is to ask a colleague or more experienced interviewer to observe a practice interview or an interview recording and offer suggestions.

In large studies, multiple interviewers may be involved in data collection. But, typically, the interviewer also is the researcher—the person who designed the study and will analyze the results. As such, the interviewer has many opportunities to interact with research participants. Each step—from initial contact, to negotiation of consent to participate, through interview and follow-up—offers the interviewer opportunities to build the research relationship and listen and learn from the research participant.

Conducting a Research Interview

Some researchers lay out the entire interview prior to the session and articulate some or all questions and their sequence in advance. Others create a plan or guide to refer to and use the list of topics to word questions during the interview. A conversational style is used by those who prefer to allow the interview to flow in its own unique way. As discussed in Chapter 2, schools of thought and practice exist for each approach, and, as discussed in Chapter 6, some level of preparation is associated with each. On the practical side, all interviewers share a common need: to begin, carry out, and end the interview. Even when researchers conduct interviews with a flexible sequence, they will want to consider the overall flow (Arthur & Nazroo, 2003; Rubin & Rubin, 2005).

> **Ethics Tip:** Make sure interview steps and approaches are consistent with the protocols laid out in pre-interview discussions and verified in the consent agreement signed by the research participants.

For simplicity's sake, four interview stages are defined here as *opening, questioning and guiding, closing,* and *following up.* While steps taken within these stages may vary depending on the purpose, structure, or approach of the interview, principles discussed here apply in most cases. Each interviewer can adapt them to fit the style and communication technology used in the study.

OPENING THE INTERVIEW

The introduction allows the interviewer to build on pre-interview communication and set the style and pace. Three main tasks should be accomplished: reintroducing the study and its purpose, establishing protocols, and developing rapport. The interviewer reminds the participant of the research parameters discussed during the recruitment and preparation stage and acknowledged in the consent agreement. Significance of the experience and the participant's perspective of the study are recognized, and appreciation for potential contribution to new understandings and knowledge is conveyed. Protocols, expectations, and ground rules for both parties are discussed. These may include confidentiality, recording or note taking during the interview, timing, or breaks.

Rapport means "an understanding, one established on a basis of respect and trust between an interviewer and respondent" (Gray, 2004, p. 22). It also means "establishing a safe and comfortable environment for sharing the interviewee's personal experiences and attitudes as they actually occurred" (DiCicco-Bloom & Crabtree, 2006, p. 316).

Interviewers may try to establish rapport before the interview, beginning warm and open communication to start building a relationship with the initial contact. Beginning the interview with some informal conversation or a simple "How are you?" check-in with the research participant can help set the stage for the interview. Inviting the participant to ask for clarification on any issues related to interview participation before beginning formal questioning can help clear away unresolved matters that could distract the participant. A reliable formula for building rapport and a perception of safety does not exist. Personal qualities, social identities, characteristics, and/or chemistry make one person seem trustworthy and another not.

QUESTIONING AND GUIDING

The interviewer may ask research participants direct or indirect questions, suggest themes for discussion, or otherwise guide the conversation. Research questions and the purpose of the study typically inform the questions, including both content and types of questions or conversation themes. Usually, interviews include several approaches to allow researchers to collect data of the depth and breadth needed to answer the research questions. Ritchie and Lewis (2003) describe questioning as a process of "mapping." To open a new topic, "ground-mapping questions" help the researcher identify relevant issues and generate multiple dimensions of the subject of inquiry. To focus the participant more narrowly on particular topics or concepts raised in response to ground-mapping questions, "dimension-mapping questions" are posed. "Perspective-mapping questions" are used to encourage interviewees to look at issues from different perspectives, to gain more richness and context. Probes for the purpose of "content mining" explore detail and allow the interviewer to "obtain a full description of phenomena, understanding what underpins the participant's attitude or behavior" (Ritchie & Lewis, 2003, p. 150). Patton (2002) looks at the process a little differently. He distinguishes between five kinds of questions, including background and demographic questions, as well as the following:

- *Opinion and values questions:* What is your opinion of _____?
- *Feeling questions:* How do you feel about _____?
- *Knowledge questions:* What do you know about _____?
- *Sensory questions:* What do you experience when you are in the _____ situation?

Patton (2002, p. 372) suggests detail-oriented follow-up questions:

- *When* did that happen?
- *Who* else was involved?

- *Where* were you during that time?
- *What* was your involvement in that situation?
- *How* did that come about?
- *Where* did that happen?

Rubin and Rubin (2005) describe using "open the locks," "tree and branch," or "river and channel" styles. An "open the locks" interview aims to create a broad picture, usually as the basis for additional interviews. One or two broad, open-ended questions are asked with the intention of unlocking a flood of responses. They suggest that the "tree and branch" style is best for exploring multiple themes, with a focus on breadth. The researcher divides the research problem (trunk) into parts, each covered by a main question (branch). When exploring one theme in depth, the researcher uses a "river and channel" approach. The researcher starts with a topic and follows it wherever it goes.

Numerous types, approaches, and styles of interview questioning exist; explaining all of them is beyond the scope of this book. The principles common to most include the use of main, follow-up, and probing questions. As explained in Chapter 6, researchers working at the most structured end of the continuum may state all in advance of the interview.

Semistructured interview researchers may state ground-mapping questions to use with all interviews (perhaps varying wording or sequence) and develop some follow-up dimension-mapping and/or perspective-widening questions to use, depending on answers and interview flow. In some cases, they may share the ground-mapping questions with interviewees prior to the interview to allow time for reflection.

Researchers using less-structured interview styles may create a guide, outline, or list of ground-mapping, dimension-mapping, and/or perspective-widening topics and create key phrases or descriptors. Such researchers may familiarize themselves with types of probes but articulate probing questions during the interview based on responses. In an unstructured interview, the researcher could discuss a ground-mapping, dimension-mapping, and/or perspective-widening framework in the context of the study, and identify themes for discussion.

CLOSING THE INTERVIEW

Closure of the interview provides a transition from the interactive event of the interview back to everyday life. Depending on the nature and subject of the interview, an emotional "cooldown" may be needed. Ritchie and Lewis (2003) suggest that shortly before the end of the agreed-on time frame, the researcher should signal the approaching close of the interview. One way is by introducing questions with phrases such as, "For the final question. . . ." Another is by closing with a summative or reflective question such as, "Is there anything we have not discussed that you would like to share before we end?" Gray (2004) says, "It is worth noting that interviewees often make some of their most interesting and valuable points once they think that the interview is over" (p. 226).

The closing phase of the interview is a time when any remaining expectations for interviewees can be discussed, including post-interview follow-up.

POST-INTERVIEW FOLLOW-UP

As you segue from closing the interview into data analysis, the post-interview follow-up is essential and should be seen as an opportunity for potentially valuable interaction with the research participant. As discussed in Chapter 6, qualitative methods generally encourage in-depth interaction with research participants at each stage of the process: preparing to collect data, collecting data, and analyzing data (see Appendix and the book's website).

After the interview, while it is fresh in your mind, reflect on what you heard and carry out a preliminary data review. Make notes on key ideas; where relevant, refine questions for subsequent interviews.

Once transcription is complete, verify data with participants and ask for clarification on missing, incomplete, or confusing statements. This step offers participants one more chance to add illuminating details and closes the circle, completing the interview contract they accepted in the consent agreement. This step strengthens the study through data triangulation—the use of a variety of data sources in a study (Patton, 2002).

Conducting a Research Interview Using Synchronous Technologies

Four main types of synchronous communication tools for online interviews are explored in this book: text based, video conferencing or video calls, multichannel, and immersive virtual environments. These types offer various degrees of media richness, meaning that they vary in the availability of instant feedback and use of multiple cues (such as facial expressions, voice inflections, and gestures). However, "richer" does not necessarily mean better. (Media richness theory is discussed in Chapter 1.) More important than richness per se is alignment with research design and with participants' usage preferences, access, and availability.

Many variations are possible within—and across—each of these online communication types, and new tools are continuously being developed. (See the book's website for updates.) Some platforms allow for combinations of text, audio, and visual forms, enabling researchers to collect data in diverse ways.

The four interview stages defined here as *opening, questioning and guiding, closing,* and *following up* characterize research interviews regardless of setting. The way they occur—and the role of the interviewer in carrying them out—will vary depending on what ICT is used. Researchers may choose to use different synchronous and asynchronous technologies for each respective stage: preparation (see Chapter 6), opening, questioning and guiding, and closing.

TEXT-BASED INTERVIEW

Text-based synchronous interviews use text messaging or chat. Several strategies introduced in Chapter 6 can help researchers conduct a text-based interview. By developing questions and key phrases in advance, the interviewer can cut and paste text into the window rather than taking the time to write out each item. Prompt response is essential; if needed, paste in a placeholder such as, "I'd like follow-up" or "Give me a second to think about what you've just shared," to signal the interviewee that you are writing a question or comment.
Suggestions for each stage are outlined in Table 10.1.

Table 10.1	Suggestions for Text-Based Interviews
Stages	**Suggestions**
Preparing	• See preparation steps in Chapter 6. • Make sure participant can use any tools needed, such as file sharing. • Confirm agreed-on uses of emoticons or abbreviations.
Opening	• Review research purpose and process, and answer any questions. • Establish expectations, including whether or not participants can choose to turn off the webcam during the interview and answer questions with audio only. • Confirm time frame, anticipated length for interview. • Offer photo through file sharing, or a link to a research project website with picture and bio. • Establish protocols for the interview. These may include agreement on signals to indicate need for more time to answer or time for a break. • Clarify/define any communication shortcuts you (or the participant) want to use.
Questioning and guiding	• Break longer questions into shorter subquestions to keep back-and-forth of dialogue moving. • Use active listening with brief paraphrased comments to keep interview flowing.

Stages	Suggestions
	• Type encouraging notes to show that you are paying attention when the participant is writing long responses. Use the written equivalent of the nod, "uh-huh," or emoticons to signal that you are listening and paying attention. Offer reassurance with short comments as appropriate. • Respond promptly. • Be prepared with follow-up questions or probes to avoid gaps in conversation. Write out core ideas or key phrases so you can cut and paste text into message window more quickly.
Closing	• Signal last question so interviewee knows you are ready to close the interview. • Make sure interviewee has finished with responses. • Reiterate any post-interview follow-up steps after the interview.

VIDEO CONFERENCE INTERVIEW

Video conferencing combines real-time sound and images of conversation partners. This kind of exchange would be considered "richer" than a text interview based on media richness theory, because social cues and visual exchange are possible. Video conferencing can give meetings and interactions a "human feeling," because participants have the ability to see people on the other side and also hear them talk, which helps develop personal relationships and a sense of immediacy (Olaniran, 2009). Some nonverbal immediacy behaviors such as physical gestures, body posture, facial expressions, and vocal expressiveness can be conveyed. (See Chapter 6 for more about video conference interview preparation.)

Studies of video conferencing in other contexts offer insights for those who want to adopt these technologies for scholarly purposes. *Good Practice Guidelines for Participatory Multi-Site Videoconferencing*, published by the Canadian National Research Council Institute for Information Technology, draws on research experience with video conferencing in education and community development work in remote and rural First Nations in Canada (Molyneaux et al., 2007; O'Donnell, Perley, & Simms, 2008). The National Research Council identified four variables to consider in the study of effective video conferencing. All these variables apply in an online research interview, albeit in a slightly different context than the studies' authors may have envisioned:

- *Social relations:* Researchers and participants must be able to relate to one another, develop trust, and create a sense of social presence.

- *Content:* The purpose for the interview and types of questions to be discussed should be appropriate for the medium.

- *Interaction between the users and the technology:* Access and ease of use should promote, not distract from, interactions between researcher and participant.

- *Technical infrastructure:* The type of video conference and the attributes of the technical infrastructure and capacity of the system to incorporate new features and elements may influence the quality of the interview communication conducted in video conference. "Clear audio and visual signals can increase participation by increasing the quality of the auditory and visual cues" (Molyneaux et al., 2007, p. 4).

Interrelationships between users, content and purpose, and the technology are discussed in business video conference examples. In an effort to cut costs in a global talent market, larger companies are using video conferencing for recruitment purposes. Employment interviews share some characteristics with research interviews. Chapman and Rowe's (2002) study of video conferencing in employer interviews found correlations between the level of structure in the interview and the choice of communication media: "The use of videoconference technology for conducting employment interviews appears to have either no effect or a positive effect on the recruiting function of the employment interview for interviewers conducting highly structured interviews" (p. 195).

Applicants reported that structured interviews "eased the anxiety" of the exchanges where video conferencing was used. "The question-answer format of the structured interview is well suited to the limitations of videoconference technologies that can interfere more with the normal flow of an unstructured conversation" (Chapman & Rowe, 2002, p. 194). However, the study showed that less-structured interactions had a negative effect on the recruiting function of the interview. The findings were opposite for face-to-face interviews, where applicants preferred the more informal, less-structured interview style (Chapman & Rowe, 2002).

In addition to framing the interaction with some level of structure, eye contact is mentioned as a dynamic of communication that merits attention when planning a video conference interview. Eye contact is a natural part of face-to-face communication and is considered by many people to be essential in building trusting relationships. Grayson and Monk (2003) describe mutual gaze as a "synchronization signal or 'hand shake'" with important functions in regulating conversation (p. 222). Failure to maintain eye contact is considered in many cultures to be a sign of deception and may lead to feelings of mistrust (Bekkering & Shim, 2006; Wegge, 2006). This is not merely a matter of the technology per se; user choices also influence perceptions. When one participant looks down at the screen and not at the camera, it appears to the other that he or she is looking away and breaking contact. This can easily happen when a researcher is trying to read a list of questions or take notes. Figures 10.2, 10.3, and 10.4 illustrate variations in a desktop video call.

Grayson and Monk (2003) describe the dilemma:

> Were they to look at the camera it would appear to the partner that they are being looked at in the eyes, but then the user can no longer judge whether their partner is looking at them (as they are looking at the camera, not the image), preventing mutual gaze from serving its purpose as a synchronization signal. (pp. 221–222)

Yuzar (2007) uses the term *virtual eye contact* to describe interactions that come as close as possible to direct visual contact. He suggests that meaningful eye contact is possible in desktop video conferencing when close-up camera views are used. Bekkering and Shim (2006) also discussed camera angles and positioning to maximize the value of visual exchange in video conferencing. Chen's (2002) study of eye contact in video conferencing suggests that simple improvements enhance participants' perceptions of eye contact:

> Because our sensitivity in the downward direction is lower than in other directions, the camera should be placed above the display to support eye contact.... A conservative solution is to make the visual angle between the camera and the eyes rendered on the display less than 5°. (p. 55)

Grayson and Monk (2003) observe that experienced users of conventional desktop video conferencing equipment soon get used to the slightly off version of mutual gaze. They point out that because video conferencing also allows for conversation, participants who

| Figure 10.2 | Seeking Eye Contact |

| Figure 10.3 | Building Rapport With "Virtual Eye Contact" Plus Text Chat |

| Figure 10.4 | Building Rapport With "Virtual Eye Contact" Plus Text Chat |

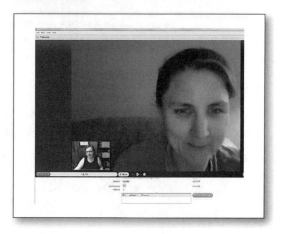

speak in a way that treats the video image of the other person as if he or she were really there offer enough information for them both to "recalibrate their expectations and to learn a new signal for mutual gaze" (p. 224). Desktop video conferencing or video calls can mesh with other technologies. Some platforms include text chat, allowing researchers to clarify interview questions or offer encouraging comments while the participant is talking.

Consumers are driving the development of these increasingly user-friendly technologies—in particular, grandparents and deployed military members' families. If experience in the medium improves interaction between the users and the technology, then as more people become accustomed to using web chats, video calls, and other desktop tools, researchers may find more interview participants willing to meet through a video conference. Integration with other interactive ICTs, as explored in the next section on multichannel groupware, can be expected as more devices include both audio and video capability. At the same time, as sophisticated video conference systems become a common fixture in office and institutional environments, they may become more accessible to researchers. Some suggestions for video conference interviews are listed in Table 10.2.

Table 10.2	Suggestions for Video Conference Interviews
Stages	**Suggestions**
Preparing	See preparation steps in Chapter 6.
	Desktop:
	• Adjust the webcam to allow for close-up view.
	• Carefully review questions or interview guide so you can minimize need to look down at notes. Take the time, before looking down to read notes, to make the best "virtual eye contact" possible.
	• Discuss options and parameters for participant's web camera. Is it acceptable for the participant to turn the camera off and use audio only?
	• Start recording.
	Facility:
	• Position microphone; mute until start time.
	• Focus and position cameras, or work with technician to do so.
Opening	• Review research purpose, process, and structure, and answer any questions.
	• Begin with broad questions to establish comfort with interview process and medium.

Stages	Suggestions
Questioning and guiding	• Stick with agreed-on structure and time frame. • Try to keep eye contact, with minimum attention devoted to taking or reading notes. • Use follow-ups and probes to keep dialogue moving.
Closing	• Signal last question so interviewee knows you are ready to close the interview. • Make sure interviewee has finished with responses. • Ask how the participant felt about the interview and about the medium. • Reiterate any post-interview follow-up steps, as well as further expectations for research participant.

INTERVIEWS IN MULTICHANNEL WEB CONFERENCING MEETING SPACES

Online researchers can take advantage of the diverse communication channels in these meeting spaces to conduct substantive online interviews. **Multichannel web conferencing meeting spaces** integrate text chat, audio, and video conferencing functions with various combinations of tools that may include shared applications and shared whiteboard. Use of text and video conference applications has been discussed in this chapter, and the visual research potential for the shared whiteboard is addressed in Chapter 6. Three other components found in most online meeting platforms are considered here: the central workspace, shared applications, and the web tour.

As noted in Chapter 6, for a structured or semistructured interview, questions or key discussion topics can be prepared in advance and presented on slides or other documents loaded into the meeting space. This allows the interviewer to focus on the conversation, without the need to cut and paste from another document or type during the interview. Interview questions or themes can be presented in the workspace, one by one, by advancing through the slides or pages. Because the medium is flexible, it is possible to move back and forth through the preset questions if a different sequence is called for.

For less-structured interviews, themes for discussion can be written or drawn on the shared whiteboard during the interview. The interviewer can speak and write the question, or pose a question related to a diagram, image, or media clip presented on the shared whiteboard. See Chapter 8 for more about the visual studies that can be conducted with these tools.

Participants have numerous options for communicating responses. They can say them, write them, draw them, and/or show examples. If an interviewee seems at a loss for words, the interviewer can encourage the participant to express the response in another way.

Given the multiple communications options in one place, the interviewer can use varied, complementary approaches at each stage of the interview. Some suggestions for meeting space interviews are listed in Table 10.3.

Table 10.3	Suggestions for Meeting Space Interviews
Stages	**Suggestions**
Preparing	• See preparation steps in Chapter 6. • Test microphone and audio; set turn-taking protocol if the system is set up for one speaker at a time. If using a webcam: • Adjust the webcam to allow for close-up view. Take the time, before necessarily looking down to read notes, to make the best "virtual eye contact" possible. • Discuss options and parameters for participant's web camera. Is it acceptable for the participant to turn the camera off and use audio only? Introduce other features participants can use to present their answers. • Demonstrate and allow participant to practice using tools for writing, drawing, and so on. • Start recording.
Opening	• Confirm time frame, anticipated length for interview. • Review research purpose, process, and structure, and answer any questions. • If webcams are available, use them to share introduction and set the tone for the interview. • Discuss how or whether to use the webcam throughout the interview—or not.
Questioning and guiding	• Use shared whiteboard to convey questions—whether prepared in advance or during interview. Say each question and ask whether clarification is needed. • Vary communication approaches, making use of visual and shared application features as relevant. • Use follow-ups and probes to keep dialogue moving.
Closing	• Signal last question so interviewee knows you are ready to close the interview. • Make sure interviewee has finished with responses. • Reiterate any post-interview follow-up steps, as well as expectations for research participant.

INTERVIEWS IN IMMERSIVE VIRTUAL ENVIRONMENTS

The preceding interview strategies involve people who communicate from the vantage point of their "real-world" identities. Interviews in immersive virtual environments are conducted by communicating through avatars in 3-D environments. An *immersive virtual environment* is defined as "one that perceptually surrounds the user, increasing his or her sense of presence or actually being within it" (Bailenson et al., 2008). The interviewer must "immigrate" into the virtual world and create an online persona that will represent the interviewer to the research participant. (See Chapter 6 for more on the creation of an avatar.)

This visual representation of the individual in virtual space creates new dimensions of communication:

> Forms of interaction need no longer be restricted to text as both proxemical and kinesical features in everyday communication can be replicated in avatar form. Social interaction becomes more complex, with the combination of the textual utterance and the corresponding avatar gesture. (Williams, 2007, p. 9)

With the addition of a microphone and speakers, voice can be added to this already complex set of interactions.

The presence of avatars and a 3-D environment is undeniably a major factor for interviewers to consider; however, the means of communication is still primarily through text. As such, some of the guidelines on text interviews apply.

At this point, scholarly research about the immersive experience and avatars' behaviors in Second Life, gaming, and other environments is beginning to emerge. So far, most of this research uses observation or laboratory simulations with limited examples of interview research. Corporations, however, are holding job fairs and conducting interviews in Second Life. When prospective employees interact in Second Life, they demonstrate technical, personal, communication, and social skills they could use to handle a real situation. As noted earlier, talent-focused companies with the resources to use innovative recruitment and interview approaches may provide useful examples for researchers. Clearly, researchers designing interview studies in immersive environments have the opportunity to conduct foundational research. Through interviews in immersive environments, the potential exists to elicit new understandings of the human presence behind the graphical presence. Some suggestions for interviews in immersive environments are listed in Table 10.4.

Table 10.4	Suggestions for Interviews in Immersive Environments
Stages	**Suggestions**
Preparing	• See preparation steps in Chapter 9. • If using text, see text interview suggestions. • If applicable, test microphone and audio. • Make sure note cards or other features are in place. • Make sure participant has all information needed, including meeting place.
Opening	• Review research purpose and process, and answer any questions. • Confirm time frame, anticipated length for interview. • Depending on the nature of the study, offer a link to a research project website with researcher's picture and bio or more background on the study. • Establish protocols for the interview. These may include agreement on signals to indicate need for more time to answer or need for a break. • Clarify/define any communication shortcuts or tools, such as note cards, that you (or the participant) want to use. • Establish whether the interview will take place in one setting or whether it will involve moving from one place to another.
Questioning and guiding	• Break longer questions into shorter subquestions to keep back-and-forth of dialogue moving. • Your avatar can display nonverbal cues, including gestures and expressions, to show listening. Brief paraphrased comments can be said or posted to keep interview flowing. Offer reassurance with short comments as appropriate. • Respond promptly. • Be prepared with follow-up questions or probes to avoid gaps in conversation. Write out core ideas or key phrases so you can cut and paste text into message window more quickly.
Closing	• Signal last question so interviewee knows you are ready to close the interview. • Make sure interviewee has finished with responses. • Reiterate any post-interview follow-up steps, as well as expectations for research participant. • Determine best follow-up contact approach.

Closing Thoughts

People are people, online or off. Interviews are successful when the researcher is able to convey warmth, sincerity, and curiosity in the role of interviewer. The online interviewer needs even more people skills than does the face-to-face interviewer. The relationship and trust building begin with the initial contact and recruiting, and the steps involved to prepare for the interview. As noted in Chapter 6, researchers should find someone willing to practice process (i.e., the technology tools) and content (i.e., the questions) before conducting an actual interview. By the time the interviewer and interviewee meet online for the interview, both individuals should be ready to proceed.

In addition to developing rapport, the online interviewer must demonstrate interest and attention throughout the interview. In interviews where only one person at a time can speak, or where the exchange is text based, short comments or use of emoticons can assure the speaker that someone is indeed listening.

Easy access to text or desktop tools makes it possible to arrange for a few short interviews instead of one or two long ones. Researchers and participants can agree to log in for one or two questions over lunch hour each day, for example. This can provide a strategic advantage, allowing researchers to collect data on events as they unfold or make observations of present experiences.

When considering the features and potential for an online communications technology, it is natural to compare it with face-to-face communication. When making decisions about selection of tools for online interviews, it may be more productive to look at online interaction as a means of communication unto itself, in a unique online environment that has its own culture. Adopting the mannerisms, norms, and attitudes of the online culture will enable the researcher to create the warm and welcoming social presence needed to make research participants feel confident and comfortable in the online interview.

Researcher's Notebook

THE E-INTERVIEW RESEARCH FRAMEWORK: CONDUCTING THE STUDY

The E-Interview Research Framework reminds us of the holistic nature of research design. Ethical issues are central to every step of the process. Key questions related to decisions about research ethics are provided in Table 10.5.

(Continued)

(Continued)

Table 10.5	Applying the E-Interview Research Framework: Collecting the Data
	Collecting the Data
Aligning purpose and design	• How does the researcher plan to work within methodological traditions and paradigms when conducting the interview and other related observations or document retrieval? • How does the researcher plan to maintain a focus on the research problem during the e-interview?
Choosing online data collection method	• Does the researcher explain the rationale for design choices to participants, as appropriate?
Handling sampling and recruiting	• Does the researcher state what will be discussed with participants during recruiting and screening processes?
Taking a position as a researcher	• Does the researcher need to explain any positional issues to participants?
Determining e-interview or observation styles	• Does the researcher need to explain any aspects of the data collection style to participants?
Selecting ICT and milieu	• Does the researcher have the skills needed to manage the ICT during the interview? • Does the researcher have a contingency plan in case there are technical difficulties?
Collecting the data	• Does the researcher have a plan for conducting the e-interview with either prepared questions or an interview guide? • Does the researcher have a plan for the four interview stages: opening, questioning and guiding, closing, and following up?

STORIES OF ONLINE INQUIRY

I conducted interviews for two related studies on collaborative e-learning. The interviews occurred on a web conferencing platform, using video conferencing, Voice over Internet Protocol (VoIP) two-way audio, text chat, and a shared whiteboard. Two studies are referenced as exemplars:

- A study about collaborative e-learning that aimed to explore instructional practices and organize results into a Taxonomy of Online Collaboration. Findings of the study were published in several articles and chapters (Diaz, Salmons, & Brown, 2010; Salmons, 2007, 2009).

- A study about women e-entrepreneurs that aimed to explore their uses of technology (Salmons, 2014).

Both sets of interviews used some common approaches. The interviews ranged from 50 minutes to 1 hour 20 minutes in length. Each interview followed the same sequence and procedure. An overview of research interview process was provided, reiterating points made in the pre-interview discussion. Using the webcam helped establish rapport and ensured that interviewees understood the steps of the interview. The research purpose and research questions were briefly explained.

This approach allowed for collection of comparable information across all participants, in relation to the stated research questions and themes of inquiry. However, because the questions were open-ended, the interviews also solicited participants' stories, thoughts, and feelings. Participants were encouraged to talk as long as they wanted and discuss the topics as fully as they wished. This approach negated some of the inflexibility associated with standardized, structured interviews. The features of the web conferencing platform enabled the research participants to respond using verbal, text, and/or visual responses. Both studies made use of the shared whiteboard to annotate and further develop visual models that represented aspects of the research phenomenon.

The second exemplar involved using some additional steps. Since this study's focus was on business uses of the Internet, I reviewed and analyzed blog posts containing text, photos and other media, projects, and crowdsourcing efforts to gain more understanding of the motivations, choices, and business practices of participating women e-entrepreneurs. I did not analyze these observations as separate data; instead, I used them as the basis for developing questions to discuss in the interview. In some cases, participants pointed to specific features of their websites or online activities, which I visited after the interview. Carried out in this way, online observations extended and complemented the online interviews.

(Continued)

(Continued)

A follow-up process allowed participants to verify and enhance data collected in the interview. The online interviews were saved, which allowed participants to review and suggest any needed modifications. Follow-up by e-mail was used to solicit additional comments or sample materials. This ensured that participants had conveyed the full extent of their experience in the context of the interview focus and scope.

Key Concepts

The four main types of online interviews are text based, video conferencing, online meeting spaces, and immersive virtual environments for communications. These tools can be combined in some online environments, or different tools can be used for the interview and for preparation and/or follow-up communications. Each has advantages and disadvantages, depending on the research purpose, context, and characteristics of the sample population.

Discussions and Assignments

1. Interviews are widely used in journalism and human resources. This means we have multiple readily available examples of interviews. Although an interview for news or entertainment has a different purpose than a scholarly interview, interviewers still must open, conduct, and close the interview. Search the Internet for a recorded one-to-one interview that lasts at least 5 minutes. Review the recording several times to identify how the interviewer conducted each step of the interview, transitioned between steps, and responded to any unexpected responses from the interviewee.

   • What worked or didn't? Why? What would you recommend?
   • If the interviewer were using this interview to collect data, what would be done differently?
   • Select one of the four synchronous modes described in this book. If the interview were conducted using that technology, what different styles or strategies would you recommend?

2. Review the planning timeline and checklist for an online interview using the ICTs you selected in the Chapter 5 assignment.

   • Based on what you learned in Chapter 10, are any changes needed? Why or why not?

- What steps would be appropriate for implementing this plan?
- What types of responses or events—including technical issues—could derail your interview? Make a contingency plan for addressing them.

On the Web

www.sagepub.com/salmons2e
Check the website for media pieces showing examples of online interview techniques. Look for updated information about conducting interviews with various technologies.

11 Contributing Quality E-Research to the Literature

Why would qualitative scholars develop criteria even as they critique it? Because criteria, quite simply, are useful. Rules and guidelines help us learn, practice, and perfect.

—Tracy (2010, p. 838)

After studying Chapter 11, you will be able to do the following:

- Identify and apply quality standards for qualitative e-research
- Use the E-Interview Research Framework to evaluate research designs and studies
- Consider ways to assess your own work or conduct peer reviews of qualitative e-research

New and emerging online methods will not gain credence unless researchers use them to generate studies that contribute to the literature. The novelty of new approaches may catch readers' attention, but quality research is what will be published and referenced—and what will inspire other scholars to extend the inquiry. Research using qualitative data collected online will be evaluated according to qualitative research guidelines and interview research criteria, as articulated by respected methodologists and by journals that publish such studies. Researchers in academic settings receive reviews from funders, dissertation supervisors, and others from within (and often across) academic disciplines. Professional socialization builds on an understanding of how the researcher's specific discipline defines and evaluates high-quality research (Loseke, 2013, p. 122).

Additionally, such studies will receive added scrutiny about how and why technology was used. Those evaluating an online study will try to understand whether the researcher made appropriate use of technology-mediated communication to collect data. Whether for external or self-assessment, when we look at a study based on data collected with online interviews and related observations, we want to know why and how the researcher made choices about the information and communications technologies (ICTs) used for the interviews, in the context of the research questions, methodology, and sample population. How did the participant respond to the process, as well as to the interview questions? Did the e-interviews proceed as planned, or were adjustments needed—why or why not? What would another researcher need to know if choosing a similar approach? What types of data were collected, and were the data adequate and appropriate given the purpose of the study? Ultimately, did the data allow the researcher to construct an analysis and generate conclusions that achieved the purpose of the study?

At the same time, researchers need to evaluate their own work throughout the designing, conducting, and analyzing stages to learn from the process and make adjustments. Mason (2002) suggests that it is essential for researchers to articulate and continuously monitor their own "internal" working designs to "facilitate the coherent and rigorous development of the researcher's project" (p. 25). Reflexivity and memoing allow researchers to take an active and vital self-evaluative stance toward their own studies.

The E-Interview Research Framework, introduced in Chapter 1 and discussed throughout the book, can be used to structure a review process, whether for use in assessing one's own research, students' proposals, theses or dissertations, or peers' work for publication purposes (Figure 11.1). In addition to the key questions offered in this chapter, templates and additional resources are available on the companion website to the book.

Using the E-Interview Research Framework to Assess Design and Research Quality

The E-Interview Research Framework includes eight interrelated categories of key questions that probe the study's methodology, ethical issues, and approach for using communications technologies to collect data from interviews and related observations. The framework is displayed as a circle to convey the sense that one angle alone will not provide the system-level view

| Figure 11.1 | The E-Interview Research Framework |

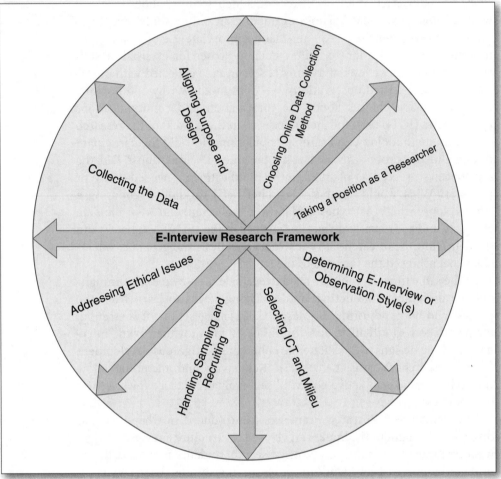

Source: Vision2Lead, Inc (2009–2014).

we need to understand the interrelated mechanisms of online interview research. The answers to one question create implications to be addressed in another category. The category listed first, Aligning Purpose and Design, is returned to at each point in the process to ensure that decisions made about interview style, communications medium, and data collection approach are appropriately reflected in the overarching design of the research.

Aligning Purpose and Design

Every qualitative study begins with a research topic, problem, or question. The researcher must clearly define the underlying basis of the research and show that the topic is relevant and significant to the scholarly discipline and/or to the practitioners who work in the field. The researcher wants to build potential readers' interest by showing that this study will look at the phenomenon in a new way, or somehow offer a fresh perspective. As Tracy (2010) observes:

> Worthy studies are interesting and point out surprises—issues that shake readers from their common-sense assumptions and practices. This is why studies of little-known phenomena or evocative contexts are intrinsically interesting. This is also why people are taken with research that turns common-sense assumptions on their head. When research merely confirms existing assumptions, people will deny its worth while acknowledging its truth. (pp. 840–841)

This basic step is foundational to any design, but for online studies it is even more critical. Other decisions—described throughout the entire E-Interview Research Framework—will depend on a clearly defined research problem, question, and purpose. If the researcher is unsure of the precise direction for the study, it will be difficult to gain support or to engage potential participants.

COHERENT BUT FLEXIBLE DESIGN

Any qualitative research design needs to show how the study will contribute by advancing wider knowledge or understanding with a defensible design and a research strategy that can address the research questions posed (Flick, 2007b, p. 20). The explanation needs to offer a "package of design elements" that shows how "research questions, data, concepts, existing understandings, data generation techniques and samples to all fit together in rational, reasonable and consistent ways" (Loseke, 2013, pp. 124–125). Tracy (2010) observed:

> Meaningfully coherent studies (a) achieve their stated purpose; (b) accomplish what they espouse to be about; (c) use methods and representation practices that partner well with espoused theories and paradigms; and (d) attentively interconnect literature reviewed with research foci, methods, and findings. . . .
> Another means toward significance is through engaging research methodology in a new, creative or insightful way—*methodological significance*. (pp. 845, 848)

In a study that uses online methods, the researcher is tasked with explaining and justifying how and where technology infuses Tracy's definition of points (a) through (d). Why and how is the technology important to the study—and where might it simply serve as a communications channel without adding to the conceptual or practical conduct of the study? How might the online approach make an innovative methodological contribution?

The research map in Figure 11.2 shows that we need to specify each element—theory or theories, epistemology, methodology, and methods—and we also have to explain what connects each of them to the research problem, questions, and purpose. The labeled arrows point to relationships that should be explicated in the research design. Where are the connecting points, and are the ways each design element influences the others clearly explained and adequately justified?

While shown in a nonlinear way, theories and epistemologies typically underpin the design of a qualitative study, since even studies that aim to generate new theory need to explain inadequacies of extant ways of thinking. How does the choice of principles, definitions, and constructs influence methodological decisions? Mason (2002) lists important questions: What role do my data play in my argument? What role does theory play in my argument? When and how does theory come into play? How can I use theoretical insights to understand and explore my data? How can I use my data to think theoretically? How can I demonstrate that my methodology is valid? How can I demonstrate that my methods are reliable and accurate? The e-researcher adds this: How do these conceptual and philosophical perspectives and considerations influence the choice of *online* methods? This question offers a segue to the next category on the E-Interview Research Framework.

Key Questions

Does the researcher . . .

- succinctly describe the research purpose in a way that someone unfamiliar with the specific phenomenon can understand?

- articulate how research purpose, theories and epistemologies, methodologies and methods are aligned?

- support decisions about the conceptual foundation and research paradigm with scholarly sources?

- summarize essential elements of the research design in ways that can be successfully communicated to peers or collaborators through brief online posts and e-mail notes?

For review questions that show how ideas, steps, and processes related to *aligning purpose and design* are relevant to every part of the E-Interview Research Framework, see Table 11.1 at the end of this chapter. For more on aligning purpose and design, see Chapter 2.

Figure 11.2   Design for Clarity and Coherence

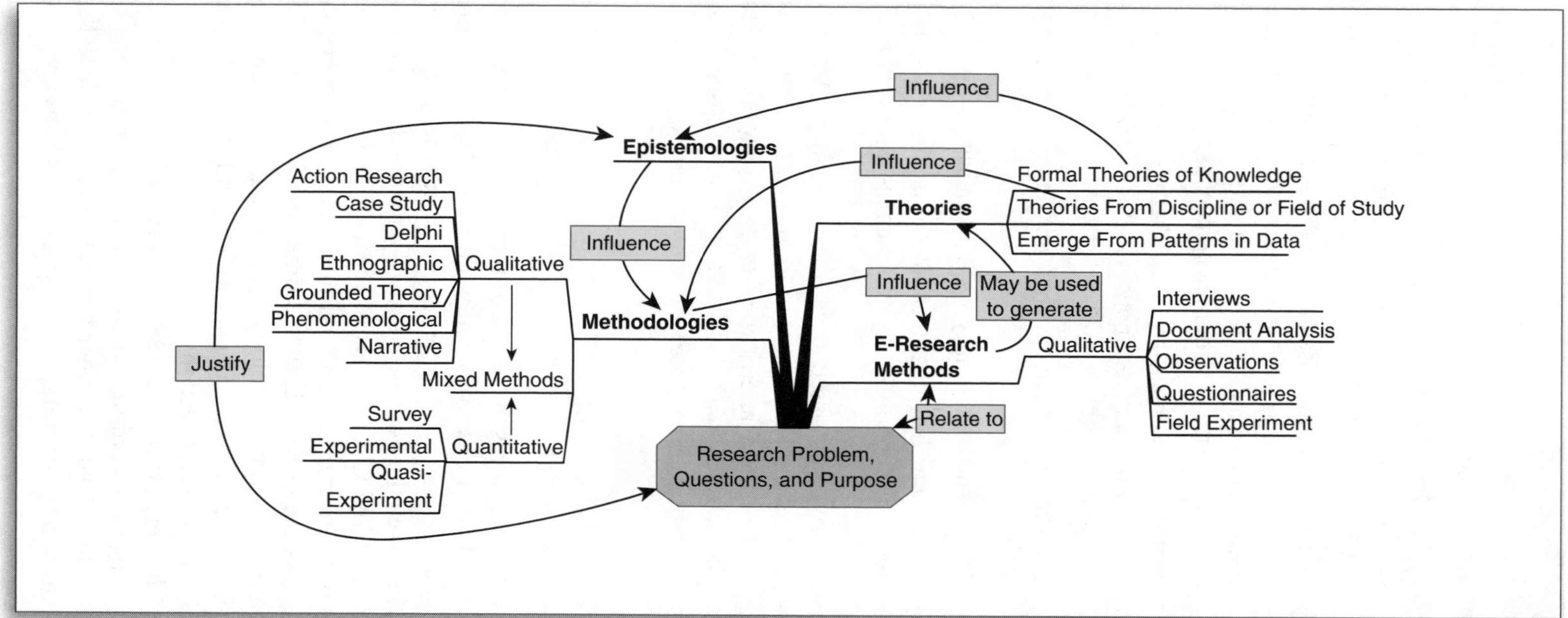

Source: Vision2lead, Inc (2009–2014).

Note: On the book website, find more examples and a template you can use to map your own study.

Key Questions

Does the researcher . . .

- explain how the online medium or setting proposed for the study allows the researcher a "holistic access" (Stenbacka, 2001) to the research phenomenon?

- describe ways the researcher will use features of the selected ICT and/or milieu to remove obstacles between the researcher and the phenomenon, and between the researcher and those who have lived experience with the phenomenon?

- disclose and address any ways that technology might limit access to the participants' responses and stories about their experiences, or create new obstacles?

- describe how the researcher will address these real or potential problems?

- disclose and address any risks to the viability or credibility to the study?

- explain whether other technology choices or alternatives to stated data collection methods would be more appropriate?

For review questions that show how designs, plans, steps, and processes related to *choosing online data collection method* are relevant to every part of the E-Interview Research Framework, see Table 11.1. For more on choosing online data collection method, see Chapter 3.

Choosing Online Data Collection Method for the Study

Hine (2013) captures the essence of this stage of the E-Interview Research Framework with one overarching question: "Is there a methodologically defensible reason why Internet-mediated interaction was deployed?" (p. 127). Given the purpose and design for the study, how does technology serve the study? Clearly, it is not adequate to describe the value of ICTs in terms of the researcher's communication preferences or convenience. Also inadequate are explanations that omit specifics about the particular types of communication technology, types of data that can be generated (e.g., verbal, text, audio, maps, images, video), and appropriateness of such data to answer research questions.

In Chapter 3, three main reasons were offered for choosing online data collection: as a communications medium, as an interview setting, or because the Internet or other technology is intrinsic to the research phenomenon. In the context of these possible options and Stenbacka's (2001) observations, the researcher needs to fully explain interrelationships between research design and choice of data collection using online interviews (and observations, documents, or other data).

Another question to consider is the availability of user-posted information, including discussion posts, media, or photographs in the online community, site, or e-mail list being studied. If such material or observations of the participant's interactions with others are to be used as data, then they must be noted in the informed consent agreement.

Taking a Position as a Researcher

Considerations related to the researcher's position in qualitative studies generally and online studies in particular should be factored into any review. These include the relationship of the researcher to the topic and the participant, the researcher's position as an insider or outsider, the influence of power dynamics on the interview, and the researcher's use of reflexivity to maintain a position of self-awareness throughout all stages of the study. Each of these matters raises questions to think through when assessing the quality of the study design—and the researcher's ability to carry it out.

INSIDER–OUTSIDER PERSPECTIVES AND INTERPRETATIONS

In Chapter 3, the concept of emic–etic and insider–outsider is treated as a continuum rather than a case of black-and-white duality. The advantages and disadvantages of some degree of insider status for online research are highlighted in that chapter. Yin (2011) observes that researchers can choose to optimize what can be gained, regardless of their positions vis-à-vis the study:

> People who do qualitative research view the *emic-etic* distinction and the possibility of multiple interpretations of the same event as an opportunity, not a constraint. In fact, a common theme underlying many qualitative studies is to demonstrate how participants' perspectives may diverge dramatically from those held by outsiders. (p. 12)

At the same time, Lincoln (2002) points out that texts generated by every researcher, as humans who come to research with their own insider-outsider experiences and notions of the world, are inherently incomplete. The crucial matter, then, is the researcher's awareness of his or her perspectives and honesty about them.

Positionality, or standpoint epistemology, recognizes the post-structural, postmodern argument that texts, any texts, are always partial and incomplete; socially, culturally, historically, racially, and sexually located; and can therefore never represent any truth except those truths that exhibit the same characteristics. . . . A text that displays honesty or authenticity "comes clean" about its own stance and about the position. (pp. 333–334)

As a reviewer then, are we able to grasp whether the researcher has "come clean" about the position he or she is taking vis-à-vis the study as a whole, the participants, and the data? Can we clearly see where the researcher falls on the continuum of etic or emic research positions? Does the researcher explain ways the perspectives of insiders and outsiders converge or diverge?

Additionally, does the researcher explain his or her role in the context of Kvale's metaphors of the researcher as a *miner* who digs for the data or the *traveler* who journeys with the participant to discover the data (Kvale & Brinkman, 2009) or the *gardener* (Salmons, 2012) who cultivates relationships with participants to develop trust and rapport online? Does the researcher discuss the significance for the study of related attitudes or perspectives?

POWER DYNAMICS

As noted in Chapter 3, the choice of online method and communications approach may offer the potential of a more open, mutual exchange between researcher and participant. Alternatively, the online interview can create or reinforce an asymmetrical power dynamic if the participant feels inept at using the technology or otherwise intimidated by the online nature of the interview. A reviewer should look closely at the rationales given for technology choices in the context of the interview and population to see whether the researcher has planned for an interview that minimizes unwanted diminishment of participants' contributions to the interview and allows participants' voices to be heard.

REFLEXIVITY

Reflexivity is an ongoing process, and in the context of research, it means more than just reflection. Hibbert, Coupland, and MacIntosh (2010) suggest that rather than simply encouraging contemplation of a situation, reflexivity generates action. "Through questioning the bases of our interpretations, reflexivity necessarily brings about change in the process of reflection—it is thereby recursive" (p. 49). Reflexivity is vital given the Lincoln (2002) directive to "come clean." The researcher, then, needs to be self-aware enough to know *what* to come clean about!

One place where researchers can start is with themselves. Tracy (2010) suggests that researchers can "practice self-reflexivity even before stepping into the field through being introspective, assessing their own biases and motivations, and asking whether they are well-suited to examine their chosen sites or topics at this time" (p. 842). Yin (2011) posits that the researchers' presence will have an unknown influence on the other persons and that their activity may directly influence the way researchers collect data. Researchers should make time to examine such potential influences before and during the conduct of the study. Kitto, Chesters, and Grbich (2008) point to the specific factor of cultural self-awareness: "Fundamentally, reflexivity requires a demonstration by the researchers that they are aware of the sociocultural position they inhabit and how their value systems might affect the selection of the research problem, research design, collection and analysis of data" (p. 245).

Others point to the value of continuously reflexive attitudes toward the research phenomenon:

> The qualitative researcher brings with him/her valuable ingredients to the process and also continuously reflects upon the phenomenon under study while proceeding in the process of generating understanding. Only a reflective researcher can make the process visible to him-/herself and thereby others and only a reflective researcher can make the gained level of understanding accessible for the relevant scientific body. (Stenbacka, 2001, p. 553)

Reflexive probes of the research design are also recommended. Mason (2002) suggests that researchers "reject the idea of a research design as a single document which is an entire advance blueprint and reject the idea of a priori strategic and design decisions made at the beginning of the research process," and instead view it as a process that is "exploratory, fluid and flexible, data-driven and context-sensitive" (p. 24). Flick (2007a) recommends that researchers "check and recheck whether a specific method or design fits your research issue and field" (p. 61).

One approach for carrying out reflexivity is through memoing—creating your own "Researcher's Notebook." Yin (2011) observes:

> Such reflexivity is unavoidable and again deserves some comment in your final methodological report. . . .
>
> Good memos can preserve what at first appear to be "half-baked" ideas that later become invaluable as well as reduce the frustration of being uncertain of whether you already had considered then rejected a certain idea. (pp. 146, 186)

In addition to writing, rereading, and working through research memos, Flick (2007b) suggests the use of "peer debriefing." Regular meetings with other people not involved in the research can help researchers disclose blind spots and consider approaches for redress (Flick, 2007b, p. 13).

For more about *taking a position as a researcher*, see Chapter 3.

Review Questions

Does the researcher . . .

- disclose any conflicts of interest, attitudes, or biases that may impair objectivity about the participants or data?
- describe how any "insider" knowledge or status may be used online to gain access to sites or communities off-limits to "outsiders"?
- make it clear whether he or she is contributing to the study any data about his or her own experiences?
- explain any reflexive practices he or she will use?
- account for any in-process changes made to the study based on ongoing, recursive reflexivity?
- make sure that any changes are covered by the informed consent agreement and, if not, renegotiate the consent agreement and as relevant any institutional review board's or other review body's understanding of the research process?

For review questions that show how characteristics and perspectives associated with *taking a position as a researcher* are relevant to every part of the E-Interview Research Framework, see Table 11.1 at the end of this chapter.

For more on taking a position as a researcher, see Chapter 3.

Determining E-Interview or Observation Style(s)

Any interview researcher needs to consider how purpose and design relate to interview structure when designing a study. As Roulston (2010) points out:

> Researchers' theoretical assumptions about qualitative interviews have implications for how research interviews are structured, the kinds of research questions made possible, the kinds of interview questions posed, how data might be analysed and represented, how research projects are designed and conducted, and how the quality of research is judged by the communities of practice in which work is situated. (p. 224)

The degree of advance preparation of questions and follow-ups correlates to the level of structure in an interview: the more preparation, the more structured the interview. The nature of communication with some technologies, such as online meeting spaces or virtual worlds, may require more pre-interview planning than would a more conversational medium such as video conferencing. A text-based interview may need forethought so a quick repartee can be sustained—and so participants do not lose interest while waiting for the researcher to craft and type each question. The issue of structure may also relate to timing factors, given that a preplanned, structured interview can be predictably conducted more quickly than an unplanned, unstructured interview.

Review Questions

Does the researcher . . .

- clearly outline what style(s) of interview will be conducted, how, and why?

- discuss how the style of interview (and, if used, observation) allows the researcher to collect the data needed to meet the purpose of the study? Does the selected style of interview align with the research purpose?

- address whether any observation is appropriate to the study and spell out parameters in the consent agreement?

- explain whether etic or emic positions influence choices of interview style? Does "insider" familiarity mean the researcher may assume a level of rapport and skip some steps in the interview? Or does an "outsider" position mean that more time is needed to develop rapport?

- identify and account for implications of the communications options with the selected ICT for the style or structure of the interview?

For review questions that show how designs, plans, steps, and processes involved with *determining e-interview or observation style(s)* are relevant to every part of the E-Interview Research Framework, see Table 11.1 at the end of this chapter.

For more on determining e-interview or observation style(s), see Chapter 4.

Selecting ICT and Milieu

Some might think that the selection of ICT and or the online setting would be a simple one, or that it might occur first, based on the researcher's preferences or intentions for types of data to collect. However, selection of the technology to use for communicating with participants and of the setting where interviews and other data collection will occur is quite complex. As noted earlier, this selection is closely intertwined with decisions about interview style and structure. This design step calls the researcher to look at implications related to every part of the E-Interview Research Framework—from research purpose to population and ethics.

One place to begin is with attention to the decision maker: researcher or participant? Hine (2013) suggests some possible considerations:

> Was the medium of interaction appropriate to the population and the topic? If it was a goal to put participants at ease and encourage them to talk on their own terms as naturally as possible, can we be convinced that the specific medium chosen enabled this to happen? (p. 125)

As noted in Chapter 3, some studies intend to uncover patterns and characteristics of online activities, while for other studies the Internet is simply a means for communication about any aspect of life. For the first type of study, the ICT may be part of the phenomenon and so it may be important to use that tool for communication with participants. If the researcher is conducting a study about how people act or interact in a game, virtual world, or social media site, then an interview in that milieu allows for informal show-and-tell about specific features. The researcher may have a specific interest in some aspect of the ICT (e.g., why community members use avatars rather than photos in their profiles), and the relevant features can be viewed while researcher and participant discuss them.

On the other hand, if we are simply picking a convenient place to meet to discuss parenting, gardening, cooking, aging, or any possible aspect of life that occurs in the physical world, then ICT features may be a lower priority. If the researcher wants a low-stress conversation about how a parent is adjusting to having the last child leave home for college, then the priority is the participant's access and convenience. If the researcher really wants to use video conferencing to capture nonverbal cues but the participant does not have a webcam, the researcher might do best to accede to the participant's choice—and sacrifice the ability to observe facial expressions.

Another related matter to ponder is the type of data needed to answer the research questions: visual, verbal, text? In addition to the interview exchange, does the researcher need to observe online interactions or collect posts, documents, or records? For example, a researcher interested in the development of online support groups may need to be able to access historical interactions over a period of time. Or if the interviewer wants to study participants' reactions to a visual model or a video clip of the phenomenon, then it will be mandatory to select a setting such as a web conferencing room where those visuals can be viewed during the interview. In these cases, the ability to read archival material or to access such a web

Key Questions

Does the researcher . . .

- make it clear how specific features of the technology relate to the research purpose and questions?
- describe the type(s) of data to be collected and relate them to ICT choices?
- spell out minimum requirements for technology access, hardware or software, etc. in the recruitment materials? Or does the researcher offer alternatives if minimum requirements cannot be met by potential participants?
- explain any issues related to participants' access to or skills needed to use the selected ICT?
- explain why the participant's choice of ICT was or was not honored?
- provide sufficient justification to support that the context is appropriate given the goals of the study (Tracy, 2010, p. 841)?

For review questions that show how designs, plans, steps, and processes involved with *selecting ICT and milieu,* including use of visual research, are relevant to every part of the E-Interview Research Framework, see Table 11.1 at the end of this chapter.

For more on selecting ICT and milieu, see Chapter 5; for more on visual methods, see Chapter 6.

conferencing room might be the priority and, as such, noted as an inclusion criterion. If a specific type of data is needed, then using an ICT or milieu that facilitates collection of those data is the top priority.

Does the researcher make it clear on what basis the ICT and milieu were selected? The following questions, and those listed in the E-Interview Framework review in Table 11.1, may be helpful for the purpose of self-assessment and/or review.

Handling Sampling and Recruiting

Deciding on a sampling strategy, locating the right people, and recruiting them to participate in a study are a challenge for any researcher. As Hine (2013) summarized, "Was the research population appropriate to the question? Did use of Internet methods impose unacceptable or unacknowledged biases?" (p. 124).

One risk for online recruiting is the ethical necessity to avoid the appearance or reality of sending or receiving unwanted messages, commonly known as spam. If the researcher posts a recruitment message or advertisement on a public website, networking community, or e-mail list, a deluge of unwanted responses may result. On the other hand, if the researcher sends unsolicited e-mail requests to potential participants, the researcher's message may be perceived as spam.

One way to avoid these pitfalls is to create a recruitment statement so all posts or requests use consistent language to describe the study and convey the same message to potential participants. The researcher can share a recruitment statement or link to a recruitment site through social media sites and/or e-mail discussion lists, and/or initiate a discussion about the nature and importance of the study. The best practice is to approach the moderator of the list or discussion group directly to get permission for the recruitment posting, and to respect any norms or guidelines.

The researcher should be transparent about sampling and recruiting approaches throughout the study, and should discuss any implications in reports of the research. As Kitto et al. (2008) observe, "simply mentioning the sampling strategy in the methods section of a qualitative research paper is not sufficient. The key findings of the research need to be evaluated in reference to the diverse characteristics of the research subjects" (p. 244). If the participants' characteristics vary from those originally intended for the study, such modifications should also be discussed and justified.

Review Questions

Does the researcher . . .

- explain how the sampling strategy aligns with the methodology?
- provide sufficient justification to support that the sample is appropriate given the goals of the study (Tracy, 2010, p. 841)?
- demonstrate that ethical recruitment procedures were used to ensure that participants are credible and of legal age to participate?
- address any special circumstances such as underage or at-risk populations?
- offer information to build participant's trust in the researcher and the researcher's approach and reliability? Verify commitment to abide by the consent agreement?

For review questions that show how designs, plans, steps, and processes associated with *handling sampling and recruiting* are relevant to every part of the E-Interview Research Framework, see Table 11.1 at the end of this chapter.

For more on handling sampling and recruiting, see Chapter 7.

Addressing Ethical Issues

Ethical researchers exhibit a self-consciousness in which they are mindful of their character, actions, and consequences for others (Tracy, 2010). *Privacy* in the research context refers to steps taken to safeguard interviewees' right to integrity and self-determination. This means research participants have the right to decide what kinds of information to share with the researcher and under what conditions (Elm, 2008). Many of the ethical issues central to a qualitative study are spelled out in the informed consent agreement.

Informed consent is the term given to the agreement between researcher and participant. Any interaction between researchers and participants that yields data, whether structured and formal or unstructured and conversational, should be preceded by a discussion of the research and expectations, and a signed letter of consent. All interview research and some observation studies need to follow these protocols.

Researchers seeking informed consent need to make clear to their subjects what material they will collect and how material about them and/or from them will be used. The specific uses of material and how their identities will be protected are part of the information subjects need to understand before signing an agreement.

When a researcher conducts an interview in a physical setting, some level of observation occurs. Would, for example, the researcher make note of the pictures on the participant's desk, books on the shelf, magazines on the coffee table? Such common objects may convey information about family or sexual orientation, hobbies or social memberships that may or may not be relevant to the study. If such observations were noted, would the researcher ask for the participant's agreement to use that information as data?

This question is even more intriguing online, since an individual may display a wide range of personal information in a profile or in pages posted on social media sites. While information on a website or blog that is accessible without registration or membership may be considered public, the situation is less obvious in regard to information posted on social media sites or online communities where registration or membership *is* required. To err on the side of ethical research behavior, participants can be given the option to allow or disallow information from online profiles or social media pages to be used as data.

Review Questions

Does the researcher . . .

- offer a clear explanation to participants about the possible future use of the research findings, such as in publications?

- spell out what data the researcher wants to collect from the interview and associated observations, as well as from the participant's website, blog, or social networking profiles or posts?

- cover all aspects of data collection in the consent agreement?

- allow participants to see transcript or notes, and to make corrections or additions?

- protect the data? If the interview is occurring on a proprietary site, does the researcher make sure it is possible to download the recording and then delete it from the server?

- respect ethical expectations established by the online community, group, site, or list? Work within any norms, community expectations/assumptions? For example, do participants in this environment assume/believe that their communication is private?

- write up findings in a way that will respect human and digital identities and preserve anonymity?

For additional review questions that show how designs, plans, steps, and processes *addressing ethical issues* are relevant to every part of the E-Interview Research Framework, see Table 11.1 at the end of this chapter. For more on addressing ethical issues, see Chapter 8.

Conducting the Interview

Finally, when the designing and planning steps are complete, reviewers have given their approvals, and the practice interviews have been conducted, the researcher must actually carry out the study! Whether face-to-face in person or through video conference, whether in writing or in a virtual world, the interviewer must be able to ask the questions, listen, and respond to an actual participant. All the preparation leads up to this real and important moment. Before the researcher heaves a sigh of relief that the research design stage is now over, there is a moment of truth: The research approach must be continuously assessed during the conduct of the study. As Flick (2007a) notes:

Adequate fit means that you check and recheck whether a specific method or design fits your research issue and field. If necessary, this would mean redesigning your study in order to make your choices adequate to what you want to study and where. More concretely, adequacy as an approach to quality means that you prepare the application of your methods as well as possible. You and your research team should become familiar with the methods you intend to apply. You also should do an interview or observation training before you approach your "real" cases. (p. 61)

The online researcher must take heed of Flick's recommendations to come prepared but also be cognizant that if all is not proceeding as planned, midresearch corrections may be needed. Naturally, any changes may need to be discussed or approved by research supervisors and verified with participants.

In addition to the review questions listed here, see the E-Interview Research Framework for additional considerations about conducting the quality study.

Review Questions

Does the researcher . . .

- use appropriate interview or observation procedures in terms of the selected ICT and online research setting?
- make an effort to ensure that the interview dialogue will be private and free of interruptions?
- adapt, as possible, to participants' preferences, access, and levels of technology literacy?
- spend enough time to gather interesting and significant data (Tracy, 2010, p. 841)?
- collect the types of data spelled out in the research design?
- use reflexive, recursive approaches for ongoing monitoring of the data collection process?

For review questions that show how designs, plans, steps, and processes related to *conducting the study* are relevant to every part of the E-Interview Research Framework, see Table 11.1 at the end of this chapter.

For more on conducting the study, see Chapters 9 and 10.

Table 11.1	An Overview of E-Interview Framework Review Questions							
	Aligning Purpose and Design	Choosing Online Data Collection Method	Taking a Position as a Researcher	Determining E-Interview or Observation Styles	Selecting ICT and Milieu	Handling Sampling and Recruiting	Addressing Ethical Issues	Collecting the Data
Does the researcher . . .	Make a coherent case for how design elements are aligned?	Offer a clear rationale for choosing online interviews?	Reveal how his or her position furthers (or conflicts with) the purpose of the study?	Explain how e-interview style (and, if used, observation) aligns with the research purpose?	Relate the approach for e-data collection to the study purpose?	Show how sampling approaches are appropriate? Explain any issues that would make the intended style or ICT problematic for the population?	Disclose any conflicts of interest or biases? Plan to protect human participants and digital portrayals? Have permission needed to access profiles or posted documents or images?	Plan to work within methodological traditions? Have the preparation and skills to conduct the e-interviews?

Source: Vision2lead, Inc (2014).

238

Closing Thoughts

While presented in a linear sequence of steps in the chapters of this book, the E-Interview Research Framework is circular, because research design is an iterative, recursive process. This way of thinking about research design is indispensable to e-researchers because changes to any aspect of research design, from interview structure to ethics, will be altered when a different ICT is selected. If the researcher plans to conduct interviews in a virtual world but then decides to carry them out using webcams and video conferencing, the nature of the exchange, the types of data, and the visual image versus representation of the participant will mean a fundamental change in research design.

The E-Interview Research Framework was originally introduced in *Cases in Online Interview Research* (Salmons, 2012) and used in that book to review a collection of studies that used data collected from interviews conducted in social media, Second Life, and web and video conferencing, as well as through e-mail. It has been used as a conceptual framework to organize *Qualitative Online Interviews*. In this chapter, suggested review considerations and questions were offered so you can carry out a thorough and robust review of your own and others' studies. A review using this framework will take into account the interconnected dimensions of a study conducted with online interviews and other qualitative data collected online. Table 11.1 presents a broad overview of review considerations in each area of the E-Interview Research Framework.

A template posted on the companion website allows you to add in your own criteria, as well as fill in comments for your own reflection or as a review document to share with the researcher.

Researcher's Notebook

STORIES OF ONLINE INQUIRY

Quality in qualitative research begins with sound design. But no matter how thoughtful the design, online qualitative research benefits from flexibility and a willingness to change if necessary to improve the study. I offer an example of using ongoing reflexivity to improve quality with changes made during the study. This story draws on the exemplar discussed in prior Researcher's Notebooks: a study of women e-entrepreneurs (Salmons, 2014).

(Continued)

(Continued)

The study began as an exploratory qualitative study. It was not designed to generate a new theory or model, as is often the goal for grounded theory; yet once the interviews were under way, it was evident that characteristics of the online milieu were very influential. To capture this trend in the data, I adopted a situational analysis, postmodern grounded theory approach (Clarke, 2005). Situational analysis is a style of grounded theory. Grounded theory is usually selected as a methodology when the study aims to generate new theory. Situational analysis looks at the social *situation,* while grounded theory typically looks at social *process* (Clarke, 2005). Situational analysts diagram elements in the research *situation* to capture the complexities and show the relationships in the data by making use of three kinds of maps: situational, social worlds/arenas, and positional maps. These maps *situate* aspects of the research phenomenon by not only mapping the data but also calling for discovery of relationships among data collected in the study and the larger scholarly and societal contexts. The researcher uses inductive reasoning to look for and compare patterns and associations in the data, and to locate linkages between sets of phenomena.

Once I introduced situational analysis to the study, I gained the lens needed to explore interrelated human (i.e., entrepreneur, partners, allies, customers, etc.) and "nonhuman" (i.e., technology) aspects of the "situation." This shift allowed for a more meaningful application of social capital theory's constructs. Social capital theory posits that businesses succeed by building mutually beneficial relationships and networks of partners, allies, and customers (Adler & Kwon, 2002; Carolis & Saparito, 2006; Nahapiet & Ghoshal, 1998; Ottósson & Klyver, 2010; Xiong & Bharadwaj, 2011; Xu, 2011). This approach allowed for a closer look at the "situation" in terms of interrelationships between the people involved (i.e., entrepreneurs and their partners, allies, and customers) and the technologies (or what Clarke, 2005, would call "nonhuman" elements) in alignment with the constructs of the relational social capital theory.

The E-Interview Framework allowed for an analysis and depiction helpful to the researcher. While it might be argued that any qualitative study benefits from reflexivity and flexibility, an online study takes place in a particular kind of milieu where unpredictable factors may emerge. This kind of assessment might be helpful to others interested in learning not only about the outcomes, as typically described in an empirical research article, but also about the research process. (See Figure 11.3 for a map of the study.)

Figure 11.3 Map of the Women E-Entrepreneurs' Study

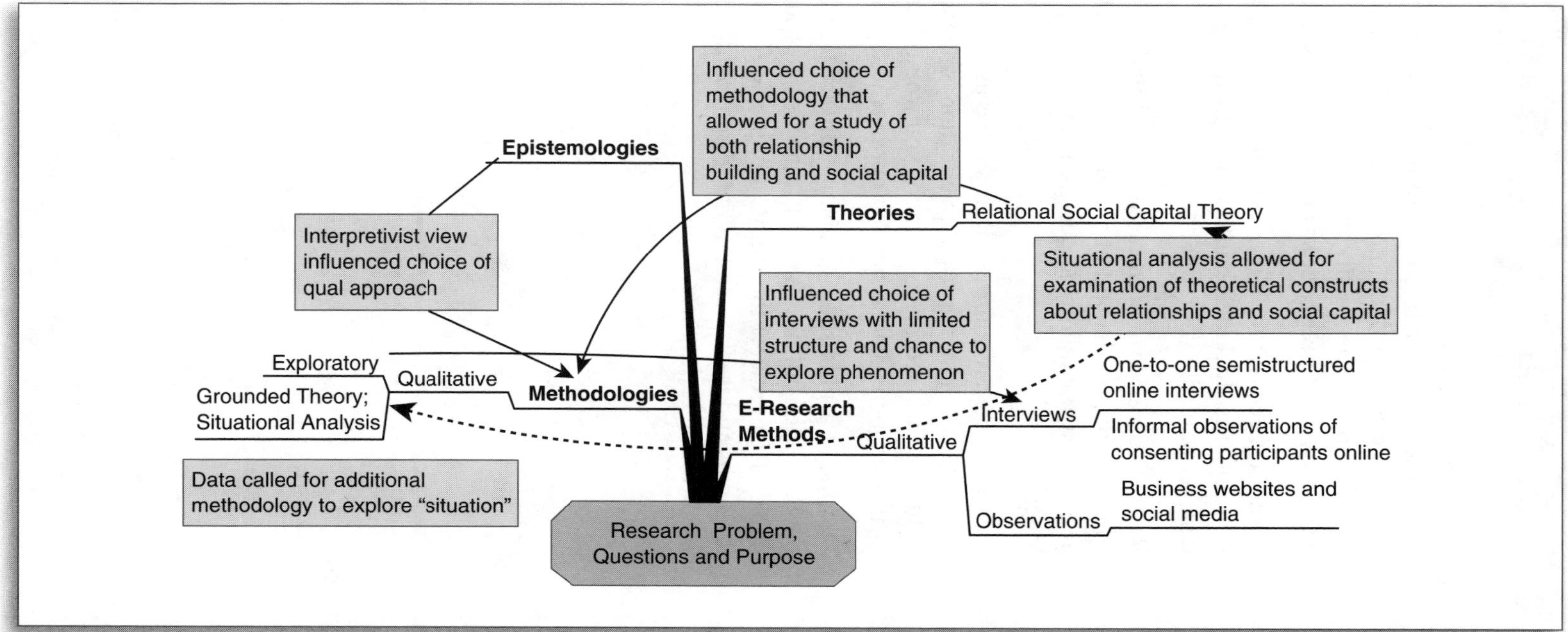

Discussions and Assignments

1. First, use the knowledge map template to show relationships among key elements of a published study or your own research design. Create a rationale for the decisions made, and suggest changes you think would improve the quality of the study. Second, working in small groups, conduct peer reviews of one another's research analyses.

2. Create a checklist for online research that articulates your own quality standards. Include or integrate ethical principles articulated in Chapter 8. Justify your choices.

3. Review at least two studies conducted with data collected online (observation, participant observation, interviews, or focus groups), and discuss the following questions in an essay three to five pages long:

   - Would you have approved the studies as a dissertation chair?
   - Would you have approved publication of the articles?
   - Identify at least three questions you would like the researchers to answer about their respective approaches.

4. Download a published qualitative dissertation or thesis that used data collected online. Use the E-Interview Research Framework and Table 11.1 to review the study's design and findings. What were the strengths and weaknesses? What recommendations would you have made to the researcher?

Online Communications and Online Interviews

12

Trends and Influences

> The future often appears strange just before it becomes ordinary.... Trying to grapple with what comes next is a deep problem. Doing so is partly a matter of science fiction, which consists, after all, of the stories we tell about the future.
>
> —Bryan Alexander (2009)

After studying Chapter 12, you will be able to do the following:

- Identify and discuss emerging trends and implications for online interview research

- Analyze and generate recommendations for further discussion and development of online interview research methodology

Trends in Internet adoption and use mean more "research" will be "e-research." As the use of information and communications technologies (ICTs) becomes ever more pervasive—meshed with and integral to our personal, social, cultural, professional, and civic lives—it will become ever more difficult to separate out and study a discrete "real" life.

As we are more accustomed to online communications, it will be more challenging to conduct qualitative research without some electronic communication with participants—if only to schedule meetings or exchange consent documents.

Other examples demonstrate that digital dualism distinction fades as the technology-enabled approach becomes widely adapted. Instead of the dualistic view, for example, of "e-business" versus "business," we now see that even small physical stores use social media and online marketing, and some enterprises that started as entirely online operations now have physical storefronts. Instead of "e-learning" versus "brick-and-mortar" institutions, we see that online programs often include face-to-face residencies and that classes taught on campuses use online resources and assignments. Instead of digital dualism, we see more of a continuum, without a firm line between what is online and off-line. What do these and other trends mean for online researchers, whose work may be seen as methodologically exemplary?

Online Communications and Online Interviews

ANYWHERE, ANYTIME COMMUNICATION

It is hard to predict what ICT, tool, or gadget will next enthrall experienced users and attract new ones. It seems likely that coming generations of ICTs will be faster, with more options for integrating visual media, audio, and text. As devices become smaller, they will go with their owners into more parts of daily personal, social, community, and professional life. More of the important events of life will be experienced in the presence of or recorded on, if not mediated through, some form of communications technology.

The "anywhere" aspect of new communications includes more emphasis on physical location, as **global positioning system (GPS)** technologies are integrated into smartphones, cameras, and other devices. We can obtain maps of our locations and destinations, and see the locations of other individuals and services.

In addition to changes in ICT tools and communication types, the use of these tools and the ways people think about them are changing. Given the focus here on the use of technology for research purposes, three phenomena that merit consideration are as follows: **online collaboration, disintermediation,** and online **privacy.**

ONLINE COLLABORATION AND SOCIAL LITERACIES

The ease of online communication allows individuals or groups to **collaborate** in new ways. Examples of online collaboration are evident across the World Wide Web. Companies, educational institutions, governmental bodies, and social-sector agencies are collaborating electronically to complete projects and solve complex problems. In these examples, collaboration occurs within an established framework or organizational structure using virtual teams, telecommuting, and mobile or remote offices. Online collaboration, though, extends beyond established organizational applications and disciplinary or geographical boundaries.

Mass collaboration occurs when people who do not know each other write, think, or work on projects together (Tapscott & Williams, 2008). People write collaboratively and edit one another's comments on social media sites or wikis; they design, implement, test, and improve on open-source software. They form social networks of new and old friends who keep in touch in online communities and on social media sites. These networks fulfill niches for people of varied ages and interests. Individuals and organizations turn to their online networks or to the collective intelligence of the wider web for input on personal or professional decisions or tasks. Using crowdsourcing, they broadcast a flexible open call to the crowd, and individuals self-select to offer solutions or assistance (Afuah & Tucci, 2012; Alexander, 2009; Estellés-Arolas & González-Ladrón-de-Guevara, 2012).

Those creating models for information or new media literacy point to a progression that aligns critical thinking with the social skills to use them in a technological environment. The concept of literacy has changed to refer not simply to a set of skills demonstrated by an individual but also to a level of competence needed to grow a personal and professional network; communicate synchronously or asynchronously with others using text, verbal, and visual modes; derive meaning and build new knowledge; and ethically share cultural productions (Koltay, 2011; Rheingold, 2012). Individuals increase their respective levels of ICT literacy by participating in active, collaborative inquiry (McKinney, Jones, & Turkington, 2011). They are not passive consumers of information found online; they are active contributors who intermingle with people known and unknown—adding, editing, and sharing ideas. In the process, they gain skills and attitudes beneficial to online research.

These trends have implications for online interview researchers and their participants. While researchers using more-structured interview approaches may be able to collect data using fairly basic online skills, higher levels of digital literacy will be important for those who want to use the kinds of dynamic, visual approaches discussed in this book. According to the Taxonomy of Online Collaboration, when the level of collaboration increases from simple dialogic transaction to higher synergistic co-creation, digital literacy skills are needed that enable contributors to develop common goals and incorporate multiple inputs into a single output (Salmons, 2007, 2011a, 2011b). The Taxonomy of Online Collaboration also posits that increased levels of collaboration call for increased levels of trust. Researchers accustomed to an embodied sensibility must find alternative ways to build presence. Kouzes and Posner (2007) observe that at the heart of online collaboration is trust, and "to build and sustain social connections, you have to be able to trust others and others have to trust you" (pp. 224–225). Researchers who are comfortable with online collaboration will be more capable of building participants' trust.

Similarly, participants who are experienced with online collaboration may find it easier to develop trusting connections with interviewers. It is reasonable to expect that people who are at ease collaborating with others "co-constructing" wikis or open-source software might also be willing to co-construct knowledge with researchers. Individuals who share photographs and video clips with Internet friends may be more willing to do so with researchers.

DISINTERMEDIATION AND APOMEDIATION

A companion trend to mass collaboration involves the increased reliance on peers, rather than experts. The term *disintermediation* refers to the removal of the middlemen between content producers and content consumers. Eysenbach (2008) discusses a progression from disintermediation to *apomediation*:

> Apomediation is a new socio-technological term that . . . characterizes the "third way" for users to identify trustworthy and credible information and services. The first possible approach is to use intermediaries (ie, middlemen or "gatekeepers"). . . . Trusted Web portals containing only information vetted by experts can also be seen as an intermediary. The second possibility is to bypass "middlemen" completely, which is commonly referred to as disintermediation. Apomediaries, such as users and friends . . . can help users navigate through the onslaught of information afforded by networked digital media, providing additional credibility cues and supplying further metainformation. (para. 22)

As Howard Rheingold (2012) observes, there are "no gatekeepers in participatory culture" (p. 53). Individuals can communicate immediately and directly with experts, people in authority, or producers of the services or products they purchase or consume. Consumers use blog and social media sites or review and comment sections on publications and company websites to convey thoughts, opinions, experiences, or preferences. Companies and content producers understand the power of criticism and peer influence. Increasingly, companies take advantage of the interaction with consumers to gain firsthand knowledge about perception of their products and to offer accurate information (Erdem, 2013, p. 39).

Although disintermediation and apomediation are occurring in some way in almost every major industry, a poignant illustration is found in the world of print media. Where before editors and publishers served as gate-keepers through editorial processes and "professional filtering of the good from the mediocre before publication; now such filtering is increasingly social, and happens after the fact" (Shirky, 2008, p. 81). Today anyone with an online connection can share news and perspectives, from the shortest posts to articles and full-length books. In this environment, self-publishing has lost much of its stigma and is no longer ghettoized as the "vanity press." In one study of 13 e-books, Laquintano (2010) explored how, through online self-publication, "authors and reader/writers have worked together to produce and sanction ebooks through sustained authorship. Sustained authorship conceptualizes authorship as sustained interaction among authors and reader/writers as the work of publishing becomes absorbed into online networks as literate activity" (p. 471).

Scholars are not immune to these trends. Hine (2013) further observes that the Internet is breaking down the "boundaries between the consumption and production of research" (p. 129) with open-access journals that are accessible to anyone. Scholars are wrestling with concepts of intellectual property and limits to ownership, when research is shared online in an open "information commons" (Borgman, 2007, p. 6). While online open-access journals retain the peer-review process, research blogs and other sources bypass traditional gatekeepers. Whether content is accurate, truthful, relevant, or worth reading will be determined by the readers and addressed by mass responses. Disintermediation and mass collaboration intersect in this use of information crowdsourcing—in the crowd, terms such as *professional, expert,* and *amateur* are no longer polar opposites.

There is an implicit sense of caveat emptor—let the online buyer, viewer, or reader beware. Without reliable professionals or experts, readers or viewers must utilize their own awareness about the topic at hand to filter the extensive volume of information now available. They may simply shut out unacceptable information, or they may suggest or enact changes as needed to correct it. Postings on a wiki site can be corrected by other site visitors, while incorrect posts to a blog may elicit readers' suggestions—or ire. If the individual's work is considered valuable and reaches its audience, the solo writer's blog or site may directly compete for readers with websites of long-established publications.

Boundaries between the researcher and the researched are changing. Hine (2013, p. 129) observes that participatory research shifts research away from a process the researcher controls with results the researcher verifies. In a discussion of medical research, O'Connor (2013) observed:

> Apomediated research . . . is research in which information about the protocol—for example, its design and conduct—is apomediated, peer-to-peer,

between individuals who may appear as both subjects and researchers. By contrast, in intermediated, or traditional medical research, researchers intermediate between subjects and information about the design, conduct, and interpretation of a given research protocol. In the new apomediated world, it is increasingly difficult to tell the difference between the researcher and the subject, begging the question: if regulations are there to protect subjects from researchers, what are regulations for when subject and research seem to be one and the same? (p. 471)

As O'Connor (2013) explains, disintermediation, apomediation, and crowdsourcing combine groups of people together to do their own research on a common problem. O'Connor cited a study conducted by an online group of crowdsourced subjects to test a series of vitamin supplements and observes an increase in these kinds of do-it-yourself approaches to studying health and medical issues—and academic publication of the results (p. 473).

Several potential implications of this trend apply to online interview research. On one hand, a culture may emerge where individuals are accustomed to communicating with strangers in very frank, personal, and self-revealing ways. If individuals associate a free and trusting sensibility with their online interactions, such expectations may transfer to the online interviewer. In this milieu of direct communication, potential interviewees may be more willing to participate in research. On the other hand, potential participants may be suspicious of "expert" researchers and distrustful about the safe keeping of data. These factors place even more responsibility on the scholarly researcher to be trustworthy and credible, and transparently accountable to high ethical standards. Researchers are more responsible for producing new knowledge and reports understandable to those beyond a specific academic discipline. In a world where casual observations can be so easily distributed, the discipline of empirical research is even more important.

PRIVACY IN ONLINE MILIEUS

The trends selected for discussion here—online collaboration and disintermediation—share a common underlying assumption. If people are going to participate in online collaborative activities as individuals or as part of the crowd, if people are going to read and write online without protective gatekeepers, then they must be willing to disclose information about themselves online. More participation in social media, online communities, multiplayer online games, and virtual worlds is occurring at the same time as increased consternation about privacy of online information. This is an area where common sense is seemingly missing, since it would seem that privacy concerns would translate into less, not more, sharing of personal information online.

Park (2013) studied this circumstance of increased access and use, and increased concern for protection of personal information. His study tied the perceptions of and actions related to privacy online to levels of digital literacy. He defined digital privacy as user awareness in three dimensions: (a) technical familiarity with the kinds of software applications that allow users to exercise control over personal information, (b) awareness of institutional practices for surveillance and data collection, and (c) understanding of privacy policies (Park, 2013). His study found that "generic technical familiarity functions as the most significant predictor of personal information control" (p. 230). He stated, "The respective predictors of technical familiarity and Internet experiences, when combined, seem to magnify existing privacy-related skill gaps" (p. 231). While one study is not adequate to fully explain or prove a connection, the findings point to the need to consider the influence of digital literacy and online privacy.

Park's (2013) study and other perspectives discussed in Chapter 8 point to implications for online researchers. Clearly, many dilemmas emerge when participants lack the literacies, awareness, and knowledge needed to understand the importance of protecting personal information. Ethical researchers do not take advantage of such circumstances; instead, they may find that consent agreement discussions offer opportunities to help participants understand how to reduce their online vulnerability.

ICT TRENDS AND IMPLICATIONS FOR RESEARCHERS

These trends and the increasingly pervasive aspects of ICT are important to online researchers for several reasons, in addition to those discussed earlier:

1. Social researchers are interested in studying human behavior and social interactions. If more behaviors and interactions occur online, then it is to be expected that researchers will be interested in studying them. Online researchers have focused on online behaviors; with new tools and broader adoption, researchers can use online interviews to explore behaviors that occur online or offline. The processes used to communicate electronically about any area of life experience, and the significance of such experiences, offer fertile ground for empirical study through online interview research.

2. Sampling possibilities enlarge as more people from diverse demographic groups become accustomed to using ICTs in everyday life. When the total pool of potential participants is larger and more ICT literate, researchers have more sampling options. Researchers can be more specific and particular about selection criteria. Or they can choose to conduct larger mixed-methods studies with varied sampling techniques.

3. The increasing variety of communication types means there are more ways to collect different types of audio, visual, and text-based data. As more people develop personal communication styles through online cultural life and mass collaboration, interview researchers will have more options in terms of type of interview and ways to conduct it.

Closing Thoughts and Recommendations for Further Research

Trends in ICT adoption and their potential for online interview research were explored in this chapter and throughout the book. But these discussions may raise more questions than they answer! Clearly, research about online research is needed. In addition, more work is needed to develop standards and criteria for excellence and integrity in online interview research. Two priorities are research ethics and online interview and observation methods.

Chapter 8 examined some of the ethical dilemmas online researchers face and proposed some guidelines. One area where greater clarity is needed is in the distinction between public and private settings.

This distinction is directly related to the determination of informed consent requirements. The public–private distinction also has implications for sampling and participant recruitment, as discussed in Chapter 7. Better understanding of the distinctions and consensus in the research field are needed to ensure that respect for privacy is upheld.

Methodological and methods issues have been explored throughout this book, and numerous areas deserve more consideration. Each stage of the interview process—and each stage of interaction with research participants—deserves more study. Which approaches for interview preparation enable researchers to develop relationships needed to conduct the type of interview that best serves the purpose of the study? What approaches motivate participants to stick with the interview—and help them resist the urge to click the window closed when some discomfort arises? Are there benefits to multiple short interviews over a more conventional approach using one longer interview? What level(s) of structure works best with which ICT? How can data best be collected when interviews are conducted in virtual—or highly visual—environments? What kinds of observation data can and should be collected during the interview? What other observations or documentation of the participant's online life will be beneficial to the study? How should such data collection be included in consent agreements? These are a few of the many questions the research community will need to answer to fulfill the potential of online interview research as a valuable approach for studying human behavior in the digital age.

Discussions and Assignments

1. In an essay of three to five pages, discuss trends that could influence online interview research. In your essay, critically review the thinking of at least three futurists. Identify at least one trend the futurists missed.

2. Compare and contrast online communication dynamics and effectiveness of two ICTs that have become available in the past year. Could these ICTs be used for data collection? How? Write an analysis of two to three pages.

3. Building on the preceding assignments and related reading, reflect on the ethical risks for researchers who conduct research with emerging ICTs, and prepare to use your analysis as the basis for leading a small-group discussion.

Appendix
Qualitative Data Analysis

There is no particular moment when data analysis begins.

—Robert Stake (1995)

There are no clearly agreed rules or procedures for analyzing qualitative data.

—Liz Spencer, Jane Ritchie, and William O'Connor (2003)

Once data have been collected from online interviews, they can be handled and analyzed much the same way as data collected through live, face-to-face interviews. That said, there is no one-size-fits-all approach for qualitative data analysis within a fully qualitative or mixed-methods study. Researchers may use inductive analysis to discover patterns, themes, or categories in the data, or a deductive analysis to analyze data according to an existing theory or framework or a hybrid approach (Fereday & Muir-Cochrane, 2006; Patton, 2002). Researchers can choose or combine elements from a number of analysis strategies. With the advent of numerous software packages for qualitative analysis, researchers also must decide which steps of the process to do by hand and which to carry out with the help of technology. This exploration of qualitative data analysis will introduce researchers to some of the many available options and resources. Additional links and updates are posted on the book's website.

A Short Survey of the Literature:
Qualitative Data Analysis by Methodology

"How do I go about finding out what the interviews tell me about what I want to know?" (Kvale & Brinkman, 2009, p. 192). Interview researchers constructing life histories are looking for different things in the data than are interview researchers constructing new theories. As noted in Chapter 3, interview approaches can be organized by degree of structure. At the analysis stage, this means some researchers begin analysis with some classifications that naturally emerge when consistent sets of questions are asked of all participants. Other researchers who conducted unstructured interviews have a wide-ranging collection of data they will need to classify. The following books offer guidance for data analysis specific to various qualitative methodologies.

Kvale and Brinkman, and Rubin and Rubin write specifically about interview research, and their respective books discuss analysis of data collected through interviews (Kvale, 2007; Kvale & Brinkman, 2009; Rubin & Rubin, 2012). Rubin and Rubin's approach builds on the semistructured **responsive interview** described throughout the book. The stages they lay out are described in Chapter 7. Kvale and Brinkman approach analysis a little differently. They look at modes of analysis focusing on meaning, language, and/or theory. In the broad category of "language analysis," they cover linguistic analysis, conversation analysis, narrative analysis, discourse analysis, and deconstruction. In *Doing Interviews,* Kvale (2007) offers an overview in one chapter, while the more comprehensive *InterViews* (Kvale & Brinkman, 2009) provides a chapter on each mode.

In *Qualitative Inquiry and Research Design: Choosing Among Five Approaches,* Creswell (2013) explores narrative research, phenomenology, grounded theory, ethnography, and case study. This volume surveys all stages of the research process for the five selected traditions. After introducing a general organizing framework, he addresses distinctive data analysis characteristics for each one. Creswell's clear explanations will be most valuable for the researcher who is trying to decide which methodology (or combination) to use. In practice, researchers will want more specific steps and examples. While Creswell deals with researchers' decisions from design to report, *Analyzing Qualitative Data: Systematic Approaches* (Bernard & Ryan, 2009) provides a multimethodology exploration of the data analysis stage for discourse analysis, narrative analysis, grounded theory, content analysis, and schema analysis.

Postmodern Interviewing (Gubrium & Holstein, 2003b) and *Inside Interviewing: New Lenses, New Concerns* (Holstein & Gubrium, 2003b) are edited collections. In *Postmodern Interviewing,* some of the contributions discuss analysis in the context of their chapters. *Inside Interviewing* offers more specific strategies, with one section of the book devoted to "Analytic Options" (Holstein & Gubrium, 2003b, pp. 311–414). The five chapters in this section discuss analysis in narrative, oral history, ethnographic, and grounded theory studies. These are critical examinations, not practical how-to steps for carrying out data analysis.

The expectations for grounded theory analysis are very specific: to generate new theoretical principles. Grounded theory researchers build on the understanding of individuals' experiences derived through phenomenological methods to generate theoretical principles (Creswell, 2013; Strauss, 1987). They look at categories discovered in the data and construct explanatory theoretical frameworks, which provide abstract, conceptual understandings of the studied phenomenon. For practical steps, one contributor to *Inside Interviewing*, Kathy Charmaz, also wrote a more in-depth book titled *Constructing Grounded Theory: A Practical Guide Through Qualitative Analysis* (Charmaz, 2006).

Situational analysis is a style of grounded theory. Situational analysis looks at the social *situation,* while grounded theory looks at social *process.* Situational analysts diagram elements in the research *situation* to capture the complexities and show relationships in the data. In *Situational Analysis: Grounded Theory After the Postmodern Turn,* Adele Clarke (2005) uses examples, illustrations, and clear explanations to promote situational and positional maps as "analytic exercises . . . provoking the researcher to analyze more deeply" (p. 83). The situational analysis approach may be useful beyond grounded theory contexts for researchers investigating policies, opinions, or other social science arenas where research participants express distinctive positions on the topic of inquiry.

Researchers who use interviews to build case studies can learn appropriate ways to analyze data from *Case Study Research* by Robert Yin (2014) or *The Art of Case Study Research* by Robert Stake (1995). The updated, more detailed text by Yin offers four different strategies for organizing the case study and five techniques for data analysis. Stake's book offers one example for analyzing data and generating naturalistic generalizations.

When researchers collect visual data, they add another set of analytic steps and concerns. Pink's (2013) *Doing Visual Ethnography* is a useful book for online researchers. She offers chapters on video as well as photographic materials and touches on uses of technology. Banks's (2007) *Using Visual Data in Qualitative Research* includes a chapter on "Presenting Visual Research" but does not specifically address analysis of visual data. Neither Pink nor Banks addresses visuals such as charts, diagrams, or illustrations. In *Qualitative Researching,* Mason (2002) offers a more comprehensive look in a chapter titled "Using Visual Methods." Although more work is needed, Mason's section on "Turning Documents and the Visual Into Data" is a start.

Each qualitative methodology may offer some specific foci for researchers; however, every research methods writer or theorist seeks resolutions to the interview researcher's common dilemma: moving from a large collection of data to some useful, well-supported answers to the research questions.

STAGES OF THE ANALYTIC PROCESS: COMPARISON

Approaches to analysis of qualitative interview data are presented here to demonstrate the general flow recommended by respected analysts. They may each use different language, but they describe a comparable process.

Rubin and Rubin, and Kvale and Brinkman write specifically about analysis of interview data; Ritchie and Lewis speak more broadly to analysis of any qualitative data but include detailed discussions of interview research (Kvale, 2007; Kvale & Brinkman, 2009; Ritchie & Lewis, 2003; Rubin & Rubin, 2012). All three research teams describe data analysis as a process that begins with research design and is ongoing throughout the research. While the researcher moves through distinct phases, analysis is iterative and deeply reflective, not linear. Some critical steps described in these three books are summarized in Table A.1.

Increasingly, researchers are using software for some of these data analysis steps. Data management and storage, text retrieval, and coding are possible with various computer-assisted qualitative data analysis software (CAQDAS) programs. One researcher observed the following:

> I found that switching from paper-based to electronic, software-based research allowed more freedom to play with ideas, because researchers can link and compare patterns within and across documents and the results can be saved, printed, or undone at will. When beginning a project, researchers create new documents or import text, numerical data, and graphics files from compatible software programs. [The software] organizes raw data (interviews, observations, etc.) and links them with memos where researchers might make codes and analytical notes, and then edit and rework ideas as the project progresses. For those involved in multiple projects, it is helpful to keep track of activities from one session to the next. Video images can also be linked to text documents. (Walsh, 2003, p. 253)

The following books offer step-by-step guidelines for using qualitative data analysis software: *Qualitative Data Analysis With NVivo* (Bazeley & Jackson, 2013), *Coding Manual for Qualitative Researchers* (Saldaña, 2013), and *Qualitative Content Analysis in Practice* (Schreier, 2012). CAQDAS options for data analysis, with links to demonstrations and reviews, can be found on the book's website.

Table A.1 Comparative Approaches to Data Analysis

Analysis Stage	Rubin and Rubin (2012)	Kvale and Brinkman (Kvale, 2007; Kvale & Brinkman, 2009)	Ritchie, Lewis, Nicholls, and Ormston (2014)
During and immediately after interviews the interviewed is attentive to and notes details in the data. Reflexivity is at play as the researcher makes memos about broad themes.	Reflection and note taking are carried out throughout the interview research.	Interviewees may "discover new relationships" . . . interviewer condenses, interprets, and sends meaning back for further reply (Kvale, 2007, p. 102).	The "framework" approach centers on a "continuous iterative approach" (p. 296). The first step is familiarization with the data and ongoing review in the context of the research questions.
In the first stage of review, the researcher reads and re-reads transcripts and notes. The researcher organizes, sorts, labels, and codes the data.	*Recognition* occurs when the researcher finds concepts, themes, events, or topical markers in the data. *Synthesis* occurs when the researcher systematically clarifies meanings of concepts and themes. Researchers *code* to label and designate themes and concepts.	Analysis can focus on meaning, language, or theoretical concepts in the data.	*Data management* refers to the process of sorting and synthesizing data to identify initial themes and construct an initial thematic framework and index.
Moving deeper, the researcher looks for trends and redefines or refines the categories accordingly. A second or third level of coding may be conducted. The researcher describes themes and selects illustrative examplars or cases.	Researchers *sort* by grouping data units with the same code or label.	*Re-interview* to allow subject the opportunity to comment on interviewer's interpretation.	The *descriptive accounts* process refers to the steps of defining elements and dimensions, refining categories, and classifying data.
The researcher clarifies and interprets the findings, answers research questions, and looks for implications and applications.	At the stage of *final synthesis*, researchers combine concepts to suggest conclusions or recommend policies.	Continue description and interpretation.	*Explanatory accounts* refers to the process of developing abstractions, explanations and applications to wider theory or practice.

Glossary of Terms

abductive reasoning: A form of reasoning that, along with inductive and deductive reasoning, shows a way to come to a conclusion. Abductive reasoning is used when the researcher has an insight or makes a guess or an assumption that a connection exists in an incomplete or seemingly unrelated set of observations. Philosopher Charles Sanders Peirce (1839–1914) is credited with the origination of this concept and for applying it to pragmatic thinking.

active interview: In an active interview, both parties to the interview are *active*, putting less focus on the interviewer as the one responsible for the interview process and focus. Meaning is actively assembled in the interview encounter (Holstein & Gubrium, 2004; Kvale, 2007).

alienation: "The appropriation of the products of somebody's action for purposes never intended or foreseen by the actor herself, drawing these products into a system of relations over which the producer has no knowledge or control" (Bakardjieva & Feenberg, 2001, p. 206)

asynchronous communication: Communications that involve a delay between message and response, meaning it is not necessary for participants to be online at the same time

The Belmont Report: The basis for protection of human subjects regulations in the United States

beneficence: To do no harm and to reduce risks involved in research; a fundamental principle of research ethics

blogs: Personal online journals where entries are posted chronologically. Users create their own weblogs as a way to share thoughts and ideas, and link to other websites and blogs to create families of sites with common interests. Microblogs use the same principle but allow for very short entries. Blogs can be text only or multichannel, with links to images or media. Some are public, and others are seen only by subscribers or friend lists. Blogs can be an asynchronous or near-synchronous form of communication.

broadband: High-speed connection that permits transmission of images, audio and video, and large files

co-constructed narratives: Researchers and interviewees share jointly created stories. Narratives are called *mediated* when the researcher monitors the exchange and *unmediated* when a researcher and interviewee, or two researchers, exchange and study their own stories (Ellis & Berger, 2003).

collaborate: The word *collaborate* has its origins in the Latin word *collaborare*, "to work together" (OED, 2005). The working definition used here is as follows: Collaboration is an interactive process that engages two or more participants who work together to achieve outcomes they could not accomplish independently (Salmons, 2008).

computer-mediated communication: Refers to human communication that occurs when messages are conveyed by computers

consequentialism: Ethical framework concerned with moral rightness of acts

constructivism: The premise of constructivism is that we construct reality based on our perceptions of the world. Subjects construct their own meanings in different ways, even in relation to the same phenomenon (Gray, 2004). The term *interpretivism* is often used synonymously with constructivism. The premise of interpretivism is that we "interpret" our experiences in the social world.

convergence: A multimedia environment and/or network where signals, regardless of type (i.e., voice, quality audio, video, data, and so on), are merged and can be accessed through the same devices (Knemeyer, 2004; Seybold, 2008, p. 11)

creative interviews: Jack Douglas's (1984) book *Creative Interviewing* introduced a life-story approach to interviews. These unstructured interviews occur on location in situational, everyday worlds of people in society (Douglas, 1984; Fontana & Frey, 2003).

criterion sampling: Selecting all participants on the basis of criteria selected to align with the research purpose

critical theory: A foundational perspective for research that entails an analysis of social action and human endeavors. Research using critical theory is organized to include stages of critique (assessment of the current state and the requirements to reach a desired state) and examination of both action and motivation; that is, it includes both what is done and why it is done.

data analysis: Approach for deriving meaning, findings, or results

deductive reasoning: Reasoning used for research in which a specific explanation is deduced from a general premise and is then tested (Schutt, 2006)

deontological ethics: Deontological ethics, building on the philosophies of Immanuel Kant (1785), views morality as the responsibility to fulfill duties and follow principles.

disintermediation: The process of cutting out the middleman so individuals communicate directly with producers and sellers of products and services

emic: Robert Stake (1995) describes emic issues as those that emerge from the actors, the insiders within the case. VanDeVen (2007) describes the inside researcher as a "participant immersed in the actions and experiences within the system being studied" (pp. 269–270).

epistemology: A branch of philosophy that considers the criteria for determining what constitutes and does not constitute valid knowledge. In research, *epistemology* refers to the study of the nature of knowledge or the study of how knowledge is justified (Gray, 2004).

Epoche: "Setting aside prejudgments and opening the research interview with unbiased, receptive presence" (Moustakas, 1994, p. 85)

etic: Robert Stake (1995) describes etic issues as those of the researcher or the larger research community outside of the case. VanDeVen (2007) describes the outside-oriented researcher as a "detached, impartial onlooker who gathers data" (pp. 269–270).

follow-up questions: Follow-up questions build on interviewee responses to get a clearer or deeper understanding of the interviewee's response.

forums: Asynchronous discussion where original comments and responses are organized by topic. Threaded discussion occurs when one user posts a message that is visible to other users, who respond in their own time. Also known as *threaded discussion*.

global positioning system (GPS): "A U.S.-owned utility that provides users with positioning, navigation, and timing services" (GPS.gov). While not a communications medium on its own, GPS can be used in conjunction with other tools in studies where the location is essential.

human subjects: Living individuals about whom an investigator (whether a professional or student) conducting research obtains the following: data through intervention or interaction with the individual, or identifiable private information (U.S. Department of Health and Human Services, 2010).

ICT literacy: Using digital technology, communications tools, and/or networks to access, manage, integrate, evaluate, and create information to function in a knowledge society (ETS, 2006).

immediacy: Communicative behaviors that reduce the physical or psychological distance between individuals and foster affiliation (Mehrabian, 1971)

in-depth interview: A qualitative research technique involving a researcher who guides or questions a participant to elicit information, perspectives, insights, feelings or behaviors, experiences, or phenomena that cannot be observed. The in-depth interview is conducted to collect data that allow the researcher to generate new understandings and new knowledge about the subject under investigation.

inductive reasoning: Reasoning used for research in which general conclusions are drawn from specific data (Schutt, 2006)

information and communications technologies (ICTs): Umbrella term describing communication devices or applications, including cellular phones, computer and network hardware and software, satellite systems, as well as the various services and applications associated with them.

institutional review board (IRB), research ethics board: Body responsible for verifying that the research design protects human subjects

interactivity: The degree of mutuality and reciprocation present in a communication setting (Kalman, Ravid, Raban, & Rafaeli, 2006)

Internet-mediated research: Research that entails gathering original data via the Internet, with the intention of subjecting these data to analysis to provide new evidence in relation to a specific research question (Hewson, 2010).

interview guide: A summary of important content the researcher intends to cover in a research interview. The interview guide for a more structured interview may include specific steps for each stage of the interview, questions, and follow-up options. For a less structured interview, it may include a list of topics or concepts for discussion with the participant.

IRB approval: The determination of the institutional review board (IRB) that the research has been reviewed and may be conducted at an institution within the constraints set forth by the IRB and by other institutional and federal requirements (U.S. Department of Health and Human Services, 2010)

main interview questions: Main interview questions are articulated to elicit overall experiences and understandings.

mass collaboration: Mass collaboration occurs when people who do not know each other write, think, or work on projects together (Tapscott & Williams, 2008). Wikis exemplify mass collaboration.

mediated immediacy: Communicative cues in mediated channels that can shape perceptions of psychological closeness between interactants; immediacy cues can be seen as a language of affiliation (O'Sullivan, Hunt, & Lippert, 2004, p. 471).

method: The practical steps used to conduct the study (Anfara & Mertz, 2006; Carter & Little, 2007)

methodology: The study of, and justification for, methods used to conduct research. The term describes approaches to systematic inquiry developed within a particular paradigm with associated epistemological assumptions (Gray, 2009). Methodologies emerge from academic disciplines in the social and physical sciences, and while considerable cross-disciplinary exchange occurs, choices generally place the study in a disciplinary context.

minimal risk: The probability and magnitude of harm or discomfort anticipated in the research are not greater in and of themselves than those ordinarily encountered in daily life or during the performance of routine physical or psychological examinations or tests (U.S. Department of Health and Human Services, 2010).

mixed methods: A research design that combines more than one method of qualitative and quantitative data collection and analysis (Creswell & Clark, 2007)

mobile access: Ability to connect to the Internet anywhere using computers, cell phones, handheld computers, and personal digital assistants

multichannel web conferencing meeting spaces: Multiple communication features are integrated into online meeting spaces. These spaces can be used for one-to-one, one-to-many, or many-to-many online gatherings. Web conferencing platforms allow for dialogue through Voice over Internet Protocol (VoIP) two-way audio, text chat, polling, shared applications, web camera desktop video conferencing, and shared whiteboard. In addition to exchange and dialogue, the shared whiteboard allows users to record meeting notes or brainstorms, illustrate, use graphic reporting, draw, or create diagrams together. Full versions allow the meeting to be archived for later viewing and transcription. Also known as *web conferencing*.

nonverbal communication: Aspects of communication that convey messages without words. Types of nonverbal communication include the following:

- *Chronemics* communication is the use of pacing and timing of speech and length of silence before response in conversation.
- *Paralinguistic* or *paralanguage* communication describes variations in volume, pitch, or quality of voice.
- *Kinesic* communication includes eye contact and gaze, facial expressions, body movements, gestures, or postures.
- *Proxemic* communication is the use of interpersonal space to communicate attitudes (Gordon, 1980; Guerrero, DeVito, & Hecht, 1999; Kalman, Ravid, Raban, & Rafaeli, 2006).

online collaboration: Constructing knowledge, completing tasks, and/or solving problems based on shared goals, through mutual engagement of two or more individuals in a coordinated effort using Internet and electronic communications

online interviews: For the purpose of this book, *online interviews,* or *e-interviews,* refer to interviews conducted with computer-mediated communication. Scholarly interviews are conducted in accordance with ethical research guidelines; verifiable research participants provide informed consent before participating in any interview.

online questionnaires: Questions delivered in a written form on an interactive website. Formal online surveys, popular with quantitative researchers, are beyond the scope of this book; however, online questionnaires or surveys can be used to screen participants or solicit demographic or other basic background information from research participants.

phenomenological approach: Research method used to investigate the meaning, structure, and essence of human experience (Patton, 2002)

positivism: A belief, shared by most scientists, that a reality exists apart from our perceptions of it that can be understood through observation and that follows general laws (Schutt, 2006). The positivist tradition's view of social reality as "knowable" relies on a concept of validity in terms of measurement (Hesse-Biber & Leavy, 2006).

postmodern interview: "Postmodern" refers to a set of "orienting sensibilities" rather than a particular kind of interviewing (Holstein & Gubrium, 2003c). These sensibilities include new ways to look at theory as "stories linked to the perspectives and interests of their storytellers" (Holstein & Gubrium, 2003c, p. 5; see also Fontana, 2003).

postpositivism: A set of "orienting sensibilities" rather than a particular kind of interviewing (Holstein & Gubrium, 2003c). These sensibilities include new ways to look at theory as "stories linked to the perspectives and interests of their storytellers" (Holstein & Gubrium, 2003c, p. 5; see also Fontana, 2003).

pragmatism: A worldview that draws on both objective and subjective knowledge (Creswell & Clark, 2007)

privacy: In the context of online interview research, *privacy* describes the ability of the individual to control access to and use of information and images.

probability sampling: A sampling method that relies on random selection so the probability of selection of population elements is known (Schutt, 2006)

probes: Probes encourage the interviewee to provide detail to flesh out and expand on the answer.

- *Attention probes* ("Okay, I understand," and so forth) let the interviewee know the researcher is listening.

- *Conversation management probes* keep the conversation focused on the research topic and help regulate the desired level of depth. Researchers use such probes to confirm answers or ask for better definition or clarification if they cannot follow the thread of the comments.

- *Credibility probes* aim to find relevant evidence to support participants' claims.

- These verbal probes are complemented with *nonverbal probes*: the eye contact or timing patterns researchers use to show participants that they are interested in hearing them continue (Rubin & Rubin, 2012, pp. 139–140).

purposive or purposeful sampling: A nonprobability sampling method in which participants or cases are selected for a purpose, usually as related to ability to answer central questions of the study

Q method: A structured approach to studying subjectivity. It is self-referential and communicable by the participants (Amin, 2000). More than 2,000 theoretical and applied Q studies have been published in a variety of disciplines, including medicine, psychology, and policy (Valenta & Wiggerand, 1997). Invented in 1935 by British physicist–psychologist William Stephenson, Q methodology is frequently associated with quantitative analysis because of its use of factor analysis (Stephenson, 1935). Q method also can be used as a qualitative technique because it concentrates on perceptions, attitudes, and values from the perspective of the person participating in the study, and relies heavily on qualitative methods in developing the Q concourse. In correlating persons instead of tests, Q method provides a holistic perspective of a participant's subjectivity in relationship to the research question.

qualitative research: Methods of inquiry directed at providing an "in-depth and interpreted understanding of the social world of research participants by learning about their social and material circumstances, their experiences, perspectives and histories" (Ritchie & Lewis, 2003, p. 3).

quantitative research: Methods of inquiry that analyze numeric representations of the world; the systematic and mathematical techniques used to collect and analyze data (Gray, 2004). Survey and questionnaire data are often analyzed in quantitative units (Yoshikawa, Weisner, Kalil, & Way, 2008).

research design: A comprehensive strategic plan for the study that "provides the glue that holds the research project together. A design is used to structure the research, to show how all of the major parts of the research project . . . work together to try to address the central research questions" (Trochim, 2006, Chapter 5).

researcher bias: In the context of interview research, *researcher bias* refers to any predetermined ideas, cultural factors, or other influences that could prejudice the researcher's understanding of participants and/or interpretation of their responses.

responsive interview: Rubin and Rubin (2005) use the term *responsive interview* to describe their approach that is characterized by a flexible design. They acknowledge the human feelings and common interests that allow interpersonal relationships to form between interviewer and interviewee. Responsive interviews aim for depth of understanding through ongoing self-reflection (Rubin & Rubin, 2005).

sample: The subjects or participants selected for the study

sample frame: Lists or collections of information about groups of people, either already existing or constructed by the researcher for the purpose of selecting the sample

sampling: Procedure for selecting cases or participants to study

saturation or redundancy: The point at which selection is ended; when new interviews seem to yield little additional information (Schutt, 2006)

shared applications: Connecting over the Internet, a user on one computer can share applications with other invited users. They view, edit, classify, and/

or work on documents, media, visuals, or technical applications. Applications sharing is generally a synchronous approach to communication.

Second Life: A massive multiplayer universe set in a 3-D virtual world created by San Francisco–based software maker Linden Labs (Wigmore & Howard, 2009)

semistructured interviews: Interviews that include some degree of planned questions, prepared approaches to questioning, and/or sequencing of questions

Skype: An IP telephony service provider that offers free video calling between computers and low-cost calling to regular telephones that are not connected to the Internet

social media: Refers to websites, online platforms, or applications that allow for one-to-one, one-to-many, or many-to-many synchronous or asynchronous interactions between users who can create, archive, and retrieve user-generated content

structured interviews: Interviewers ask fixed-choice questions and record responses based on a coding scheme. All interviews ask the same questions in the same order, and interviewers aim to maintain a consistent, neutral approach to questioning and responding to all participants (Fontana & Frey, 2003; Schaeffer & Maynard, 2003; Schutt, 2006).

surveys: Investigations into one or more variables in a population that may involve collection of qualitative and/or quantitative data (Gray, 2004). Data may be analyzed with qualitative or quantitative methods.

synchronous communication: Communications that occur in real time, with no delay between message and response. It is necessary for participants to be online at the same time.

text messaging, instant messaging, and chat: People can communicate online by exchanging short written messages. The term *text message* is used when people write back and forth over mobile phones or devices, while *instant messaging* or *chat* refers to the same kind of communication on computers or smartphones. Chat or messaging may require registration and/or log-in to enter and post; it may be private or open to the public. One-to-one, one-to-many, or many-to-many individuals can converse in writing. This kind of communication can reach synchronicity or can be synchronous or near-synchronous.

theory: An explanation of a phenomenon that is internally consistent, is supportive of other theories, and gives new insights into the phenomenon.

Some qualitative researchers frame the study in theoretical terms, while others aim to discover and "ground" theoretical principles in the data. In quantitative research, theory "is an inter-related set of constructs (or variables) formed into propositions, or hypotheses, that specify the relationship among variables" (Creswell, 2014, p. 54).

unstructured interviews: Interviews that do not follow a prepared set of procedures with questions that have been articulated in advance. Researchers devise questions during the interview or allow topics to emerge in a naturalistic fashion from the participants' own explanations of their experiences.

utilitarianism: Ethical view that actions should provide the most good or do the least harm

variables: Characteristics that are measurable (Gray, 2004)

video conferencing or video calls: Video conferencing is a live session between two or more users who are in different locations. Options include room systems that allow individuals or groups to see each other in an office, meeting room, or studio. Web conferencing, desktop conferencing, or video calls allow users to see each other using a web camera and computer. Typically, the desktop web conferencing allows viewing participants face-to-face, in contrast to the broader camera range and potential of video conferencing to show group activities and events, creating a sense of presence and being.

virtual worlds: Synchronous, persistent networks of people, represented by avatars, facilitated by computers (Bell, 2008)

virtue ethics: Ethical actions ought to be consistent with certain ideal virtues that provide for the full development of our humanity (Velasquez et al., 2008).

visual literacy: The ability to recognize, draw meaning from, and convey ideas through visible symbols, pictures, or images

Voice over Internet Protocol (VoIP): A generic term used to describe the techniques used to carry voice traffic over the Internet (infoDev, 2008)

webinar: A workshop or lecture delivered over the web. Webinars may be a one-way webcast or may allow for interaction between participants and presenters. Voice over Internet Protocol (VoIP) audio, shared whiteboard, and shared applications may be used.

whiteboards: The equivalent of a blackboard, but on a computer screen. A whiteboard allows one or more users to draw on the screen while others on the network watch, and can be used for instruction the same way a blackboard is used in a classroom (*Computer User High Tech Dictionary*, 2008).

wikis: Web applications designed to allow multiple authors to add, remove, and edit content (infoDev, 2008)

wireless: Generic term for mobile communication services that do not use fixed-line networks for direct access to the subscriber (infoDev, 2008)

References

Adler, P. S., & Kwon, S. W. (2002). Social capital: Prospects for a new concept. *Academy of Management Review, 27*, 17–40.

Afuah, A., & Tucci, C. L. (2012). Crowdsourcing as a solution to distant search. *Academy of Management Review, 37*(3), 355–375.

Alexander, B. (2009). Apprehending the future: Emerging technologies, from science fiction to campus reality. *EDUCAUSE Review, 44*(3), 12–29.

Amaghlobeli, N. (2012). Linguistic features of typographic emoticons in SMS discourse. *Theory and Practice in Language Studies, 2*(2), 348–354.

Amin, Z. (2000). Q methodology: A journey into the subjectivity of the human mind. *Singapore Medical Journal, 41*(8), 410–414.

Anarbaeva, S. M. (2012). Samarita Ibanez: An identity journey from first life to Second. *Journal for Virtual Worlds Research, 5*(1), 1–14.

Anfara, V. A., & Mertz, N. T. (Eds.). (2006). *Theoretical frameworks in qualitative research.* Thousand Oaks, CA: Sage.

Arthur, S., & Nazroo, J. (2003). Designing fieldwork strategies and materials. In J. Ritchie & J. Lewis (Eds.), *Qualitative research practice: A guide for social science students and researchers* (pp. 109–137). London: Sage.

Atkinson, P., & Silverman, D. (1997, September). Kundera's immortality: The interview society and the invention of the self. *Qualitative Inquiry, 3*, 304–325.

Ayling, R., & Mewse, A. J. (2009). Evaluating Internet interviews with gay men. *Qualitative Health Research, 19*(4), 566–576. doi:10.1177/1049732309332121

Ayyagari, R., Grover, V., & Purvis, R. (2011). Technostress: Technological antecedents and implications. *MIS Quarterly, 35*(4), 831–858.

Baggini, J., & Fosl, P. S. (2007). *The ethics toolkit: A compendium of ethical concepts and methods.* Malden, MA: Blackwell.

Bailenson, J. N., Yee, N., Blascovich, J., Beall, A. C., Lundblad, N., & Jin, M. (2008). The use of immersive virtual reality in the learning sciences: Digital transformations of teachers, students, and social context. *Journal of the Learning Sciences, 17*, 102–141.

Bakardjieva, M. (2005). *Internet society: The Internet in everyday life.* London: Sage.

Bakardjieva, M., & Feenberg, A. (2001). Respecting the virtual subject, or how to navigate the private/public continuum. In C. Werry & M. Mowbray (Eds.), *Online communities: Commerce, community action, and the virtual university* (pp. 195–213). Upper Saddle River, NJ: HP Prentice Hall.

Bamford, A. (2003). *The visual literacy white paper*. Uxbridge, Australia: Adobe Systems.

Bampton, R., & Cowton, C. J. (2002). The e-interview. *Forum: Qualitative Social Research, 3*(2). Retrieved from http://www.utsc.utoronto.ca/~kmacd/IDSC10/Readings/interviews/e-interview.pdf

Banks, M. (2007). *Using visual data in qualitative research*. London: Sage.

Baños, R. M., Botella, C., Rubió, I., Quero, S., García-Palacios, A., & Alcañiz, M. (2008). Presence and emotions in virtual environments: The influence of stereoscopy. *CyberPsychology & Behavior, 11*(1), 1–8.

Baron, N. S., & Ling, R. (2011). Necessary smileys and useless periods. *Visible Language, 45*(1–2), 45–67.

Baym, N. K. (2009). What constitutes quality in qualitative Internet research? In A. N. Markham & N. K. Baym (Eds.), *Internet inquiry: Conversations about method* (pp. 173–190). Thousand Oaks, CA: Sage.

Bazeley, P., & Jackson, K. (2013). *Qualitative data analysis with nVivo* (2nd ed.). London: Sage.

Bekkering, E., & Shim, J. P. (2006). Trust in videoconferencing. *Communications of the ACM, 49*(7), 103–107.

Bell, L., & Nutt, L. (2012). Consenting to what? Issues of access, gate-keeping and 'informed' consent. In T. Miller, M. Birch, M. Mauthner, & J. Jessop (Eds.), *Ethics in qualitative research* (pp. 53–69). London: Sage.

Bell, M. (2008). *Definition and taxonomy of virtual worlds*. Paper presented at New Digital Media (Audiovisual, Games and Music): Economic, Social and Political Impacts, Sao Paulo, Brazil.

Beneito-Montagut, R. (2011). Ethnography goes online: Towards a user-centred methodology to research interpersonal communication on the internet. *Qualitative Research, 11*(6), 716–735. doi:10.1177/1468794111413368

Bernard, H. R., & Ryan, G. (2009). *Analyzing qualitative data*. Thousand Oaks, CA: Sage.

Berry, D. M. (2004). Internet research: Privacy, ethics and alienation: An open source approach. *Journal of Internet Research, 14*(4), 323–332.

Bishai, S. (2012). Blog like an Egyptian. In J. Salmons (Ed.), *Cases in online interview research* (pp. 37–56). Thousand Oaks, CA: Sage.

Bjerke, T. N. (2010). When my eyes bring pain to my soul, and vice versa: Facing preconceptions in email and face-to-face interviews. *Qualitative Health Research, 20*(12), 1717–1724. doi:10.1177/1049732310375967

Blaikie, N. (2004). Interpretivism. In M. S. Lewis-Beck, A. Bryman, & T. F. Liao (Eds.), *The SAGE encyclopedia of social science research methods* (pp. 509–511). Thousand Oaks, CA: Sage.

Bloomberg, L. D., & Volpe, M. (2012). *Completing your qualitative dissertation: A roadmap from beginning to end* (2nd ed.). Thousand Oaks, CA: Sage.

Boothby, D., Dufour, A., & Tang, J. (2010). Technology adoption, training and productivity performance. *Research Policy, 39*(5), 650–661. doi:10.1016/j.respol.2010.02.011

Borgman, C. L. (2007). *Scholarship in the digital age: Information, infrastructure, and the Internet*. Cambridge: MIT Press.

Brewer, J., & Hunter, A. (2006). Collecting data with multiple methods. In J. Brewer & A. Hunter (Eds.), *Foundations of multimethod research* (pp. 59–78). Thousand Oaks, CA: Sage.

British Educational Research Association. (2011). *Ethical guidelines for educational research*. London: Author. Retrieved from http://www.bera.ac.uk/publications/Ethical%20Guidelines

Brown, S. R. (1980). *Political subjectivity: Applications of Q methodology in political science*. New Haven, CT: Yale University Press.

Brown, S. R. (1993). A primer on Q methodology. *Operant Subjectivity, 16*, 91–138.

Browne, K. (2005). Snowball sampling: Using social networks to research nonheterosexual women. *International Journal of Social Research Methodology, 8*(1), 47–60.

Bruckman, A. (2002). Studying the amateur artist: A perspective on disguising data collected in human subjects research on the Internet. *Ethics and Information Technology, 4*(3), 217.

Bryman, A. (2006). Integrating quantitative and qualitative research: How is it done? *Qualitative Research, 6*(1), 97–113.

Bryman, A., & Cassell, C. (2006). The researcher interview: A reflexive perspective. *Qualitative Research in Organizations and Management, 1*(1), 41–55.

Buchanan, E. (2011). Internet research ethics: Past, present, future. In M. Consalvo & C. Ess (Eds.), *The handbook of Internet studies* (pp. 83–108). New York: Wiley-Blackwell.

Buckley, C. A., & Waring, M. J. (2013). Using diagrams to support the research process: Examples from grounded theory. *Qualitative Research, 13*, 148–172. doi:10.1177/1468794112472280

Budd, J. M. (2008). Critical theory. In L. M. Given (Ed.), *The SAGE encyclopedia of qualitative research methods* (pp. 174–179). Thousand Oaks, CA: Sage.

Cabiria, J. (2008). *A Second Life: Online virtual worlds as therapeutic tools for gay and lesbian people*. Doctoral dissertation, Fielding Graduate University, Santa Barbara, CA.

Cabiria, J. (2012). Interviewing in virtual worlds: An application of best practices. In J. Salmons (Ed.), *Cases in online interview research* (pp. 109–123). Thousand Oaks, CA: Sage.

Carolis, D. M. D., & Saparito, P. (2006). Social capital, cognition, and entrepreneurial opportunities: A theoretical framework. *Entrepreneurship: Theory & Practice, 30*(1), 41–56. doi:10.1111/j.1540-6520.2006.00109.x

Carter, S. M., & Little, M. (2007). Justifying knowledge, justifying method, taking action: Epistemologies, methodologies, and methods in qualitative research. *Qualitative Health Research, 17*(10), 1316–1328.

Carusi, A. (2008). Data as representation: Beyond anonymity in e-research ethics. *International Journal of Internet Research Ethics, 1*(1), 37–65.

Castaños, C., & Piercy, F. P. (2010). The wiki as a virtual space for qualitative data collection. *The Qualitative Report, 15*(4), 948–955.

Chapman, D. S., & Rowe, P. M. (2002). The influence of videoconference technology and interview structure on the recruiting function of the employment interview: A field experiment. *International Journal of Selection and Assessment, 10*(3), 185–197.

Charmaz, K. (2003). Qualitative interviewing and grounded theory analysis. In J. A. Holstein & J. F. Gubrium (Eds.), *Inside interviewing: New lenses, new concerns* (pp. 311–330). Thousand Oaks, CA: Sage.

Charmaz, K. (2006). *Constructing grounded theory: A practical guide through qualitative analysis.* Thousand Oaks, CA: Sage.

Chen, M. (2002). *Leveraging the asymmetric sensitivity of eye contact for videoconference.* Paper presented at the Special Interest Group on Computer-Human Interaction Conference on Human Factors in Computing Systems, Minneapolis, MN.

Chen, P., & Hinton, S. M. (1999). Realtime interviewing using the World Wide Web. *Sociological Research Online, 4.*

Chin-Sheng, W., & Wen-Bin, C. (2006). Why are adolescents addicted to online gaming? An interview study in Taiwan. *CyberPsychology & Behavior, 9*(6), 762–766.

Chou, C. (2001). Internet heavy use and addiction among Taiwanese college students: An online interview study. *CyberPsychology & Behavior, 4*(5), 573–585.

Clandinin, D. J., & Connelly, F. M. (2000). *Narrative inquiry: Experience and story in qualitative research.* Thousand Oaks, CA: Sage.

Clarke, A. (2005). *Situational analysis: Grounded theory after the postmodern turn.* Thousand Oaks, CA: Sage.

Computer user high tech dictionary. (2008). Retrieved September 8, 2008, from http://www.computeruser.com

Consalvo, M., & Ess, C. (Eds.). (2011). *The handbook of Internet studies.* West Sussex: Wiley-Blackwell.

Couture, A. L., Zaidi, A. U., & Maticka-Tyndale, E. (2012). Reflexive accounts: An intersectional approach to exploring the fluidity of insider/outsider status and the researcher's impact on culturally sensitive post-positivist qualitative research. *Qualitative Sociology Review, VIII*(i), 86–105.

Coyne, I. T. (1997). Sampling in qualitative research. Purposeful and theoretical sampling; merging or clear boundaries? *Journal of Advanced Nursing, 26,* 623–630.

Creswell, J. W. (1998). *Qualitative inquiry and research design: Choosing among five traditions.* Thousand Oaks, CA: Sage.

Creswell, J. W. (2003). *Research design: Qualitative, quantitative and mixed methods approaches* (2nd ed.). Thousand Oaks, CA: Sage.

Creswell, J. W. (2007). *Qualitative inquiry and research design: Choosing among five approaches* (2nd ed.). Thousand Oaks, CA: Sage.

Creswell, J. W. (2013). *Qualitative inquiry and research design: Choosing among five approaches* (3rd ed.). Thousand Oaks, CA: Sage.

Creswell, J. W. (2014). *Research design: Qualitative, quantitative and mixed methods approaches* (4th ed.). Thousand Oaks, CA: Sage.

Creswell, J. W., & Clark, V. L. P. (2007). *Designing and conducting mixed methods research* (2nd ed.). Thousand Oaks, CA: Sage.

Crilly, N., Blackwell, A. F., & Clarkson, P. J. (2006). Graphic elicitation: Using research diagrams as interview stimuli. *Qualitative Research, 6*(3), 341–366.

Crotty, M. (1998). *The foundation of social research: Meaning and perspectives in the research process.* London: Sage.

Daft, R. L., & Lengel, R. H. (1986). Organizational information requirements, media richness and structural design. *Management Science, 32*(5), 554–571.

Davis, M. (1999). *Ethics in the university.* Florence, Italy: Routledge.

Davis, M., Bolding, G., Hart, G., Sherr, L., & Elford, J. (2004). Reflecting on the experience of interviewing online: Perspectives from the Internet and HIV study in London. *AIDS Care, 16*(8), 944–952.

Day, S. (2012). A reflexive lens: Exploring dilemmas of qualitative methodology through the concept of reflexivity. *Qualitative Sociology Review, VIII*(i), 61–84.

Debes, J. (1968). Some foundations of visual literacy. *Audio-Visual Instruction, 13*, 961–964.

Dennis, A. R., Fuller, R. M., & Valacich, J. S. (2008). Media, tasks, and communication processes: A theory of media synchronicity. *Management Information Systems Quarterly, 32*(4), 575–600.

Denzin, N. K. (1989). *Interpretive biography* (Vol. 17). Newbury Park, CA: Sage.

Denzin, N. K. (2001). The reflexive interview and a performative social science. *Qualitative Research, 1*(23), 23–25.

DeVault, M., & McCoy, L. (2002). Institutional ethnography: Using interviews to investigate ruling relations. In J. F. Gubrium & J. A. Holstein (Eds.), *Handbook of interviewing: Context and method* (pp. 751–755). Thousand Oaks, CA: Sage.

Dewey, J. (1916). *Democracy and education*. New York: Macmillan.

Diaz, V., Salmons, J., & Brown, M. (2010). *ELI Discovery Tool: Guide to collaborative learning*. Retrieved from http://www.educause.edu/library/resources/eli-discovery-tool-guide-collaborative-learning

DiCicco-Bloom, B., & Crabtree, B. F. (2006). The qualitative research interview. *Medical Education, 40*, 314–321.

Douglas, J. D. (1984). *Creative interviewing*. Thousand Oaks, CA: Sage.

Duncombe, J., & Jessop, J. (2012). 'Doing rapport' and the ethics of 'faking friendship.' In T. Miller, M. Birch, M. Mauthner, & J. Jessop (Eds.), *Ethics in qualitative research* (pp. 107–122). London: Sage.

Dunn, R. A., & Guadagno, R. E. (2012). My avatar and me—Gender and personality predictors of avatar-self discrepancy. *Computers in Human Behavior, 28*(1), 97–106. doi:http://dx.doi.org/10.1016/j.chb.2011.08.015

Dwyer, T. (2010). *Media convergence*. Maidenhead, UK: McGraw-Hill Professional.

Educational Testing Services. (2006). *ICT literacy assessment preliminary findings*. Retrieved February 25, 2007, from http://www.ets.org/Media/Products/ICT_Literacy/pdf/2006_Preliminary_Findings.pdf

Ellis, C., & Berger, L. (2003). Their story/my story/our story. In J. F. Gubrium & J. A. Holstein (Eds.), *Postmodern interviewing* (pp. 157–186). Thousand Oaks, CA: Sage.

Elm, M. S. (2008). How do various notions of privacy influence decisions in qualitative Internet research? In A. N. Markham & N. K. Baym (Eds.), *Internet inquiry: Conversations about method* (pp. 69–87). Thousand Oaks, CA: Sage.

Elwell, J. S. (2013). The transmediated self: Life between the digital and the analog [Electronic version]. *Convergence: The International Journal of Research Into New Media Technologies*. doi:10.1177/1354856513501423

Emerson, R. W. (1838). *Literary ethics*. Hanover, NH: Dartmouth College.

Erdem, S. A. (2013). Moving from intermediaries to apomediaries: A study of the ongoing changes in marketing channels. *Review of Business Information Systems, 17*(1). Retrieved from http://journals.cluteonline.com/index.php/RBIS/article/view/7582/7648

Erickson, T., & Herring, S. C. (2005). *Persistent conversation: A dialog between research and design*. Paper presented at the International Conference on System Sciences, Manoa, Hawaii.

ESOMAR. (2011). *ESOMAR guideline on social media research*. Retrieved from http://www.esomar.org/uploads/public/knowledge-and-standards/codes-and-guidelines/ESOMAR-Guideline-on-Social-Media-Research.pdf

ESOMAR & International Chamber of Commerce. (2008). *ICC/ESOMAR international code on market and social research*. Retrieved from http://www.esomar.org/uploads/public/knowledge-and-standards/codes-and-guidelines/ICCESOMAR_Code_English_.pdf

Ess, C. (2002). *Ethical decision making and Internet Research: Recommendations from the AOIR ethics working committee*. Retrieved December 10, 2003, from http://www.aoir.org/reports/ethics.pdf

Estellés-Arolas, E., & González-Ladrón-de-Guevara, F. (2012). Towards an integrated crowdsourcing definition. *Journal of Information Science, 38*(2), 189–200. doi:10.1177/0165551512437638

ETS. (2006). *ICT literacy assessment preliminary findings*. Retrieved February 25, 2007, from http://www.ets.org/Media/Products/ICT_Literacy/pdf/2006_Preliminary_Findings.pdf

Eysenbach, G. (2008). Medicine 2.0: Social networking, collaboration, participation, apomediation, and openness. *Journal of Medical Internet research, 10*(3). doi:10.2196/jmir.1030

Eysenbach, G., & Till, J. (2001). Ethical issues in qualitative research on Internet communities. *British Medical Journal, 323*(7321), 1103–1105.

Fereday, J., & Muir-Cochrane, E. (2006). Demonstrating rigor using thematic analysis: A hybrid approach of inductive and deductive coding and theme development. *International Journal of Qualitative Methods, 5*(1), 80–92.

Fielding, N. (2007). *New technologies, new applications: Using access grid nodes in field research and training*. Swindon, UK: Economic & Social Research Council.

Flick, U. (2007a). Quality in qualitative research. In U. Flick (Ed.), *Designing qualitative research* (pp. 61–67). London: Sage.

Flick, U. (2007b). Standards, criteria, checklists and guidelines. In U. Flick (Ed.), *Managing quality in qualitative research* (pp. 11–26). London: Sage.

Fontana, A. (2003). Postmodern trends in interviewing. In J. F. Gubrium & J. A. Holstein (Eds.), *Postmodern interviewing* (pp. 51–66). Thousand Oaks, CA: Sage.

Fontana, A., & Frey, J. H. (2003). The interview: From structured questions to negotiated text. In N. K. Denzin & Y. S. Lincoln (Eds.), *Collecting and interpreting qualitative materials* (pp. 61–106). Thousand Oaks, CA: Sage.

Fox, N. (2008a). Induction. In L. M. Given (Ed.), *The SAGE encyclopedia of qualitative research methods* (pp. 430–431). Thousand Oaks, CA: Sage.

Fox, N. (2008b). Postpositivism. In L. M. Given (Ed.), *The SAGE encyclopedia of qualitative research methods* (pp. 660–665). Thousand Oaks, CA: Sage.

Frankel, M. S., & Siang, S. (1999). *Ethical and legal aspects of human subjects research on the Internet*. Washington, DC: American Association for the Advancement of Science.

Franklin, B. (2004). *The autobiography of Benjamin Franklin*. NewYork: Simon & Schuster. (Original work published in 1757)

Freeman, R. (2007). Epistemological bricolage: How practitioners make sense of learning. *Administration & Society, 39*(4), 476–496.

Gardner, H. (1983). *Frames of mind: The theory of multiple intelligences.* New York: Basic Books.

Garg, A. (2008). Sampling hurdles: "Borderline illegitimate" to legitimate data. *International Journal of Qualitative Methods, 7*(4), 59–67.

Garrison, D. R., Anderson, T., & Archer, W. (2004). Critical thinking and computer conferencing: A model and tool to assess cognitive presence. *American Journal of Distance Education, 15*(1), 7–23.

Gehling, R., Turner, D., & Rutherford, B. (2007). Defining the proposed factors for small business online banking: Interviewing the IT professionals. *Financial Services Marketing, 12*(3), 189–196.

Geiser, T. (2002). Conducting online focus groups: A methodological discussion. In L. Burton & D. Goldsmith (Eds.), The medium is the message: Using online focus groups to study online learning (Vol. 2003, pp. 1–14). New Britain: Connecticut Distance Learning Consortium.

Gergle, D., Kraut, R. E., & Fussell, S. R. (2004). Language efficiency and visual technology minimizing collaborative effort with visual information. *Journal of Language and Social Psychology, 23*(4), 491–517.

Goldstein, B. M. (2007). All photos lie: Images as data. In G. C. Stanczak (Ed.), *Visual research methods: Image, society, and representation* (pp. 61–81). Thousand Oaks, CA: Sage.

Gordon, R. L. (1980). *Interviewing: Strategy, techniques and tactics.* Homewood, IL: Dorsey.

Gray, D. (2004). *Doing research in the real world.* London: Sage.

Gray, D. (2009). *Doing research in the real world* (2nd ed.). London: Sage.

Grayson, D. M., & Monk, A. F. (2003). Are you looking at me? Eye contact and desktop video conferencing. *Transactions on Computer-Human Interaction, 10*(3), 221–243.

Gruber, T., Szmigin, I., Reppel, A. E., & Voss, R. (2008). Designing and conducting online interviews to investigate interesting consumer phenomena. *Qualitative Market Research, 11*(3), 256–274. doi:http://dx.doi.org/10.1108/13522750810879002

Gubrium, E., & Koro-Ljungberg, M. (2005). Contending with border making in the social constructionist interview. *Qualitative Inquiry, 5*(11), 689–715.

Gubrium, J., & Holstein, J. (2003a). From the individual interview to the interview society. In J. F. Gubrium & J. A. Holstein (Eds.), *Postmodern interviewing* (pp. 21–50). Thousand Oaks, CA: Sage.

Gubrium, J., & Holstein, J. (Eds.). (2003b). *Postmodern interviewing.* Thousand Oaks, CA: Sage.

Guerrero, L. K., DeVito, J. A., & Hecht, M. L. (Eds.). (1999). *The nonverbal communication reader: Classic and contemporary readings.* Prospect Hills, IL: Waveland Press.

Hanna, P. (2012). Using Internet technologies (such as Skype) as a research medium: A research note. *Qualitative Research, 12*(2), 239–242. doi:10.1177/1468794111426607

Hargrove, R. (2001). *E-leader: Reinventing leadership in a connected economy.* Cambridge, MA: Perseus.

Hayles, N. K. (2006). Unfinished work: From cyborg to cognisphere. *Theory, Culture & Society, 23*(7–8), 159–166. doi:10.1177/0263276406069229

Heeter, C. (2003). Reflections on real presence by a virtual person. *Presence: Teleoperators & Virtual Environments, 12*(4), 335–345.

Hesse-Biber, S. N. (2010). *Mixed methods research: Merging theory with practice.* New York: Guilford Press.

Hesse-Biber, S. N., & Leavy, P. (2006). *The practice of qualitative research.* Thousand Oaks, CA: Sage.

Hewson, C. (2010). Internet-mediated research and its potential role in facilitating mixed methods research. In S. N. Hesse-Biber & P. Leavy (Ed.), *Handbook of emergent methods* (pp. 543–570). New York: Guilford Press.

Hibbert, P., Coupland, C., & MacIntosh, R. (2010). Reflexivity: Recursion and relationality in organizational research processes. *Qualitative Research in Organizations and Management, 5*(1), 47–62. doi:10.1108/17465641011042026

Hine, C. (Ed.). (2000). *Virtual ethnography.* Oxford, UK: Berg.

Hine, C. (2013). *The Internet: Understanding qualitative research.* Oxford, UK: Oxford Press.

Holstein, J. A., & Gubrium, J. F. (1995). *The active interview.* Thousand Oaks, CA: Sage.

Holstein, J. A., & Gubrium, J. F. (2003a). Active interviewing. In J. F. Gubrium & J. A. Holstein (Eds.), *Postmodern interviewing* (pp. 67–80). Thousand Oaks, CA: Sage.

Holstein, J. A., & Gubrium, J. F. (Eds.). (2003b). *Inside interviewing: New lenses, new concerns.* Thousand Oaks, CA: Sage.

Holstein, J. A., & Gubrium, J. F. (2003c). Postmodern sensibilities. In J. F. Gubrium & J. A. Holstein (Eds.), *Postmodern interviewing* (pp. 3–20). Thousand Oaks, CA: Sage.

Holstein, J. A., & Gubrium, J. F. (2004). The active interview. In D. Silverman (Ed.), *Qualitative research: Theory, method and practice* (pp. 140–161). Thousand Oaks, CA: Sage.

Hsu, C., & Sandford, B. (2010). Delphi technique. In N. Salkind (Ed.), *Encyclopedia of research design* (pp. 344–347). Thousand Oaks, CA: Sage.

Huang, R., Kahai, S., & Jestice, R. (2010). The contingent effects of leadership on team collaboration in virtual teams. *Computers in Human Behavior, 26*(5), 1098–1110. doi:http://dx.doi.org/10.1016/j.chb.2010.03.014

Hughes, J. (2012a). Editor's introduction: Internet research methods. In J. Hughes (Ed.), *SAGE Internet research methods.* London: Sage.

Hughes, J. (2012b). *Web-based network sampling: Efficiency and efficacy of respondent-driven sampling for online research.* London: Sage.

Hull, C. L. (1943). *Principles of behavior.* New York: Appleton-Century-Crofts.

Hunt, N., & McHale, S. (2007). A practical guide to the email interview. *Qualitative Health Research, 17*(10), 1415–1421.

Husserl, E. (1931). *Ideas: General introduction to pure phenomenology.* London: Allen & Unwin.

infoDev. (2008). Glossary. In *ICT regulation toolkit.* Washington, DC: Author.

Jacobsen, M. M. (1999). *Orality, literacy, cyberdiscursivity: Transformations of literacy in computer-mediated communication.* Unpublished doctoral dissertation, Texas A&M University.

James, N., & Busher, H. (2006). Credibility, authenticity and voice: Dilemmas in online interviewing. *Qualitative Research, 6*(3), 403–420.

James, N., & Busher, H. (2009). *Online interviewing*. London: Sage.

Johnson, R. B., & Onwuegbuzie, A. J. (2004). Mixed methods research: A research paradigm whose time has come. *Educational Researcher, 33*(7), 14–26.

Johnson, R. B., Onwuegbuzie, A. J., & Turner, L. A. (2007). Toward a definition of mixed methods research. *Journal of Mixed Methods Research, 1*(2), 112–133. doi:10.1177/1558689806298224

Joinson, A. (2001). Self-disclosure in computer-mediated communication: The role of self-awareness and visual anonymity. *European Journal of Social Psychology, 31*, 177–192.

Kahai, S. S., & Cooper, R. B. (2003). Exploring the core concepts of media richness theory: The impact of cue multiplicity and feedback immediacy on decision quality. *Journal of Management Information Systems, 20*(3), 263–299.

Kalman, Y. M., Ravid, G., Raban, D. R., & Rafaeli, S. (2006). Pauses and response latencies: A chronemic analysis of asynchronous CMC. *Journal of Computer-Mediated Communication, 12*(1), 1–23.

Kant, I. (2008). *Grounding for the metaphysics of morals* (T. K. Abbott, Trans.). Radford, VA: Wilder Publications. (Original work published in 1785)

Kaplan, H. B. (1975). The self-esteem motive. In H. B. Kaplan (Ed.), *Self-attitudes and deviant behavior* (pp. 10–31). Pacific Palisades, CA: Goodyear.

Kehrwald, B. (2008). Understanding social presence in text-based online learning environments. *Distance Education, 29*(1), 89–106.

King, N., & Horrocks, C. (2010). *Interviews in qualitative research*. London: Sage.

Kitchin, R. M. (1998). Towards geographies of cyberspace. *Progress in Human Geography, 22*(3), 385–406.

Kitto, R. J., & Barnett, J. (2007). Analysis of thin online interview data: Toward a sequential hierarchical language-based approach. *American Journal of Evaluation, 28*(3), 356–368.

Kitto, S. C., Chesters, J., & Grbich, C. (2008). Quality in qualitative research: Criteria for authors and assessors in the submission and assessment of qualitative research articles for the Medical Journal of Australia. *Medical Journal of Australia, 188*(4), 243–246.

Knapik, M. (2006). The qualitative research interview: Participants' responsive participation in knowledge making. *International Journal of Qualitative Methods, 5*(3), 1–13.

Knemeyer, D. (2004). Digital convergence: Insight into the future of web design. *Digital Web Magazine*. Retrieved from http://www.digital-web.com/articles/digital_convergence/

Koerber, A., & McMichael, L. (2008). Qualitative sampling methods: A primer for technical communicators. *Journal of Business and Technical Communication, 22*(4), 454–473.

Koltay, T. (2011). The media and the literacies: Media literacy, information literacy, digital literacy. *Media, Culture & Society, 33*(2), 211–221. doi:10.1177/0163443710393382

Kouzes, J. M., & Posner, B. Z. (2007). *The leadership challenge* (4th ed.). San Francisco: Jossey Bass.

Kozinets, R. V. (2010). *Netnography: Doing ethnographic research online.* Thousand Oaks, CA: Sage.

Kress, G. (2003). *Literacy in the new media age.* London: Routledge.

Kress, G. (2005). Gains and losses: New forms of texts, knowledge, and learning. *Computers and Composition, 22*(1), 5–22. doi:http://dx.doi.org/10.1016/j.compcom.2004.12.004

Kress, G., & Selander, S. (2012). Multimodal design, learning and cultures of recognition. *The Internet and Higher Education, 15*(4), 265–268. doi:http://dx.doi.org/10.1016/j.iheduc.2011.12.003

Kvale, S. (2006). Dominance through interviews and dialogues. *Qualitative Inquiry, 12*(3), 480–500.

Kvale, S. (2007). *Doing interviews.* Thousand Oaks, CA: Sage.

Kvale, S., & Brinkman, S. (2009). *InterViews: Learning the craft of qualitative research interviewing* (2nd ed.). Thousand Oaks, CA: Sage.

LaBanca, F. (2011). Online dynamic asynchronous audit strategy for reflexivity in the qualitative paradigm. *The Qualitative Report, 16*(4), 1160–1171. doi:10.1080/13645570802156196

Laflen, A., & Fiorenza, B. (2012). "Okay, my rant is over": The language of emotion in computer-mediated communication. *Computers and Composition, 29*(4), 296–308. doi:http://dx.doi.org/10.1016/j.compcom.2012.09.005

Laquintano, T. (2010). Sustained authorship: Digital writing, self-publishing, and the ebook. *Written Communication, 27*(4), 469–493. doi:10.1177/0741088310377863

Lee, N., & Lings, I. (2008). *Doing business research: A guide to theory and practice.* London: Sage.

Lehdonvirta, V. (2010). Virtual worlds don't exist: Questioning the dichotomous approach in MMO studies. *Journal for Virtual Worlds Research, 10*(1). Retrieved from http://gamestudies.org/1001/articles/lehdonvirta

Lévi-Strauss, C. (1983). *The raw and the cooked: Mythologiques, Volume 1.* Chicago: University of Chicago Press.

Licoppea, C., & Smoredab, Z. (2005). Are social networks technologically embedded? How networks are changing today with changes in communication technology. *Social Networks, 27*(4), 317–335.

Lillie, J. (2012). Nokia's MMS: A cultural analysis of mobile picture messaging. *New Media & Society, 14*(1), 80–97. doi:10.1177/1461444811410400

Lincoln, Y. S. (2002). Emerging criteria for quality in qualitative and interpretive research. In N. K. Denzin & Y. S. Lincoln (Eds.), *The qualitative inquiry reader* (pp. 327–346). Thousand Oaks, CA: Sage.

Lincoln, Y. S., & Guba, E. G. (1985). *Naturalistic inquiry.* Thousand Oaks, CA: Sage.

Locke, K. (2010). Abduction. In A. Mills, G. Durepos, & E. Wiebe (Eds.), *Encyclopedia of case study research* (pp. 2–4). Thousand Oaks, CA: Sage.

Lombard, M., & Ditton, T. (1997). At the heart of it all: The concept of presence. *Journal of Computer-Mediated Communication, 3*(2). Retrieved from http://onlinelibrary.wiley.com/doi/10.1111/j.1083-6101.1997.tb00072.x/full

Lomborg, S. (2013). Personal internet archives and ethics. *Research Ethics, 9*(1), 20–31. doi:10.1177/1747016112459450

Loseke, D. R. (2013). *Methodological thinking: Basic principles of social research design.* Thousand Oaks, CA: Sage.

Loue, S. (2000). *Textbook of research ethics: Theory and practice*. Hingham, MA: Kluwer Academic.

Madge, C. (2006). *Online research ethics*. Retrieved from http://www.restore.ac .uk/orm/ethics/ethcontents.htm

Mann, C., & Stewart, F. (2000). *Internet communication and qualitative research: A handbook for researching online*. San Francisco: Sage.

Markham, A. N. (2005). Disciplining the future: A critical organizational analysis of Internet studies. *Information Society, 21*, 257–267.

Markham, A., & Buchanan, E. (2012). *Ethical decision-making and Internet research: Recommendations from the AoIR Ethics Working Committee* (Version 2.0). Retrieved from http://aoir.org/reports/ethics2.pdf

Martey, R. M., & Shiflett, K. (2012). Reconsidering site and self: Methodological frameworks for virtual-world research. *International Journal of Communication, 6*, 105–126.

Mason, J. (2002). *Qualitative researching* (2nd ed.). Thousand Oaks, CA: Sage.

McDermott, E., & Roen, K. (2012). Youth on the virtual edge: Researching marginalized sexualities and genders online. *Qualitative Health Research, 22*(4), 560–570. doi:10.1177/1049732311425052

McKinney, P., Jones, M., & Turkington, S. (2011). Information literacy through inquiry. *Aslib Proceedings, 63*(2–3), 221–240. doi:http://dx.doi.org/10.1108/00012531111135673

Meek, D. (2012). YouTube and social movements: A phenomenological analysis of participation, events and cyberplace. *Antipode, 44*(4), 1429–1448. doi:10.1111/j.1467-8330.2011.00942.x

Meho, L. I. (2006). E-mail interviewing in qualitative research: A methodological discussion. *Journal of the American Society for Information Science & Technology, 57*(10), 1284–1295. doi:10.1002/asi.20416

Mehrabian, A. (1971). *Silent messages*. Belmont, WA: Wadsworth.

Messinger, P. R., Ge, X., Stroulia, E., Lyons, K., & Smirnov, K. (2008). On the relationship between my avatar and myself. *Journal of Virtual Worlds Research, 1*(2), 1–17.

Metros, S. E. (2008). The educator's role in preparing visually literate learners. *Theory Into Practice, 47*, 102–109.

Miles, M., & Huberman, A. M. (1994). *Qualitative data analysis: An expanded sourcebook* (2nd ed.). Thousand Oaks, CA: Sage.

Mill, J. S. (1985). *The collected works of John Stuart Mill: Essays on ethics, religion, and society* (Vol. X). London: Routledge.

Miller, J., & Glassner, B. (2004). The "inside" and the "outside": Finding realities in interviews. In D. Silverman (Ed.), *Qualitative research: Theory, method and practice* (pp. 125–139). Thousand Oaks, CA: Sage.

Milliou, C., & Petrakis, E. (2011). Timing of technology adoption and product market competition. *International Journal of Industrial Organization, 29*(5), 513–523. doi:10.1016/j.ijindorg.2010.10.003

Molyneaux, H., O'Donnell, S., Liu, S., Hagerman, V., Gibson, K. B. M., Matthews, B., et al. (2007). *Good practice guidelines for participatory multi-site videoconferencing*. Fredericton, Canada: National Research Council.

Morgan, D. L. (2007). Combining qualitative and quantitative methods. Paradigms lost and pragmatism regained: Methodological implications. *Journal of Mixed Methods Research, 1*(1), 48–76.

Moustakas, C. (1994). *Phenomenological research methods*. Thousand Oaks, CA: Sage.

Nahapiet, J., & Ghoshal, S. (1998). Social capital, intellectual capital, and the organizational advantage. *Academy of Management Review, 23*(2), 242–266.

Näykki, P., & Järvelä, S. (2008). How pictorial knowledge representations mediate collaborative knowledge construction in groups. *Journal of Research on Technology in Education, 40*(3), 359–387.

Neuman, W. L. (1994). *Social research methods: Qualitative and quantitative approaches*. Needham Heights, MA: Allyn & Bacon.

Newton, J. (2006). *Action research. The SAGE dictionary of social research methods*. Thousand Oaks, CA: Sage.

O'Connor, D. (2013). The apomediated world: Regulating research when social media has changed research. *Journal of Law, Medicine & Ethics, 41*(2), 470–483. doi:10.1111/jlme.12056

O'Connor, H. (2006). Online interviews. *Exploring online research methods: Online interviews*. Leicester, UK: University of Leicester.

O'Donnell, S., Perley, S., & Simms, D. (2008). *Challenges for video communications in remote and rural communities*. Paper presented at the IEEE International Symposium on Technology and Society, New Brunswick, Canada.

OED. (2005). *Oxford English dictionary*. Retrieved May 29, 2005, from http://www.askoxford.com

O'Hara, P. (2005). *Strategic initiative for developing capacity in ethical review (SIDCER)*. Paper presented at the International Conference on Ethical Issues in Behavioural and Social Sciences Research, Montreal, Canada.

Olaniran, B. A. (2009). Organizational communication: Assessment of videoconferencing as a medium for meetings in the workplace. *International Journal of Technology and Human Interaction, 5*(2), 63–84.

Ong, W. (1990). *Writing and reading texts are speech events: Language as hermeneutic*. St. Louis, MO: St. Louis University.

Onwuegbuzie, A. J., & Leech, N. L. (2007). Sampling designs in qualitative research: Making the sampling process more public. *The Qualitative Report, 12*(2), 238–254.

Opdenakker, R. (2006). Advantages and disadvantages of four interview techniques in qualitative research. *Forum: Qualitative Social Research, 4*(11). Retrieved from http://www.qualitative-research.net/index.php/fqs/article/view/175/391

O'Reilly, M., & Parker, N. (2012). 'Unsatisfactory saturation': A critical exploration of the notion of saturated sample sizes in qualitative research [Electronic version]. *Qualitative Research*. doi:10.1177/1468794112446106

O'Sullivan, P. B., Hunt, S. K., & Lippert, L. R. (2004). Mediated immediacy: A language of affiliation in a technological age. *Journal of Language and Social Psychology, 23*(4), 464–490.

Otondo, R. F., Scotter, J. R. V., Allen, D. G., & Palvia, P. (2008). The complexity of richness: Media, message, and communication outcomes. *Information & Management, 45*, 21–30.

Ottósson, H., & Klyver, K. I. M. (2010). The effect of human capital on social capital among entrepreneurs. *Journal of Enterprising Culture, 18*(4), 399–417.

Paechter, C. (2013). Researching sensitive issues online: Implications of a hybrid insider/outsider position in a retrospective ethnographic study. *Qualitative Research, 13*(1), 71–86. doi:10.1177/1468794112446107

Park, Y. J. (2013). Digital literacy and privacy behavior online. *Communication Research, 40*(2), 215–236. doi:10.1177/0093650211418338

Pascale, C.-M. (2011). *Cartographies of knowledge: Exploring qualitative epistemologies*. Thousand Oaks, CA: Sage.

Patton, M. Q. (2002). *Qualitative research and evaluation methods* (3rd ed.). Thousand Oaks, CA: Sage.

Pauwels, L. (2011). An integrated conceptual framework for visual social research. In E. Margolis & L. Pauwels (Eds.), *The SAGE handbook of visual research methods* (pp. 3–23). London: Sage.

Pedroni, J. A., & Pimple, K. D. (2001). *A brief introduction to informed consent in research with human subjects*. Bloomington, IN: Poynter Center for the Study of Ethics and American Institutions.

Penslar, R. L., & Porter, J. P. (2009). Basic IRB review. In *Institutional review guidebook* (Chap. 3). Retrieved from http://www.hhs.gov/ohrp/archive/irb/irb_chapter3.htm

Pink, S. (2007). *Doing visual ethnography* (2nd ed.). London: Sage.

Pink, S. (2013). *Doing visual ethnography* (3rd ed.). London: Sage.

Porter, J. P. (1993). *Institutional review board guidebook*. Washington, DC: U.S. Department of Health and Human Services Office for Human Research Protections.

Pryke, M. (2003). *Using social theory: Thinking through research*. London: Sage.

Rallis, S. F., & Rossman, G. B. (2012). *The research journey: Introduction to inquiry*. New York: Guilford Press.

Reppel, A., Gruber, T., Szmigin, I., & Voss, R. (2008). Conducting qualitative research online: An exploratory study into the preferred attributes of an iconic digital music player. *European Advances in Consumer Research, 8*, 519–525.

Rheingold, H. (2012). Stewards of digital literacies. *Knowledge Quest, 41*(1), 52–55.

Ritchie, J., Lewis, J., Nicholls, C. M., & Ormston, R. (Eds.). (2014). *Qualitative research practice: A guide for social science students and researchers* (2nd ed.). London: Sage.

Ritchie, J., Lewis, J., & Elam, G. (2003). Designing and selecting samples. In J. Ritchie & J. Lewis (Eds.), *Qualitative research practice: A guide for social science students and researchers* (pp. 77–108). London: Sage.

Rogers, R. (2009). *The end of the virtual: Digital methods*. Amsterdam: Amsterdam University Press.

Rogers, R. (2010). Internet research: The question of method. *Journal of Information Technology and Politics, 7*(2), 241–260.

Roper, J. M., & Shapira, J. (2000). *Ethnography in nursing research*. Thousand Oaks, CA: Sage.

Rose, G. (2012). *Visual methodologies: An introduction to researching with visual materials*. London: Sage.

Rosenblatt, P. C. (2003). Interviewing at the border of fact and fiction. In J. F. Gubrium & J. A. Holstein (Eds.), *Postmodern interviewing* (pp. 225–242). Thousand Oaks, CA: Sage.

Ross, D. N. (2001). Electronic communications: Do cultural dimensions matter? *American Business Review, 19*, 75–81.

Roulston, K. (2010). Considering quality in qualitative interviewing. *Qualitative Research, 10*(2), 199–228. doi:10.1177/1468794109356739

Rubin, H. J., & Rubin, I. S. (2005). *Qualitative interviewing: The art of hearing data* (2nd ed.). Thousand Oaks, CA: Sage.

Rubin, H. J., & Rubin, I. S. (2012). *Qualitative interviewing: The art of hearing data* (3rd ed.). Thousand Oaks, CA: Sage.

Saldaña, J. (2013). *Coding manual for qualitative researchers* (2nd ed.). London: Sage.

Salmons, J. (2007). Expect originality! Using taxonomies to structure assignments that support original work. In T. Roberts (Ed.), *Student plagiarism in an online world: Problems and solutions* (pp. 208–227). Hershey, PA: IGI Reference.

Salmons, J. E. (2008). Taxonomy of collaborative e-learning. In L. A. Tomei (Ed.), *Encyclopedia of information technology curriculum integration* (pp. 839–942). Hershey, PA: Information Science Reference.

Salmons, J. (2009). E-Social constructivism and collaborative e-learning. In J. Salmons & L. A. Wilson (Eds.), *Handbook of research on electronic collaboration and organizational synergy* (Vol. II, pp. 280–294). Hershey, PA: Information Science Reference.

Salmons, J. (2010). *Online interviews in real time.* Thousand Oaks, CA: Sage.

Salmons, J. (2011a). *An overview of the Taxonomy of Online Collaboration* [Media]. Vision2Lead, Inc. Boulder, CO. Retrieved from http://connect.capellauniversity.edu/p32182738/?launcher=false&fcsContent=true&pbMode=normal

Salmons, J. (Producer). (2011b). A taxonomy of collaboration with Dr. Janet Salmons. *On Teaching Online* [Podcast]. Retrieved from http://onteachingonline.com/oto-17-a-taxonomy-of-collaboration-with-dr-janet-salmons/

Salmons, J. (Ed.). (2012). *Cases in online interview research.* Thousand Oaks, CA: Sage.

Salmons, J. (2014). Putting the "E" in entrepreneurship: Women entrepreneurs in the digital age. In L. Kelley (Ed.), *Entrepreneurial women: New management and leadership models.* Westport, CT: ABI-Clio Praeger.

Schaeffer, N. C., & Maynard, D. W. (2003). Standardization and interaction in the survey interview. In J. F. Gubrium & J. A. Holstein (Eds.), *Postmodern interviewing* (pp. 51–66). Thousand Oaks, CA: Sage.

Schreier, M. (2012). *Qualitative content analysis in practice.* London: Sage.

Schutt, R. K. (2006). *Investigating the social world: The process and practice of research* (5th ed.). Thousand Oaks, CA: Pine Forge Press.

Schwandt, T. A. (Ed.). (2007). *The SAGE dictionary of qualitative inquiry* (3rd ed.). Thousand Oaks, CA: Sage.

Seidman, I. (2006). *Interviewing as qualitative research: A guide for researchers in education and the social sciences* (3rd ed.). New York: Teachers College Press.

Seybold, A. M. (2008). The convergence of wireless, mobility, and the Internet and its relevance to enterprises. *Information Knowledge Systems Management, 7,* 11–23.

Shank, G. (2008). Deduction. In L. M. Given (Ed.), *The SAGE encyclopedia of qualitative research methods* (pp. 208–209). Thousand Oaks, CA: Sage.

Shin, N. (2002). Beyond interaction: The relational construct of "transactional presence." *Open Learning, 17*(2), 121–137.

Shirky, C. (2008). *Here comes everybody: The power of organizing without organizations.* New York: Penguin Press.

Silverman, D., & Marvasti, A. (2008). *Doing qualitative research: A comprehensive guide.* Thousand Oaks, CA: Sage.

Sixsmith, J., & Murray, C. D. (2001). Ethical issues in the documentary data analysis of Internet posts and archives. *Qualitative Health Research, 11*(3), 423–432.

Smith, R. C. (2003). Analytic strategies for oral history interviews. In J. F. Gubrium & J. A. Holstein (Eds.), *Postmodern interviewing* (pp. 203–224). Thousand Oaks, CA: Sage.

Soanes, C., & Stevenson, A. (Eds.). (2004). *Concise Oxford English dictionary* (Vol. 2005, 11th ed.). Oxford, UK: Oxford University Press.

Spencer, L., Ritchie, J., & O'Connor, W. (2003). Analysis: Practices, principles and processes. In J. Ritchie & J. Lewis (Eds.), *Qualitative research practice: A guide for social science students and researchers* (pp. 199–218). London: Sage.

Stake, R. E. (1995). *The art of case study research.* Thousand Oaks, CA: Sage.

Stanczak, G. C. (2007a). Observing culture and social life: Documentary photography, fieldwork, and social research. In G. C. Stanczak (Ed.), *Visual research methods* (pp. 23–61). Thousand Oaks, CA: Sage.

Stanczak, G. C. (2007b). *Visual research methods: Image, society, and representation.* Thousand Oaks, CA: Sage.

Stebbins, R. A. (2001). What is exploration? In R. A. Stebbins (Ed.), *Exploratory research in the social sciences* (pp. 1–30). Thousand Oaks, CA: Sage.

Stenbacka, C. (2001). Qualitative research requires quality concepts of its own. *Management Decision, 39*(7), 551–555.

Stephenson, W. (1935). Correlating persons instead of tests. *Character and Personality, 4,* 17–24.

Stern, S. R. (2009). How notions of privacy influence research choices: A response to Malin Sveningsson. In A. N. Markham & N. K. Baym (Eds.), *Internet inquiry: Conversations about method* (pp. 94–98). Thousand Oaks, CA: Sage.

Strauss, A. L. (1987). *Qualitative analysis for social scientists.* Cambridge, UK: Cambridge University Press.

Streeton, R., Cooke, M., & Campbeii, J. (2004). Researching the researchers: Using a snowballing technique. *Nurse Researcher, 12*(1), 35–45.

Suler, J. (2003). Presence in cyberspace. In *Psychology of cyberspace* [Electronic version]. Retrieved from http://www-usr.rider.edu/~suler/psycyber/presence.html

Sumner, M. (2006). Epistemology. In V. Jupp (Ed.), *The SAGE dictionary of social research methods* (pp. 93–95). Thousand Oaks, CA: Sage.

Sung, E., & Mayer, R. E. (2012). Five facets of social presence in online distance education. *Computers in Human Behavior, 28*(5), 1738–1747. doi:http://dx.doi.org/10.1016/j.chb.2012.04.014

Sutherland-Smith, W. (2002). Weaving the literacy web: Changes in reading from page to screen. *Reading Teacher, 55*(7), 662–669.

Swann, W. B., Jr. (1987). Identity negotiation: Where two roads meet. *Journal of Personality and Social Psychology, 53,* 1038–1051.

Swann, W. B., Jr., Pelham, B. W., & Krull, D. S. (1989). Agreeable fancy or disagreeable truth? Reconciling self-enhancement and self-verification. *Journal of Personality and Social Psychology, 57*(5), 782–791.

Tapscott, D., & Williams, A. D. (2008). *Wikinomics: How mass collaboration changes everything.* New York: Portfolio Hardcover.

Thygesen, M. K., Pedersen, B. D., Kragstrup, J., Wagner, L., & Mogensen, O. (2011). Utilizing a new graphical elicitation technique to collect emotional narratives describing disease trajectories. *The Qualitative Report, 16*(2), 596–608.

Tracy, S. J. (2010). Qualitative quality: Eight "Big-Tent" criteria for excellent qualitative research. *Qualitative Inquiry, 16*(10), 837–851. doi:10.1177/1077800410383121

Trochim, W. (2006). *Research methods knowledge base.* Retrieved August 6, 2009, from http://trochim.human.cornell.edu/kb/index.htm

Ueda, Y., & Nojima, M. (2011). Effect of dispositional factors on perception of text messaging by cell phone. *Interdisciplinary Journal of Contemporary Research in Business, 3*(6), 606–614.

U.S. Department of Health and Human Services. (2010). Protection of human subjects. In U.S. Department of Health and Human Services, *Code of federal regulations* (Title 45, Part 46). Washington, DC: Government Printing Office. Retrieved from http://www.hhs.gov/ohrp/humansubjects/guidance/45cfr46.html

U.S. Department of Health and Human Services. (2013). Protection of human subjects. In U.S. Department of Health and Human Services, *Code of federal regulations* (Title 21, Part 50). Washington, DC: Government Printing Office. Retrieved from http://www.accessdata.fda.gov/scripts/cdrh/cfdocs/cfcfr/CFRSearch.cfm?CFRPart=50

Valenta, A. L., & Wiggerand, U. (1997). Q methodology: Definition and application in health care informatics. *Journal for the American Medical Informatics Association, 6*(6), 501–510.

VanDeVen, A. H. (2007). *Engaged scholarship.* Oxford, UK: Oxford University Press.

Varnhagen, C. K., McFall, G. P., Pugh, N., Routledge, L., Sumida-MacDonald, H., & Kwong, T. E. (2010). Lol: New language and spelling in instant messaging. *Reading and Writing, 23*(6), 719–733.

Velasquez, M., Moberg, D., Meyer, M. J., Shanks, T., McLean, M. R., DeCosse, D., et al. (2008). *A framework for thinking ethically.* Retrieved August 31, 2008, from http://www.scu.edu/ethics/practicing/decision/framework.html

Waldron, J. (2013). YouTube, fanvids, forums, vlogs and blogs: Informal music learning in a convergent on- and offline music community. *International Journal of Music Education, 31*(1), 91–105. doi:10.1177/0255761411434861

Walsh, M. (2003). Teaching qualitative analysis using QSR NVivo. *The Qualitative Report, 8*(2), 251–256.

Walther, J. (1999). *Research ethics in Internet-enabled research: Human subjects issues and methodological myopia.* Retrieved December 10, 2003, from http://www.nyu.edu/projects/nissenbaum/ethics_wal_full.html

Walther, J. B., Loh, T., & Granka, L. (2005). Let me count the ways: The interchange of verbal and nonverbal cues in computer-mediated and face-to-face affinity. *Journal of Language and Social Psychology, 24*(1), 36–65.

Webb, B., & Webb, S. (1932). *Methods of social study.* London: Longmans, Green.

Wegerif, R. (1998). The social dimension of asynchronous learning networks. *Journal of the Asynchronous Learning Networks, 2*(1). Retrieved from http://sloanconsortium.org/jaln/v2n1/social-dimension-asynchronous-learning-networks

Wegge, J. (2006). Communication via videoconference: Emotional and cognitive consequences of affective personality dispositions, seeing one's own picture, and disturbing events. *Human-Computer Interaction, 21*, 273–318.

Weiss, R. S. (1994). *Learning from strangers: The art and method of qualitative interview studies.* New York: Free Press.

Wigmore, I., & Howard, A. B. (2009). *Whatis.com: The leading IT encyclopedia and learning center.* Retrieved August 6, 2009, from http://whatis.techtarget.com

Wiles, R. (2013). *What are qualitative research ethics?* London: Bloomsbury Academic.

Williams, M. (2007). Avatar watching: Participant observation in graphical online environments. *Qualitative Research, 7*(1), 5–24.

Wilmot, A. (2008). *Designing sampling strategies for qualitative social research.* Newport, UK: Office for National Statistics.

Wilson, L. A. (2009). Collaboration in the service of knowledge co-creation for environmental outcomes, science and public policy. In J. E. Salmons & L. A. Wilson (Eds.), *Handbook of research on electronic collaboration and organizational synergy* (pp. 599–614). Hershey, PA: Information Science Reference.

Wortham, J. (2013, March 10). Online emotions, in hundreds of new flavors. *New York Times.* Retrieved from http://www.nytimes.com/2013/03/10/technology/sticker-apps-adding-more-variety-to-the-emoticon-world.html?_r=0

Xiong, G., & Bharadwaj, S. (2011). Social capital of young technology firms and their IPO values: The complementary role of relevant absorptive capacity. *Journal of Marketing, 75*(6), 87–104. doi:10.1509/jmkg.75.6.87

Xu, Y. (2011). How important are entrepreneurial social capital and knowledge structure in new venture innovation? *Journal of Management Policy and Practice, 12*(5), 11–24.

Yin, R. K. (2009). *Case study research: Design and methods* (4th ed.). Thousand Oaks, CA: Sage.

Yin, R. K. (2011). *Qualitative research from start to finish.* New York: Guilford Press.

Yin, R. K. (2014). *Case study research: Design and methods* (5th ed.). Thousand Oaks, CA: Sage.

Yoshikawa, H., Weisner, T. S., Kalil, A., & Way, N. (2008). Mixing qualitative and quantitative research in developmental science: Uses and methodological choices. *Developmental Psychology, 44*(2), 344–354.

Yu, C.-S., & Tao, Y.-H. (2009). Understanding business-level innovation technology adoption. *Technovation, 29*(2), 92–109. doi:10.1016/j.technovation.2008.07.007

Yuzar, T. V. (2007). Generating virtual eye contacts through online synchronous communications in virtual classroom applications. *Turkish Online Journal of Distance Education, 8*(1), 43–54.

Zalta, E. N. (2008). *Stanford encyclopedia of philosophy.* Retrieved August 31, 2008, from http://plato.stanford.edu/

Index

⑤SAGE research**methods**

The essential online tool for researchers from the world's leading methods publisher

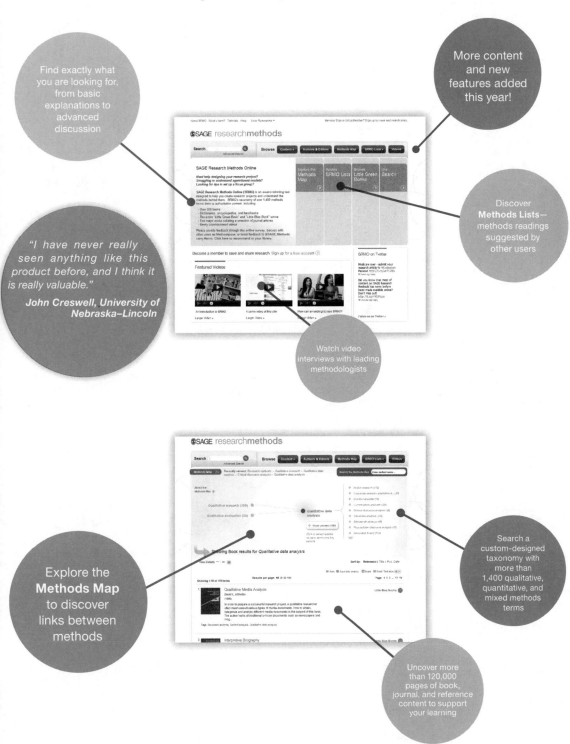

Find exactly what you are looking for, from basic explanations to advanced discussion

More content and new features added this year!

Discover **Methods Lists**—methods readings suggested by other users

"*I have never really seen anything like this product before, and I think it is really valuable.*"
John Creswell, University of Nebraska–Lincoln

Watch video interviews with leading methodologists

Explore the **Methods Map** to discover links between methods

Search a custom-designed taxonomy with more than 1,400 qualitative, quantitative, and mixed methods terms

Uncover more than 120,000 pages of book, journal, and reference content to support your learning

Find out more at
www.sageresearchmethods.com